THE CAT'S MIND

THE CAT'S MIND

Understanding Your Cat's Behaviour

Bruce Fogle DVM, MRCVS

PELHAM BOOKS

To Ratbag

PELHAM BOOKS

Published by the Penguin Group
Penguin Books Ltd, 27 Wrights Lane, London w8 5tz, England
Viking Penguin, a division of Penguin Books USA Inc.
375 Hudson Street, New York, New York 10014, USA
Penguin Books Australia Ltd, Ringwood, Victoria, Australia
Penguin Books Canada Ltd, 10 Alcorn Avenue, Suite 300, Toronto, Ontario, Canada m4v 3b2
Penguin Books (NZ) Ltd, 182–190 Wairau Road, Auckland 10, New Zealand

Penguin Books Ltd, Registered Offices: Harmondsworth, Middlesex, England

First published in Great Britain in November 1991
First published in this edition May 1995
3 5 7 9 10 8 6 4 2

Copyright © Dr Bruce Fogle, 1991

Typeset in Monophoto Photina
Printed in England by Clays Ltd, St Ives plc

A CIP catalogue record for this book is available from the British Library

Library of Congress Catalog Card Number 91–28793

ISBN 07207 2050 8 (paperback)

Illustrations by Dianne Breeze
Graphs by K. S. Smith

Contents

Acknowledgements

Libraries are, of course, essential for researching a book such as this, but what turns enjoyment into sheer pleasure is using a library where the staff are actively interested in your project. Benita Horder and her staff at the Royal College of Veterinary Surgeons Library in London held my hand as they taught me to use their latest technology for information retrieval and, as well as finding the most obtuse articles I requested, they frequently nipped in to where I was researching to show me articles in journals that had just arrived that morning. Thanks and gratitude to them all.

Introduction

Let me first of all say that there is no way of writing about cats that allows you to be thought of as a sane and sensible person. The reason, or at least the probable reason, is that in a multitude of ways cats evoke strongly differing emotions in different people. In an American survey conducted in the 1980s one out of every four people questioned were shown actively to dislike cats, a larger percentage than for any other animal apart from snakes and spiders. Yet other surveys show that cat owners are willing to invest more money in their pet feline's health and well-being than are dog owners. While H. P. Lovecraft described the cat as the symbol of perfect beauty, Johannes Brahms sat at his bedroom window, bow and arrow in hand, taking pot shots at his neighbour's cats.

Combined with the fact that my sanity will be questioned because of what follows is the undeniable fact that thousands of authors have already chosen to write on the subject. The public library in Glendale, California, for example, has over 1500 books about the cat on its shelves and Yale University's library is not far short of that number. Everyone, it seems, has a firm opinion on the animal and writes about it. Why add more?

My answer is simple. Most of the books on cats that I have read have been written by ardent cat lovers. From Jean Burden, who said that 'A dog is prose; a cat is a poem', to Robertson Davies, who revels in what he calls cat's 'rampant egotism, their devil-may-care attitude towards responsibility, their disinclination to earn an honest dollar', books about cats are books with passion.

That passion can cloud common sense even among scientists. Several years ago I attended a scientific meeting at which a professor of psychology described his research showing that if children are raised in households with cats, these children will grow up to be more responsible and reliable adults. Fascinating results, but the good professor had fudged them; he was so convinced that cats are wonderful he came to conclusions that were in no way justified by his research. Now it may well be that those of us who were raised in families with cats actually are more reliable and responsible. I would certainly like to think so, yet what I hope to do in the following chapters is to recount the research in cat behaviour that has been carried out recently but to avoid the type of biased conclusions the professor of psychology made. That will be difficult because we all – including me – have our own notions about cat behaviour.

In his dictionary Noah Webster described the cat as 'a deceitful animal and when enraged extremely spiteful'. I disagree. I don't think that the cat's mind is capable of deceit, but this brings into question whether it is at all appropriate to use words applied to human emotions when describing how the cat's mind works. Is it correct to use words like 'gregarious' or 'jealous' or 'lonely' to describe a cat's behaviour or feelings? To put the point more philosophically, is our image of the cat a true reflection of reality?

My training as a veterinarian puts me firmly in the camp of the biologist and ethologist. That training says that I should use the methods of science to examine the cat's mind. I should measure what I can measure, analyse data, probe into the genetics and physiology of the cat's mind. A purely scientific approach to cat behaviour is based upon the premise that everything a cat does is simply a passive result of predetermined biological laws. A scientific approach assumes that the social and the cultural simply don't exist at the level of the cat's mind. But is this true or is it a human conceit?

I can't answer the question but have raised it now because, although most of what follows is based upon scientific observation, there will be a handsome dollop of my interpretation of these scientific findings and I will use human-emotion words to describe the cat's mind. Fortunately I'm in quite acceptable company. Konrad Lorenz was happy to use the word 'jealous' to describe bird behaviour, explaining that the survival value which caused jealousy behaviour to evolve in birds is more or less identical to its survival value in humans.

Cats, of course, can't speak their minds. We know they think, but only through indirect evidence. To understand their minds involves an exercise in imagination over and above simple scientific reporting and this can be difficult for the scientist to perform, especially the scientist who wants to be taken seriously. Living outside the 'ivory tower', I don't have to worry about scientifically justifying each and every word I say as does the professional academic. I can state that I think cats are dignified, supercilious, graceful, modest, urbane, beautiful, clean, tactful or independent – all adjectives that I am happy to apply to them and which I don't feel the need to justify scientifically. Some of these words are wholly anthropomorphic, but rather than feeling it is wrong to attribute human emotions to other animals I think it's an absolute positive. Of course, if I describe a cat as lonely or jealous, I am making a value judgement. I'm also saying something about my moral view of the animal, but this isn't necessarily bad science. After all, for thousands of years we have been making emotional value judgements to predict the behaviour of first the prey we hunted and later the stock we domesticated, and we have been quite successful at that.

In examining the cat's mind we can perhaps use even more words that we usually apply only to human personalities. Hans Eysenck first developed the definitions of the words extravert and introvert to describe human behaviour and then later expanded his theory to describe the differences between the neurotic personality and the emotionally stable personality. The words that he used to compare extravert people with neurotic or psychotic individuals are, technically, only ever used to describe human behaviour, but think about your cat when you read his definitions.

An extravert is sociable, lively, active, assertive, sensation-seeking, carefree, dominant, surgent, venturesome. This sounds like a typical

Extraverts are venturesome. Introverts are tense.

Abyssinian or Somali to me. (Breed differences are discussed in more detail in Chapter Eleven.) The neurotic is shy, moody, emotional, tense, anxious, irrational; the psychotic is aggressive, cold, impersonal, anti-social, unempathetic and tough-minded; both of these characters sound like poorly socialized cats. (How the cat's mind is affected through socializing is examined in Chapters Six, Seven and Ten.)

According to Eysenck, extraverts are slower to condition – and gregarious cats are certainly more difficult to train than their calmer relatives. He also says, somewhat controversially, that it's possible that personality differences are actually quantifiable on electro-encephalographs (EEGs).

If I were to take a strictly mechanical approach to the cat's mind, looking only at genetics, instinct, imprinted behaviour, Pavlovian conditioning and other hard facts – and that is what perhaps the majority of hard scientists would do – I would be depriving us of a wealth of subjective information. A mechanical approach is inherently wrong. Many scientists, for example, know that a dog salivates at the sound of a bell after it has been conditioned to do so by being fed whenever a bell rings, *but they think it doesn't know why it salivates.* This is classic Pavlovian conditioning, but the interpretation is probably wrong. It is far more likely that conditioning is not the acquisition of a new reflex but rather the acquisition of new knowledge. That's a very simple idea but an extremely difficult one for many scientists to accept.

The cat's mind comprehends the environment. It has needs and knows how to satisfy them. Cats do things intentionally, not simply by instinct. The cat's mind holds knowledge and beliefs, has intentions and almost undoubtedly perceives the world in much the same way we do, even if it can't convert those perceptions into symbols or language. After all, the scientifically acceptable principle of continuity means that the human mind has precedent over the cat's mind. (Its perceptions are probably the same because its brain set-up is so similar to ours; this is described in Chapter One.) Language isn't absolutely necessary for good communication either. Just as, over a period of time, humans who are close to each other develop sensitive 'antennae' which pick up the emotions of their fellows, we do so with our cats too. We don't need scientific evidence to tell us that our cats are happy or sorrowful, tired or exhilarated. And just as we pick up these non-verbal messages from them, cats are excellent at communicating with each other. (Detailed information on how cats communicate follows in Chapter Four.)

Our notions as to what goes on in cats' minds are deeply coloured by the reasons we keep them as companions. At any given time, throughout the world, there are probably over 200 million domestic cats living with human beings. There are over 50 million in the USA alone, where they are now the most popular pet, outnumbering dogs, and 7 million in the UK where they are only slightly less numerous than dogs, many of them regarded as honorary members of the family, given personal names, fed specially prepared food, equipped with toys and bedding, worried over when they are unwell and grieved over when they die. Cats do make ideal companions. They are not as intrusive as dogs. They don't upset routine, are clean and relatively independent, but still send us the signals we want to receive. The most important fact is that there seems to be a mutual liking between certain domestic cats and domestic cat owners, a rewarding and fulfilling dialogue based upon the fact that both parties are content that neither will take advantage of the other. This is not always the case and the consequences when the equilibrium is upset are the behaviour disorders that veterinarians are increasingly being asked for advice upon.

Through their non-verbal messages of attachment cats have been particularly adept at moving into human territories without our becoming deeply upset at this intrusion. It isn't simply their intelligence or adaptability that has permitted this to happen but rather our perception of cats. After all, rats are highly intelligent and more adaptable than almost any other mammal, yet other than in the case of a few 'rataholics' we have not actively chosen to share our homes with them. Millions of people from a multitude of cultural backgrounds have chosen to do so with cats, however. The reason lies in our interpretation of their behaviour.

Cats parasitize our inherent need to care for living things. When a cat solicits a stroke or a caress by rubbing its body against its owner's leg, many owners simply melt. But cats are equally adept at influencing our attitude towards them in more subtle ways.

Countless studies have shown that, although we are unaware that we do it, we look at people we like more than people we don't like. A corollary to that is that being looked at is interpreted as a signal of interest and attraction. In one experiment in which people were interviewed in pairs, the ones who were looked at more frequently by the interviewer believed that they were preferred. Cats, of course, are brilliant unblinking starers. Pet cats routinely maintain eye-to-eye contact with their owners and, as do dogs, spend a considerable proportion of their time looking at us.

For some people the cat's stare can be disconcerting. It can suggest a lack of deference or even hostility. These people are among the one in four who actively dislike cats. For the majority, however, the wide-eyed look is interpreted to mean 'I like you and am interested in you.' In return, when we stare back at our pet cats, their behaviour reinforces our often misconceived perception of what they are thinking. A typical pet cat's response to a direct stare from its owner is eventually to half-close its eyes a few times and then slowly turn away. Combining the appearance of the large eyes relative to the size of its head, the roundness of the head and the upturned corners of the mouth, we interpret its expression as a smile. The visual signals are indeed a reasonably good facsimile of a human smile, but in feline terms the cat's response is really one of submission. Closing the eyes and turning the head away is what an adult cat will do when it has a demarcation dispute with another cat.

We are probably more accurate in our assessment of what dilated pupils mean. Because cats have vertical pupils they can open their eyes much wider than we can and when they do the effect is more dramatic. When we open our eyes wide it usually means that we are looking at something attractive or exciting, and the same rule probably applies to cats too. When a cat sits on your lap, gently kneads with its feet and stares up at you with wistful almond-shaped eyes, its behaviour denotes contentment and attraction.

Cats are not as good at expressing their emotions with their faces as dogs are. Although they can move their whiskers and ears in a variety of ways, they don't have the facial muscles that are necessary for the range of expressions that canines and simians possess. We don't find it difficult to interpret when a cat is angry or frightened, but otherwise all we usually see is a serene inscrutability, an expression of detached contentment that we find soothing and appealing. That interpretation may be right or wrong, but it is in our minds rather than the cat's.

Although cats are capable of a variety of sounds, they are far quieter than our other domestic pet, the dog, and this relative muteness further influences how we interpret their minds. Aaron Katcher, a psychiatrist at the University of Pennsylvania, has compared the one-way dialogue between cat owner and cat as similar to the exchange between a patient and a Rogerian or non-interventive empathic psychiatrist. Because cats are relatively reserved and mute, we unconsciously look upon their affection towards us as innocent, unconditional, reliable, sincere and without pretence.

Compared to the dog, the cat is infinitely better studied. There are thousands of scientific articles describing feline behaviour. Research workers have always taken cats seriously. They are 'real' animals, self-domesticated rather than domesticated through our intervention. But in these hundreds of thousands of pages of learned writing there is still no accurate answer to the question why a cat will lie on your lap. Is it fondness? Or is it simply to obtain warmth? Mark Twain once described the behaviour of a cat at the Marseille Zoo. Each day it would climb up an elephant's hind leg to roost on his back. With his trunk the elephant would remove it, but the cat would simply climb back. Fondness or warmth? Cats don't wear their emotions on their sleeve as dogs do and that is what makes it such a difficult question to answer. It is also probably the reason why so many scientists find cats so fascinating.

The cat is our most recently domesticated animal. While the dog was domesticated from the wolf at least 12,000 and probably over 25,000 years ago, the domestic cat emerged from wild obscurity only 3000 to 4000 years ago in Egypt and perhaps Mesopotamia. There is still today a healthy scientific argument concerning exactly what a domestic cat is. Certainly the domestic cat (whose scientific name is *Felis domesticus*) is directly related to the North African wild cat (*Felis lybica*). Just as the wolf (*Canis lupus*) is the progenitor of the dog (*Canis domesticus*), it is from the wild cat that the domestic cat has

The domestic cat (above) is closely related to the North African wild cat.

descended. The argument is over whether there is any *real* difference between the wild cat and the domestic cat. And where does the European wild cat (*Felis sylvestris*) fit in?

Anatomically there are few differences. The domestic cat has a slightly longer intestinal tract than the wild cat – it eats a wider variety of food and needs more room to digest. The wild cat is slightly larger than the domestic cat and has a dense coat, and there is a genetic logic here too. Cats that survive by capturing live prey adapt to catch what is available. Both the Norwegian Forest Cat and the Maine Coon, breeds of domestic cat that evolved to survive harsh winters, have dense coats and are larger than average – a result of simple genetic shift (discussed in more detail in Chapter One).

Because there is an indigenous wild cat in Europe it would seem logical that this species has had a dominant role to play in the evolution of the domestic cat. Facts, however, argue against *Felis sylvestris* being anything other than a marginal influence. Although both the European and North African wild cats possess similar and unique tabby-pattern coats, the North African cousin has a wider variety of coat colours and a greater affinity to humans. This last point can be dramatically observed by comparing the natural behaviour of both types.

Although there has been one report from Scotland of a male hybrid European wild cat being 'as tame as a fireside cat', all other reports describe these animals as untameable. The naturalist Frances Pitt described how she lavished attention on wild cat kittens, handling that she said would have transformed a fox or an otter into a house pet but did not enable her to get farther than 'armed neutrality' with the felines. Her greatest success was with Satan, a wild cat who spat and hissed indomitably as a kitten but whom she kept at her home in Scotland. Pitt described how hybrid crosses between her wild cat and domestic cats could not be trusted after they were half-grown and described them as 'nervous and queer-tempered'. Consistently the hybrids were rusty-hued striped tabbies with thick tails ringed in black. In other words the coat colour and texture of the wild cat predominated.

The North African wild cat has been described differently by a number of naturalists. Neil Todd has told how even today, in the southern part of the Sudan, the North African wild cat exists in a symbiotic relationship with the local Azande tribe who, despite this long-standing history, have made no effort to domesticate it. While the European wild cat shuns contact with humans, its North African cousin is content to live in close proximity to us.

At the end of the last century the British found over 300,000 mummified cats at Beni Hassan in Egypt. Virtually all of them were shipped to England where they were crushed and used as fertilizer, but eventually the British Museum acquired 190 mummified cat skulls dating from 600 to 200 BC and examined them. Nearly all were skulls of *Felis lybica*, the North African wild cat, but three were from *Felis chaus*, the small jungle cat. This adds one more dimension to the evolution of the domestic cat's mind.

The usual explanation for the domestication of the cat in Ancient Egypt is that it was needed to protect grain stores from rodents. There is a natural logic to the equation that grain attracts rodents and rodents attract cats, but this is an over-simplification of the process of domestication. After all, grain had been stored in Mesopotamia and Egypt for at least 7000 years before cats were domesticated. It seems an unnaturally long time to wait before choosing this method of control for an age-old problem.

At around the same time the cat was allegedly being domesticated it also became venerated as a religious cult in Egypt, and its attainment of such a status could infer a more long-standing and familiar, if undocumented, relationship with human beings. The modern-day bond between the wild cat and the tribes of the southern Sudan, mentioned above, adds further weight to this argument. In other words cats have very likely lived in intimate association with humans ever since there was any advantage for them to do so.

This means that the process of self-domestication, evolving to fit into a new ecological niche, has gone on for quite some time. Cats were uninvited but not unwelcome guests in human communities, and those with the least fear of humans were the most successful. This is why *Felis lybica* is the originator of our domestic cat; and because it can breed successfully with other feline species, such as *Felis chaus* (the jungle cat), there have been throughout its history continuing introductions of new genetic material. The consequence is that the domestic cat today behaves differently from its wild creator. Before we look at how a pet cat thinks, however, we should examine where it came from.

Domesticated cats spread slowly out of Egypt, taken by merchants and armies around the world. They were transported via Babylonia to India and on to China between 2000 and 3000 years ago. The Greeks brought cats to Europe at the same time, but it was not until AD 999 that they arrived in Japan (and not until AD 1620 that they were allowed off their leads). All of these cats shared behaviour, instinct and thoughts with their wild cousins in Africa. Domestic cats are simply the result of a little natural biological tinkering and a little planned biological change. A Burmilla or a Devon Rex or even a blotched tabby today is simply the latest version of the original, *Felis lybica*, with four-wheel drive and a superior paint job. And the original was and still is the best mammalian carnivore that biological evolution ever produced.

Cats are the world's most specialized land predators, the sharks of grasslands and scrub. In the cat, evolution created an animal that kills its prey through a single bite which severs the spinal cord. Pet cats today seldom do this because we have tinkered with their minds, exaggerating or simply enhancing but certainly perpetuating life-long kitten-like behaviour in most of them, but the originals – the European and North African wild cats – still kill in this way.

A cat has short but very powerful jaws with generous attachment areas on the skull for the neck muscles. This means that it can hold and manipulate surprisingly large prey. Its carnassial teeth (those on the sides) are blade-like, virtually serrated, and allow the cat to slice into its food; but, more important, the canine teeth are somewhat flattened. Using film and photographs the German ethologist Paul Leyhausen carefully studied how the domestic cat kills its prey and has described how its flattened canine teeth actually enter between two vertebrae in the neck, severing the spinal cord and killing instantly: the chance-in-a-million bite. Moreover, evolution has given the cat's canine teeth a massive bed of nerve receptors, so that it can actually feel with these teeth. Evolution has also equipped the cat with nerve fibres that conduct information very quickly, which means that its jaw muscles have a fast contraction time. And finally the chances of evolution have resulted in the cat having an anatomical structure that transmits the stresses of the powerful and fast bite back along the smoothly curving, strengthened, bony arches of the skull.

The result of these physical attributes is that mature and experienced wild cats are able to capture prey, feel for the right place with their teeth and with great speed bite home with their canines, specially adapted to a flattened shape that will penetrate between even a small rodent's neck vertebrae. Long before Paul Leyhausen had explained the cat's ability to kill its prey instantly, the naturalist Francis Pitt had observed this in her captive wild cat, Satan. So prompt and efficient was he at dispatching mice that all mice caught in the Pitt household were carried to Satan's cage where he dealt with them with 'lightning swiftness'. (Pitt describes how she used to go on walks with one of her hybrids which caught rabbits like a dog, killed them instantly and carried them home. She stopped the walks after her hybrid went out on her own one evening and Pitt found three of her hens decapitated the following morning.) Our pet cats too could behave in this way if they chose.

Before describing how pet cats think and behave in more detail, it is helpful to summarize the behaviour of their forebears. In this summary and elsewhere the term 'wild cat' refers to the European or North African wild cats described above; 'domestic cat' or 'pet cat' means a cat raised in association with humans; and 'feral cat' refers to a domestic cat raised in the absence of contact with humans – a feral cat is a domestic cat that lives in the wild.

Wild cats are loners, solitary hunters who meet others of their kind only for the five or six days of the year when the female is in oestrus. They are reclusive animals that hunt at dawn and dusk, searching out rodents, rabbits, hares, birds, reptiles and insects. Both individual males and females will take over a territory and then defend it. This is their 'protected area' and it provides them with food and shelter. In both Czechoslovakia and Scotland the territory of the European wild cat is usually between 250 and 500 acres (100 and 200 hectares), females being content with the smaller and males the larger areas. The size of the territory depends upon the food supply. The more food there is, the smaller the territory that the wild cat will defend.

Wild cats mark their territory with urine spray, faecal deposits and secretions from glands on their bodies. Faeces are left unburied at the limits of the territory but are buried within it. Conspicuous objects within the territory such as rocks or fallen trees are visually marked with claw marks. Territories are too large to mark in their entirety and so only the important bits – feeding areas, resting places and connections between them – are marked. Wild cats increase their scent-marking behaviour when transient cats, wild, feral or domestic, cross their territory. Scent marking itself, however, is not a deterrent to other cats, for once a territory is vacated another wild cat will take it over regardless of the number of scent posts.

Both males and females will defend their territories against intrusions from both sexes, but females are less tolerant of other females entering their territory (probably because of the protective behaviour that produces maternal aggression) than males are of other males. Females have only one oestrus cycle per year, in January or February, experience a sixty-eight-day gestation period and usually produce three kittens. If these kittens die (and although it is rare, they can sometimes be cannibalized by a male cat), the female will have another heat cycle and can produce another litter that year. The kittens have their first solid food when thirty to forty days old, stay with their mother for ninety to 120 days, then go off on their own to set up territories. They are sexually mature by the time they are a year old and physically mature by two years.

Wild cats have a tendency to monogamy and this still appears to be true when they are in captivity and even when a harem of females is available. Francis Pitt's Satan 'never cast a covetous eye on any female other than his Persian-type mate'. When a wild cat gives birth, she simply scratches the ground and gets on with the procedure, but then almost daily moves the kittens to a new nest until they are about four weeks old. This is naturally an excellent defence ploy, an adaptive survival strategy for the kittens.

Most of us will see much of our pet cats' behaviour mirrored in that of their wild relatives, but even more can be learned from the behaviour of feral cats (domestic cats that have reverted to the wild). The striking difference between wild and domestic cats is the solitary nature of the former and the sociability of the latter, and studies of feral cats in various habitats have thrown light on this. The studies have shown that the amount of food available is the most important factor influencing sociability among feral cats – an important finding, for it means that, contrary to what was once believed, cats are not simply a species of mutually intolerant individuals. Far from it: when circumstances permit, they are highly tolerant of each other and even have an established rank order.

The studies of feral cats were conducted in gloriously diverse surroundings ranging from the warm Sacramento Valley in California, USA, to the dockyards of Portsmouth, England, to the Outer Hebrides islands of Scotland to Marrion Island in the sub-Antarctic. They revealed that sociability depended not only on the food supply but also on climate. Cats on cold Marrion Island, for instance, will sleep together to keep warm and hunt either singly or in groups for burrowing birds. Feral cats in the warmer Sacramento Valley in California have a population density only slightly less than the average on Marrion Island, about twelve cats per 250 acres (100 hectares), yet seldom have any contact with each other other than for mating.

While male and female wild cats might have territories that overlap each other, females seldom do. Females are more sedentary and territorial than males. The same is true of feral cats, but the rule is not as strictly followed. Both male and female ferals don't seem to mind having overlapping territories, and when natural food is scarce they are willing to live communally for hand-outs from human beings. Feral cats in the Outer Hebrides, where there are approximately nineteen cats per 250 acres (100 hectares), live off rabbits during the summer and hand-outs from islanders during the winter. The feral cats in the Portsmouth dockyards, on the other hand, where their density is approximately 200 cats per 250 acres, live totally off hand-outs and by scavenging among human refuse. In these circumstances a system of social behaviour has evolved with stable groups of two to nine females sharing communal nursing, kitten guarding, defence and food. As their kittens mature, the young males emigrate while the young females remain. This shows that domestic cats are capable of creating a sophisticated group similar in size and structure to the lion pride, which is also all-female. Both groups clump around food sources, and while one has evolved to occur around a herd of herbivores on the savannah of East Africa, there should be no less respect given to the fact that the other has evolved to occur around a different food source that happens to exist in a piazza in Venice or a park in Paris.

Where their population is of low density, then, feral cats are solitary and territorial, but where it is high they are capable of forming a social group. And naturally there are a multitude of intermediate stages and still further ones when cats are raised in close and constant proximity to humans.

Cats, much more than dogs, provoke extremes of emotional reaction in people. In a bar in Galway on the west coast of Ireland a man raised his glass and toasted: 'God save all here, barring the cat' – humorous to some, but deeply offensive to cat lovers. Today, in what has been a dog's world, the increasing popularity of cats is resulting in misconceived notions about what goes on in a cat's mind and exactly what it is capable of doing. Twenty years ago only 10 per cent of my patients were felines; today they represent just over 50 per cent. These new cat owners very often did not grow up with cats, but were dog owners who have chosen cats as pets because they want the companionship that a pet brings but no longer have a lifestyle that permits the ownership of a dog. They mistakenly apply their understanding of canine behaviour to their new feline, believing that their cat should be as responsive as the dog they formerly owned or that its social needs are the same. This is one of the reasons why there is such a significant new interest in feline behaviour. So many people are simply getting it wrong. And the custard-pie prize for getting it the most gloriously wrong has got to go to the United States Army.

During the Vietnam war, some bright spark, almost undoubtedly an owner of Coon Hounds who had never issued a command to a cat in his life, decided that the Army should experiment with using cats as night-time guides for soldiers. After all, he must have said to himself, dogs have good noses and we use them to sniff out ordnance. Cats have good night vision, so we should use them too. He forgot, or perhaps simply never knew, that it is easy to train cats – as long as you pick something they like doing. In this project cats were issued harnesses and told to lead soldiers through the jungle at night. After a month of night manoeuvres a report was filed; here are some extracts from it:

> A squad, upon being ordered to move out, was led off in all different directions by the cats . . . . On many occasions the animals led the troops racing through thick brush in pursuit of field mice and birds . . . . Troops had to force the cats to follow the direction of the patrol; the practice often led to the animals stalking and attacking the dangling pack straps of the soldier marching directly in front of the animal . . . . If the weather was inclement or even threatening inclemency, the cats were never anywhere to be found.

The project was suspended.

Before we get into the genetics of the cat's mind let me give a final example of my prejudices. Sometimes art can be better than science in trying to explain the phenomena of life. This was written by Dilys Laing:

> I put down my book
> The Meaning of Zen
> And see the cat smiling into her fur
> as she delicately combs it with her rough pink tongue.
> 'Cat, I would lend you this book to study
> but it appears that you have already read it.'
> She looks up and gives me her full gaze.
> 'Don't be ridiculous,' she purrs. 'I wrote it.'

PART ONE

The Anatomy and Physiology of the Cat's Mind

Chapter One

The Genetics of the Mind

Millie, my Maine Coon, has a passion for smoked salmon and dill sauce. My neighbour's stout tabby-and-white tom prefers chicken bones from our garbage. Yet wild cats, the progenitors of Millie and the tom, would eat fish or scavenge decomposing meat only if their lives depended upon it. Wild cats eat only live prey but feral and domestic cats will beg, steal or scavenge almost anything. This change of behaviour is a result of natural genetic selection, a simple process that has gone on for centuries and is still continuing.

The North African wild cat carried, and still carries, the genetic flexibility allowing for domestication. That flexibility can be seen today in its behaviour in the Sudan where it willingly lives in close proximity to humans and survives on a diet of live prey and scavenged food. The European wild cat, confronted with the same environmental situation (nearby or encroaching human habitation), does not apparently have the genetic malleability to modify its behaviour to live near and, in part, off us.

Changes of behaviour such as this are a result of subtle genetic alterations, or genetic shift, and are constantly occurring. Until recently most genetic shift occurred either naturally or was unwittingly caused by our intervention. The wild cats of southern Sudan have experienced a natural genetic shift. In the survival of the fittest, those that were least afraid of humans, and which could therefore eat our left-overs, were likeliest to survive and multiply.

Our unwitting intervention produces similar genetic shifts. When, at the turn of the century, cold-storage warehouse operators in the Chicago area put cats in their cold storage to keep the rat population under control, over 80 per cent of the cats died. The survivors bred and within a few years all the cold-storage cats were smaller animals with shorter tails and thick fur. A similar genetic shift produced the Norwegian Forest Cat and the Maine Coon. In both circumstances we transplanted an animal that was native to a temperate climate, plentiful with small rodents, to a cooler one where there were fewer small rodents but more larger game. In these circumstances genetic shift produced thick protective coats, fluffy tails and larger cats capable of capturing rabbits and hares. The Singapura, on the other hand, evolved from cats taken to a tropical climate. In a warm environment, where there was a plentiful supply of mice, there was no advantage of either bulk in weight or thickness of fur. And because the local human population at best only tolerated the presence of these cats, there was a natural selection process mitigating against having a strong, powerful voice like that of the Siamese. The consequence is a small, quiet, short-haired cat.

The evidence from mummified Egyptian cats suggests that although today's domestic cat is a direct descendant of the North African wild cat, and most of the behaviour differences between the two are the result of genetic shift, there is another reason why the mind of the modern pet cat is different from that of the wild cat and that is a process called hybrid vigour.

All members of the cat family are genetically so closely related that they can successfully breed with each other. Cross a tiger with a lion and the kittens that result are tigons. If natural crosses such as this continue to occur, the descendants eventually incorporate the best features from both species, although they continue to look most like the one with the dominant body features. (In my book *The Dog's Mind* I describe how the wolf has been replaced in New England by an animal that looks exactly like a wolf but is part-wolf, part-coyote, part-domestic dog. The hybrid vigour of this cross has produced an animal with the hunting ability of the wolf and the domestic dog's lack of fear of humans. The same change is occurring in Australia where dingos freely cross-breed with domestic sheep dogs and cattle dogs.) We can judge from mummified remains that the Ancient Egyptians kept a number of different cats, mostly *Felis lybica* (the North African wild cat) but also *Felis chaus* (the jungle cat). It is most likely that these different but related species interbred and, through hybrid vigour, the best features – the aspects of behaviour that allowed their descendants to survive and multiply in proximity to us – were perpetuated.

Genetic shift and hybrid vigour are the processes that have created the variety of cats in existence today. Yet, compared to dogs, cats outwardly appear to carry only a small potential to produce different body shapes and temperaments. The largest breed of dog is almost

200 times larger than the smallest breed of dog; the largest breed of domestic cat, the Maine Coon, however, is only four or five times as large as the smallest breed of cat, the Singapura. It is doubtful whether the cat carries the genetic plasticity to produce miniature and massive breeds, but it certainly has enough latent genetic variation to produce different body types (from the compact, cobby, British types to the sensuous, elongated, oriental physique), and a range of coat colours and densities equal to those of the dog. But do these have any relationship to the cat's mind? The answer is 'yes' and is a consequence of a genetic phenomenon called 'linkage'.

Linkage is a phenomenon by which, when one characteristic is selected for, say, coat or eye colour, another characteristic is also unwittingly selected for, because the gene that controls this second characteristic is linked to the gene you are initially perpetuating. For example, white cats with blue eyes are frequently deaf because the gene causing deafness is linked to the genes necessary to produce this combination of coat and eye colour.

The process affects behaviour too. The Abyssinian cat's coat colour is genetically a mutant of the tabby coat colour, but linked to this mutation is a genetic variation that produces a cat with a high energy level. The Abyssinian is a classic 'over-the-top' breed, more active than average, highly inquisitive and demanding more attention. Personality traits such as these are inherited, although they have been best studied in dogs where personality traits have been intentionally exaggerated and perpetuated to create specific breeds. Dr Bonnie Beaver, professor of animal behaviour at the Veterinary College of Texas A&M University, says, however, that timid, social and aggressive personalities have shown evidence of heritability in the Texas A&M cat colony. For generations we have used this type of knowledge in dog breeding, but are only now just starting to use it in cats.

Generally speaking, professional cat breeders are much more knowledgeable about the genetics of coat colour and texture than are dog breeders. Books dedicated to the genetics of cat breeding are readily available. Animal behaviourists have also studied cats in more detail, producing arcane but still peripherally interesting information. Michael Warren at the Pennsylvania State University Animal Behaviour Laboratory observed that cats snatch food using their left paw 50 per cent of the time and their right paw 50 per cent of the time; interesting but perhaps not the most important aspect of cat behaviour. Detailed information on genetics is readily available but, even though I have always found the mathematics of genetics almost painfully unamusing, I should at least mention some basics.

The simplicity of genetics is that it operates on the 'all-or-none' principle. For example, if red sweet peas are crossed with white sweet peas (an experiment practised by the father of genetics, the Austrian monk Gregor Mendel), the results are not pink sweet peas but rather sweet peas that are the dominant colour (red) yet carry the potential to produce white sweet peas. In the diagram below the red sweet pea is called RR and the white one WW. Crossing them produces RW and is represented this way:

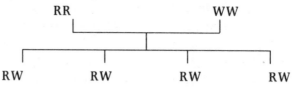

RW is red but carries the potential to produce white. Now, if we take two of these red descendants and cross them, we end up with three red flowers but one white one and it is represented this way:

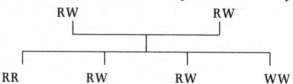

The same 'all-or-none' law of genetics applies to cats, and although in the case of these animals genetics almost always looks at coat colour and conformation it is equally applicable to behaviour.

The data bank of information for all the characteristics of the cat's mind as well as its body is carried in the chromosomes in every cell. There are thirty-eight chromosomes in each cell of the cat's body and they are just large enough to see using a powerful but standard microscope. Each chromosome contains thousands of genes threaded out in a bead-like fashion. When the cell reproduces, as most cells constantly do, the chromosomes are copied exactly, producing a complete genetic library in each new cell. A copying enzyme anchors itself at one end of the chromosome and moves along to the other end using the chromosome's sequence of genes to make a new chromosome. The end result is a pair of chromosomes and the copying is so faithfully accurate that geneticists calculate that there might be one mistake in a single gene for every million copies. There are about as many genes as there are words in this chapter. If my typing were as accurate as copying enzymes it would mean that if I retyped this chapter a million times I would type only one error in one word once.

The gene itself is a mathematically neat four-state storage system. A computer or word processor uses two-state information storage. The computer I use stores all information in two states it calls A and O. By holding long strings of As and Os it creates a data bank or memory. And when I unlock this memory, the data can be retrieved in a form I can understand. In the data bank of my computer this chapter is nothing but strings of A and O. But when it is retrieved, at the push of a button, it is faithfully reproduced as I have written it. And if I have written it correctly, it is reproduced correctly. If I have made any errors along the way, these errors are faithfully reproduced too.

Genes work in the same way but they use four sites or states usually called A, T, C and G. The mathematical combinations of four states is mind-boggling compared to the two states of computers, and this tremendous storage capacity is available in almost every cell of the body. It is so great that all the information of the entire set of the *Encyclopaedia Britannica* could be stored in one cell of my cat's body.

The gene's four-state information technology train is called deoxyribonucleic acid or DNA. This is what is so faithfully copied and scorched into the memory of each new cell. But if the copying is so superb, why are all cats not clones of each other, identical replicas? The answer, of course, is in the germ cells, the egg and the sperm.

In each of the cat's thirty-eight chromosomes, its string of genes is laid out in the same way, with specific sites (or addresses or locations) that handle certain aspects of life. Site number 926 on the chain might, for example, be the site for coat colour and although the site is the same in every chromosome in every cat, the contents can be different.

All chromosomes come in pairs; all except the germ cells' chromosomes, the egg's and sperm's. These cells have single chromosomes and it is the mixing (or matching) of the different contents at gene sites that creates the uniqueness of each and every kitten that is produced. Some contents at gene sites can be dominant over the contents at the same site on the connecting gene, which is why certain coat colours or behaviours are dominant. An example is tabby colour, but the same principle applies to behaviours.

Many of the characteristics of the cat are labelled dominant or recessive. The most common coat colour of the wild cat is the tabby colour of yellow/brown and black. The geneticist labels this A A and it is dominant. (Capital letters denote dominance.) The colour black, on the other hand, is called recessive and is labelled aa. If a genetically pure tabby cat is bred with a (genetically simple) black cat, the results will be tabby-coloured cats that carry a recessive gene for black. The cross is written this way:

Now, if two of these descendants are mated, we will get three tabbies and one black cat:

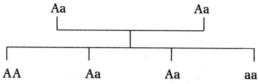

One tabby (AA) is pure tabby, two (Aa) are tabby colour but carry the recessive gene for black, and one (aa) is black.

This law of genetics applies to the cat's mind too. To give a simplistic example, wild cats might carry a dominant gene that dictates that live prey should be eaten but also carry a recessive gene that lets them scavenge from human settlements. Through natural selection pressures, this recessive gene can, as a result of genetic drift, become so prevalent that the new behaviour becomes the norm. Yet the new behaviour, while now common, never completely replaces the former one which usually remains at a fixed incidence of about 10 per cent in the cat population. This is the field of population genetics, one in which no animal has been more intensively studied than the cat.

For changes in behaviour, temperament or conformation to occur, sub-populations of animals should ideally be isolated, allowed to inter-breed only among themselves and then, on a limited and infrequent basis, allowed to meet with other isolated sub-populations and inter-breed with them. At first by sheer happenstance, and now through planned breeding, this is exactly what has occurred in the case of cats. Populations became isolated in eastern Turkey, producing orange-and-white, water-loving cats. Other populations were isolated in South-east Asia, producing vocal and gregarious felines. Yet other populations became isolated in northern Russia and in Japan, creating cats with stumpy tails or that preferred to eat fish. These isolated populations bred true. They consistently produced offspring that looked and behaved like their parents. Today breeders are actively crossing breeds to create new breeds. The Burmese, for example, has been crossed with the long-haired Chinchilla to produce the Burmilla, a surprisingly attractive, even-tempered and active cat. But let's first look at those isolated sub-populations and speculate on how they got there.

The domestic cat is undoubtedly the most successful feline today, surviving in most parts of the world. Technically it has been success- ful at adaptive radiation – at modifying its behaviour so that its descendants survive in new environments. The cold-storage cats of Chicago mentioned earlier are a clear example but so too are the feral cats on Marrion Island in the sub-Antarctic that survive on bird eggs and sleep together, the Monach Island cats whose food is rabbit, the Outer Hebrides cats that rabbit in the summer and live off hand- outs in the winter, the Coliseum cats in Rome that exist solely on hand-outs, and Millie, my Maine Coon, the epitome of the contented house cat, with her penchant for gravad lax. All of these cats have been successful but it is only through our passive help that this has been so: we took the animals to these continents and islands in the first place, an action the consequence of which has fascinated the population geneticist Neil Todd.

Until recently we have left cats (unlike all the other animals we have domesticated) largely to themselves to reproduce. The result has been true random breeding with very few selective breeding pressures from us. Cats haven't migrated around the world by them- selves. We've taken them everywhere and then let them breed randomly, and in doing so we have unwittingly carried out unique population genetics experiments.

Working from the Carnivore Genetics Research Center in Massa- chusetts, Todd became interested in the domestic cat because it is a species that has moved, and is still in the process of moving, from one ecological niche to another; from a predatory lifestyle to a sub- sidized one. From being a relatively asocial and retiring animal living in grassland and scrub, the cat is actively evolving into a more gregariously sociable species, sociable with its own kind and with others (us and dogs, for example) and willing to live in a new urban habitat.

Research in the 1960s and 1970s revealed that in such species as foxes, mink, mice and rats, behaviours such as fear and aggression could be manipulated simply by crossing different coat colours. In other words, fear and aggression were linked to coat colour. (By manipulating coat colour the Russians were able to produce 'tame' foxes within a few generations.) Although similar studies have not been carried out in cats, Todd is convinced that the same effect would almost certainly be revealed in cats and probably in all other mammals. (As I mentioned in *The Dog's Mind*, the 'avalanche of rage syndrome' in cocker spaniels appears to be related to blond or golden hair colour.)

It appears that as soon as men commenced commercial navigation, cats became members of the ship's company. But which cats? As human beings have always had a penchant for the odd and unusual, it seems likely that mariners of the past chose according to their personal tastes. This could explain a curiosity of population genetics. The only place where orange and dominant-white cats occur in remarkably large numbers is in the Van district of eastern Turkey. But strangely, and against the laws of genetics, cats of similar colouring are found in high numbers on the northern and western coasts of Scotland, in rural Iceland and on the Faroe Islands. Todd argues that 1000 years after they were introduced to these outposts of European civilization, these cats may still, because of their genetic isolation, reflect the aesthetic preferences of the Vikings who took them there – or the preferences of the Vikings' Black Sea contacts.

Our influence on coat colour can be expected, but have we also unconsciously influenced the cat's mind? Todd thinks we have and his argument is this.

Unlike most other domestic species, the cat is 'self-domesticated' – the result of a natural evolutionary transition to exploit the new ecological situation created when humans settled in communities. The most obvious difference between wild and domestic cats today is the uniformity of coat colour of the former and the dramatic variety of coat colour of the latter. Todd believes there are two reasons for this difference: self-selection and the fact that we artificially enhanced the initial self-selection.

In the transition from wild to domestic, one of the most obvious changes is the increase in the density of cat populations. Wild cats have a population density of perhaps five per square mile (2.5 square km) while that of urban cats might be up to 1000 per square mile. To survive in the urban human environment cats had to evolve to a state where they would put up with such crowding. This means that, as domestication occurred, territorial imperatives were modified or suppressed or displaced. At the same time active hostility towards other cats was suppressed and replaced by tolerance or indifference.

This reduction of aggression and hostility was also extended to humans and to their livestock, for in order to be accepted in a human community cats could not attack the humans' poultry or the young of other domesticated species. A dramatic demonstration of this change can still be observed today on islands of the Great Barrier Reef in Australia where feral cats live commensally with chickens without attacking them many generations after either species was kept in a domestic context.

As I have mentioned, behaviours such as fear and aggression can be selectively bred for or against, and it seems that in their domestication cats naturally bred against these behaviours in order to enhance their position in their new ecological niche. This natural selection for reduced fear and aggression also selected for a greater variety of coat colours.

In many species of animals there is a relationship between coat colour and reduced fear and aggression.

In foxes there is a correlation between three mutant coat colours and reduced fear and aggression. These three mutant colours are non-agouti, blue and chocolate. (Agouti hairs have the pigment melanin distributed in the hair shaft in such a way that there is a reduced band of pigmentation just below the tip of the hair. This creates a 'salt-and-pepper' or brindle effect. Non-agouti hair has more or less uniform pigment along its length.) When fox breeders selected for these colours, they found they unwittingly also selected for reduced fear and aggression. The reason is that there is a linkage between these coat colours and body hormone function. When the colour is selected for, a change in hormone production is also selected for. (See Chapter Two for more details.) These three colours occur in cats too, and together with the colours blotched tabby and sex-linked orange – tortoiseshell, calico and marmalade – are also probably associated with altered body-hormone activity and reduced fear and aggression. (From a British focus, the blotched tabby colour has spread throughout the world and is so successful that, with time, it will possibly engulf all available feral cat populations.)

It seems reasonable to assume that the cats which were best at adapting to exploit their new environment were those that inhibited their fear of and aggression towards other cats and towards other species. This was the primary natural selection pressure and along with it came an increase in mutant coat colour. Tolerance and tameness exaggerated the rainbow of colours of the cat's coat.

This first genetic shift was natural but what followed was more directly under our control. In choosing appropriate shipmates, sailors would choose cats that were most tolerant of living in close quarters with humans. And it was sailors who spread cats around the world. The Greeks and Phoenicians began their movement, after which cats were spread step by step across Europe and then on to the Americas and to Australasia. At each stage of this man-made migration there would be a selective pressure for transporting the most amenable and tame.

Because the non-agouti-coat mutant is known to show reduced fear and aggression, Neil Todd calculated the distribution of this colour throughout Europe to see if his hypothesis was true, and in doing so he created a map strikingly similar to that of the ancient trade routes. He found high concentrations of non-agouti-coat cats throughout the areas of the western Mediterranean to the Straits of Gibraltar and from Rabat in Morocco round to the Atlantic coast of North Africa. These areas, the Balearics, Alicante, Algeciras, Tangier and even Rabat, were all once dominated by the maritime Phoenicians. As he got farther away from where the Phoenicians traded, the incidence of non-agouti colour dropped, except in one area, the trade routes of the Rhône and Seine Rivers through Europe. Here the incidence of non-agouti colour increased. Todd argues that at each stop on trade routes, human selection pressure favoured the tamest cats. Finally, in Britain, the end of the old trade routes, he found the highest concentrations of non-agouti-coloured cats.

The most tolerant and playful cats were most likely to become sailors' shipmates.

Cats have been successful at populating the corners of the world because they have the genetic ability to modify their behaviour to suit the environment. Domestic cats are more manageable, more docile and more fertile than their wild cousins. They are easier to handle and have a reduced fight-or-flight response. We have unwittingly given a helping hand to the creation of the mind of the domestic cat, although in doing so we have also unintentionally brought about some of the feline behaviour problems that occur today. Modern pet owners want playful cats, active, sociable creatures. But in order to create a playful and sociable adult cat we must perpetuate juvenile behaviours, for both play and sociability are greater in the young than in the mature cat. Genetic manipulation of the cat's mind is only just beginning. The potential is there for us to create as much variety, but also as many problems, as we have with our manipulation of the dog's mind.

Chapter Two

The Brain, Hormones and Biofeedback

Cats are among the most versatile of all mammals. They learn quickly, are highly adaptive, have purpose, are self-programmed and recall almost instantly. They are successful as a species because they have been superbly designed, but design of course is not everything. A Ferrari might be brilliantly designed, but if you give it an 1100cc Lada engine the design is rendered useless. The cat's brain is equipped to meet the needs of a streamlined body. Gram for gram it is immensely powerful, and when the weight of the brain is compared to the weight of the body it controls, cats have larger brains than all mammals other than primates and Cetacea such as dolphins.

The brain is the command centre for all body functions. It is the site of memory and intelligence, the repository of 'instinct' or what is now preferably called 'energy' or 'drive'. It receives sensory messages through touch, sight, smell, taste and hearing, decides on the actions to be taken and then controls the responses. The brain is the site of consciousness and consciousness is what attaches the cat to the outside world. Consciousness is biologically advantageous because through it the animal is able to control and manage its social behaviour. It is this facility that has allowed the cat to charm its way into our lives.

The brain is a furnace of activity and needs vast amounts of energy to keep it functioning. A cat that weighs $8\frac{1}{2}$ lb (4 kg) has a brain that weighs around 1 oz (30 g), yet it is so greedy for energy that over 20 per cent of the blood the heart pumps out goes directly to it.

It used to be thought that the brain was the repository for two different types of knowledge. One was called 'instinct' and this was pre-wired into the brain. This 'fixed wiring' was thought to be genetic in origin and meant that the cat always responded to certain circumstances in a fixed and mechanical way. The other type of knowledge was 'learned'. A cat would acquire skills or knowledge, would learn and remember.

Today behaviourists know that it is really impossible to differentiate between these two types of knowledge. A kitten has an 'instinct' or 'drive' to hunt and will pounce and leap and swipe frenetically, but might become an efficient hunter only if its mother shows it how to hunt. A kitten has an 'instinct' or 'drive' to bury its faeces and will scrabble about in a litter tray, but will only bury its faeces successfully if it sees its mother doing so. Learning and 'instinct' are not two separate areas of the brain but are intimately related.

In order for the cat to have a consciousness it must have the ability to store and retrieve information from a vast library or memory of every sensation it experiences, every emotion it feels, every idea it has – and cats certainly have ideas. All are processed in its brain.

The cat's brain is made up of billions of cells, each of which has thousands of connections, or synapses, with other cells. There is really no beginning and no end. There are probably over 100 trillion inter-connections between brain cells. The old idea that different parts of the brain are solely responsible for different activities is now known to be inaccurate. The same memory can be stored in a number of different locations, which is why there can be massive injuries to one area of the brain yet there are not the losses that one would expect. Certain areas are, however, primarily responsible for certain functions.

At birth the cat's brain is not yet completely developed and it still has an overwhelming ability to repair itself. If the visual cortex, the part of the brain that is responsible for registering sight, is surgically removed from an adult cat, as has been done experimentally, that cat will be blind. But if the same area is removed from a new-born kitten, it will still be able to see when it grows up. The reason is that just before and after birth there are far more cells in the brain than there will be in the finished product but they are not as yet organized. They also have more widespread connections. The genetic programme that is responsible for creating the brain plays safe and provides extra building blocks. This programme creates exploratory networks that are finally sculpted into the brilliant synthesizer that the brain becomes. But the creation of the smoothly functioning brain does not rest on genetic inheritance alone. It also relies on experience. If a new-born kitten is kept in total darkness, again as has been done experimentally, when the kitten is mature and exposed to light it will not be able to see. It hasn't received the necessary sensory stimulation to create the integrated networks of synapses that are responsible for vision.

The number of brain cells that a cat uses at any one time will vary dramatically and virtually all information is routed either into short-term or long-term memory. Some new evidence from the University of Illinois suggest that memories are not simply passively stored in the brain but rather develop as part of an active response which produces measurable physical changes in the brain. This could be why some learned behaviours such as using a cat flap are never forgotten even though a cat might only use a flap as a kitten and then, because of house changes, not have the opportunity to use one again for years.

The cat's brain has the ability to discretely categorize all the information it receives; to ignore what it isn't interested in and to retain the rest. If the information is new, it is routed into the short-term memory system. This is rather like a computer screen. There is a limit to the amount of information that can be kept there and to the length of time it can be kept. If it is important information, it can then be routed into long-term memory, but it usually has to be worked on. A reward is a potent way of converting a short-term memory into a long-term memory. For my cat, Millie, a taste of smoked salmon and bagels, initially a new memory, was converted and incorporated rapidly into her long-term memory system by the reward of the taste. That taste is now tucked away in her brain in her general body of knowledge.

Not all bits of long-term memory are of equal value, however. There are factors that influence the absorption of new memories and other factors that influence their retrieval. Using Hans Eysenck's definitions, extravert people, impulsive outgoing individuals, have more difficulty building up libraries of long-term memories than do others. Studies certainly show that extraverts tend to confuse left and right more frequently than do others, forget appointments more frequently, are more often late and try to do too many things at once. Does that sound like a Somali cat to you? Concentration is certainly necessary for the creation of long-term memory and must be one of the reasons why some cats are so much better at learning than are others. Anxiety will also affect the ability to learn and store memories, as will old age.

The actual way that information is passed through the vast networks of inter-connected brain cells is now reasonably well understood, although the shape and form of the networks themselves is still unknown. Chemicals, mostly amino acids, act as transmitter substances and either 'light up' or 'turn off' networks of brain cells. Over thirty different neuro-transmitter substances exist in the cat's brain and they are all either excitatory (E) or inhibitory (I). They excite or inhibit nerve cells within webs or networks of cells. Stimulate some and the brain lights up, as it were, like a Christmas tree. Stimulate others and the lights go out. Among the most fascinating of the recently discovered neuro-transmitter substances are the encephalins or endorphins, the body's own opiates. These are manufactured in the cat's brain and, among other functions, regulate the cat's conscious perception of pain. Cats have either more powerful or more efficient endorphin systems than us or dogs, which is why a cat can suffer serious injuries such as bone fractures after a fall or a car accident but will run off and hide rather than scream in agony. A perverse consequence of the cat's highly efficient brain endorphin system is that practising veterinarians such as myself consistently see cats that are in more advanced stages of injury or illness, not because the owners are lax but simply because a cat does not give the outward signals of distress or discomfort that a dog will.

As all learning is ultimately stored in the brain there can be problems with both the filing system itself and with searching out and retrieving the right information. Some learning is robust and enduring. Other learning is fragile and fleeting. Learning can get lost in many ways and ageing is one of them. At one time it was thought that memory deteriorated in the elderly because of a lack of storage space in the brain, but that has proved not to be true. The brain has an almost infinite capacity to store information. It now seems likely that information retrieval becomes impaired. It certainly slows down with age.

The speed of transmission of information from brain cell to brain cell and throughout the cat's nervous system depends upon whether the nerves have developed a fatty substance called myelin to protect them. The kitten's brain and nervous system is virtually unmyelinated at birth but that changes very quickly. An unmyelinated nerve transmits impulses at around 4.5 miles per hour (2 m per second), which is why the kitten's response to its environment is so slow. At birth the kitten's brain is sufficiently developed to control only the heartbeat, breathing, balance and equilibrium. The new-born kitten has no temperature control but its facial nerve is mature and it uses its head as a probe, avoiding cold, hard surfaces and liking soft, warm ones, such as its mother. It already has a sense of smell, however, and once it finds a teat and sucks, it recognizes that teat and will always try to go back to the same one for further feeding. By two to three weeks of age the kitten's brain is sufficiently developed to control its body temperature and metabolism. It can, for example, urinate and defecate without the need for its mother to stimulate these activities by licking the anogenital region. By four weeks it has a conscious perception of space and of its body being touched, and by five weeks it can control when it falls asleep and when it is awake. All of these functions are possible because its brain is maturing, the networks of cells are forming and the nerves themselves are myelinating. Compared to the transmission speed of 4.5 miles per hour (2 m per second) of an unmyelinated nerve, a large myelinated nerve fibre transmits impulses at 270 miles per hour (120 m per second). But then, with age, the nerves start to demyelinate – under the microscope the myelin looks moth-eaten. As demyelination occurs, nerve transmission slows down. That's why it takes old cats longer to respond to sensory stimulation.

The developing ability to control sleep is an example of how neurotransmitter substances affect the cat's mind. Cats sleep away almost two thirds of their lives, spending almost twice as much time asleep as most other mammals, and the amount of time they sleep will vary with how hungry they are, the weather, how old they are or whether there is a chance for any sexual activity. Warmth, security and a full stomach, the hallmarks of most house cats, will provoke sleep at almost any time.

Cats sleep almost two-thirds of their lives, more than any other domestic species.

In the brain there is a sleep centre, urged into action by inhibitory (I) neuro-transmitters and a waking centre. In fact there are really two sleep centres, one present in the hindbrain from birth, which is responsible for deep sleep, and one that develops at four to five weeks of age in the forebrain, which is responsible for light sleep.

Sleep is a curious activity. It seems to be an active rather than a passive process, and because cats are such superstars when it comes to sleep, much research into this behaviour has been carried out on them. During sleep the brain seems to increase its activity in certain areas. This increased activity produces tiny electrical impulses that provide a simple and reliable method for monitoring sleep. The electrical activity is recorded on an electroencephalograph (EEG).

The EEG of the awake cat has no regular pattern but rather is influenced by the state of arousal of the animal. If it sees or hears or even thinks something, there is increased electrical activity which can be measured on the EEG. But as the cat becomes drowsy and falls into a light sleep, the wave pattern on the EEG changes to one of slow, irregular, high-amplitude waves. After around thirty minutes of light sleep, the EEG pattern changes, as very often does the position of the cat itself. This is the period of deep or active sleep. During this period my cat Millie 'chases rabbits'. Under her closed or partially closed eyelids her eyes flick about rapidly, which is why this deep sleep is often called rapid eye movement (REM) sleep. Her body becomes flaccid but she flexes her paws and twitches her whiskers, ears and tail. Sometimes she mutters in 'cat mutter'.

The EEG pattern for REM sleep suggests that the brain is as active as it is when a cat is awake and the reasonable conclusion is that cats dream just as we do in this kind of sleep. After six or seven minutes of this deep sleep a cat returns to a twenty- to thirty-minute period of slow-wave sleep and these cycles continue until the cat wakes up. Healthy adult cats spend around 15 per cent of their lives in deep sleep, 50 per cent of their lives in slow-wave or light sleep and only 35 per cent of their lives awake.

The actual anatomy of the cat's brain is like that of most other mammals. It consists of a series of swellings around a hollow tube that runs from the head through the backbone to the tail. The tube itself is fluid-filled and the entire organ is surrounded by further fluid, then a tough membrane and the skull. The front of the brain (the cerebrum) is involved with conscious behaviour, the senses and body movement. Long-term memory is also stored here. The next swelling, smaller than the cerebrum, is the cerebellum. This part of the cat's brain is exceptionally large and well developed, which seems logical as it is responsible for co-ordinating balance and movement. A common virus infection in cats, panleucopenia virus, damages this part of the brain in foetuses if a pregnant female contracts the disease during the first few weeks of pregnancy. The consequence is that the new-born kitten has no balance; it can't right itself or orient to its mother. But because the new-born's brain still has enormous re-cuperative powers, if a kitten without a cerebellum is helped to feed and helped to orient itself correctly it can still grow up to have control over its body, although not the superb control of a cat with a normal cerebellum.

The underlying core of the brain is called the brainstem and it is here that the reticular formation, responsible for consciousness, and the sleep and wake centres are located. The hypothalamus and limbic systems are also situated here, with their responsibilities for the feelings of hunger, fear, aggression, pleasure or sexual and maternal activity.

And, once more, it isn't anthropomorphic to state that cats experience emotions as we do. In fact it's absolutely logical to believe that they do, because there is virtually no difference between their brainstems and limbic systems and ours. Over the years researchers have inserted electrodes into certain areas of cats' brainstems and so have turned docile animals into ferocious demons wanting to attack anything that comes near their cage. They have stimulated other areas, provoking the pleasure centre, and have implanted tiny pellets of hormone to bring castrated cats back to full sexual vigour. The experiments have been unpleasant, at times thoughtless and at other times unwarranted and cruel, but it would be foolish to disregard the results.

Finally, attached to the hypothalamus is the pituitary gland, the master gland of the body's hormonal system. The brain sends signals through the hypothalamus to the pituitary, which in turn transmits signals to the various glands throughout the body. These in turn send signals back to the pituitary which transmits hormonal information back to the brain. This fascinating system is called biofeedback.

Through biofeedback, hormones have a profound influence on the cat's behaviour, but equally the cat's behaviour has a profound influence on the production of hormones. Take male sex hormone (testosterone), for example. This plays an active role in aggression. Cats with higher levels of testosterone are likely to be more aggressive. But tomcats aren't born with the genetic potential to produce lots of testosterone. Rather than its being genetic, the 'reward' of producing an abundance of testosterone is earned through the behaviour of the cat from the time he is a kitten. Did he bag the best teat? Was he the best learner? Most important, has he coped well with life? The cat that deals with stress most effectively is the cat that is entitled to increase his testosterone level. And coping with stress involves an efficient biofeedback mechanism between the brain, the pituitary gland and the adrenal glands.

Kittens that are exposed to sensory stimulation when they are young, kittens that use their balance, hearing, sight, taste and smell, grow up to be bigger cats with bigger brains that have more connections between the cells than kittens which are denied these sensory stimuli. The brain receives this sensory information in the cerebrum and passes it on into the hypothalamus, which in turn produces substances such as corticotrophin-releasing hormone (CRH), which are transported to the pituitary gland. The pituitary then produces stimulating hormones that direct the glands around the body (the adrenal gland, the thyroid gland and the testicles or ovaries) to produce their hormones. Stress or coping with difficult situations involves an efficient biofeedback between the brain and the adrenal gland.

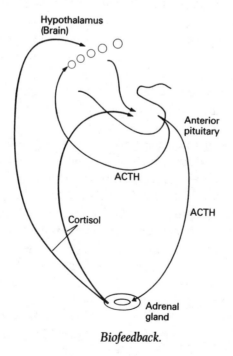

Biofeedback.

The two adrenal glands are located near the kidneys and one of their functions is to produce corticosteroids. The adrenal is instructed to release corticosteroid by the pituitary gland which sends a releasing hormone called adrenocorticotrophic hormone (ACTH). When a cat is anxious or excited, the pituitary releases and sends out ACTH. ACTH stimulates the adrenal gland to release corticosteroids which in turn reduce the cat's excitability. The released corticosteroids circulate back to the pituitary gland and dampen down ACTH production. This is biofeedback. It has a dramatic effect on the cat's mind, but the question still remains as to how early experience influences this system.

The greatest likelihood is that if this system is frequently and gently stimulated when the cat is young, and that means before myelinization is even complete, the feedback system will actually affect how the brain develops. The consequence is that ACTH production is finely tuned to corticosteroid stimulation.

Other pituitary hormones are also stimulated by the outside world. The cry of the new-born kitten is heard by the mother and stimulates her cerebrum, which sends messages to the hypothalamus which in turn sends signals to the pituitary gland to release the hormone oxytocin. The hormone then flows via her blood stream to her mammary glands and allows her to release milk. Growth hormone is also produced in the pituitary and is released only when the kitten is asleep. This is perhaps one of the reasons why kittens need to sleep so much more than adult cats.

As well as stimulating the adrenal gland into action, the pituitary also stimulates the thyroid gland in the neck to release its hormones. Over-activity of the thyroid gland has a considerable effect on the behaviour of the cat and as a clinical entity it is being diagnosed increasing frequently. Cats with over-active thyroids are usually elderly and owners first notice a weight loss but voracious appetite. The hyperthyroid cat's heart rate is much faster than normal and it behaves in a jerky, 'can't-settle-down' manner. The total effect of thyroid and adrenal gland hormones on the cat's mind is very poorly understood but research in foxes suggests it might be quite significant.

Researchers in the 1970s discovered that those foxes with the three mutant coat colours – non-agouti, blue and chocolate – exhibited less fear and aggression than foxes with dominant coat colours. When 'startle tests' were used, mutant-coloured foxes startled less readily and took flight over shorter distances. But the researchers discovered even more. There were apparent changes in pituitary, thyroid and adrenal gland functions. Foxes with mutant coat colours had smaller pituitary glands, relative to their body weight, than did foxes with dominant colours. There was less thyroid hormone in their circulation; not so little as to cause clinical hypothyroidism (illness resulting from insufficient thyroid hormone production), but rather less than in foxes with dominant coat colours. And finally their adrenal glands were also smaller on an adrenal:body weight ratio than those of dominant-coloured foxes, and there was a reduction in the production of the precursor substance that is necessary to produce the adrenal hormones adrenalin and melanin.

These findings complement Neil Todd's hypothesis that there was a natural selection for mutant coat colours in cats that allowed them to cope better in their new, more sociable ecological niche, living in close proximity to other cats, other animals and to us. There is an apparent linkage between hormone production and coat colour.

The pituitary gland is also responsible for producing the hormones that stimulate the ovaries and testicles into activity. Although wild cats breed only once in the spring, domestic cats are more fertile but are still 'seasonally polyoestrous'. They are more likely to come into season during the spring, as daylight increases. The reason is simple. Sensory stimulation from increasing daylight provokes neuroendocrine changes in the cerebrum. The activated cerebrum lights up networks in the hypothalamus and these in turn stimulate the pituitary to produce follicle-stimulating hormone (FSH). This hormone enters the bloodstream, reaches the ovaries and stimulates the onset of oestrus. (This is discussed in more detail in Chapter Seven.)

In a similar fashion the scent of a cat in oestrus or the sound of her calling enters the nostrils or the ears of the local tom. This ignites the same 'Christmas tree' of networks in the brain. The hypothalamus secretes releasing factors that stimulate the pituitary to increase its production of leutenizing hormone (LH) and this in turn stimulates the testicles to produce more testosterone. The tom is now ready to fight for the queen and to mate successfully (also discussed more fully in Chapter Seven).

On the question of exactly what a cat can learn to do, the brain structures that are of most interest are the networks of cells called the limbic structures and the activation and motivation systems or networks of the hypothalamus. All of these must function smoothly for learning to occur. It was once thought that the cerebrum and, more specifically, the cerebral cortex were responsible for the highest level of learning, but it now seems that this part of the brain has the more limited function of information storage, although of course it is also responsible for sensory discrimination.

If we look at the brain's influence on the mind in a less anatomical way, it is possible broadly to describe its function in a simple form. The highest level of brain activity could be called the executive level. This is where the basic decisions are made; for example, *'Catch that mouse!'* The executive level of the cat's brain is responsible for goal-oriented activity. Beneath the executive level is the supervisory level which is responsible for continually evaluating how things are going. The supervisory level is constantly being bombarded with sensory and hormonal information and must separate the important from the unimportant. In doing so, the supervisory level makes sure that the brain is sensitive only to factors that are important in achieving the goal – catching the mouse. The supervisory level determines overall priorities and makes sure that other sensory input is disregarded. How all of this gives rise to consciousness in humans or cats is still a mystery.

The information that we have on how the brain functions can, however, help us to create pet cats whose minds work to the best of their abilities. The answer is to give them mental stimulation when they are young and to continue to stimulate them mentally throughout their lives. The supercats of this world are born to conscientious, intelligent, resourceful mothers. They are well nourished as kittens and handled frequently by humans who play with them regularly. They are provided with interesting and ever-changing environments and are allowed to continue to use their senses, their bodies and their minds throughout life.

Medical researchers in Japan studying the human brain carried out an interesting survey. Their findings can probably be applied to cats' brains too. Doctors took brain scans of all the executives over fifty-five years old in a large electronics firm in Tokyo. They were divided into two groups, A and B, of equal education, age, intelligence, social class, level of seniority and responsibility in the company. There was one key difference. The executives in Group A were required, by the nature of their jobs, to interact with other people significantly more often than those in Group B. The results of the brain scans showed that Group A's brains were in significantly better shape, showing less age-related atrophy than their exact peers in Group B.

One of the fascinating aspects of the mind is that learning, memory and memory retention increase when the emotion of interest is aroused. Supercats are those that find life interesting. Understimulated cats have smaller brains than those that lead more active lives. If we are to keep them as house pets, we owe it to them to make their lives as interesting and as fulfilling as possible. If we do, we satisfy both the cats' need for mental stimulation and our enjoyment of seeing them behave to the maximum of their potential.

Chapter Three

The Senses

It can be difficult to imagine the sensory world of another animal. We have to go by our own sensory capacities: how *we* see, hear, taste, smell and feel. Cats can't see red, but what do they see instead? Cats can hear the high-pitched sounds of the mouse's squeak: what do these noises sound like to them? Cat's can't taste sweet, so what do they taste when they eat sugar? Cats don't feel a burning sensation with temperatures that are painful to us, but what do they feel?

Even more difficult to describe are their sensory capacities for which there are no equals in humans. Do cats actually 'see' with their whiskers? Do they really have a homing sense, an ability to know in which direction to travel to find their way home? The cat's senses are an integral part of its mind, for it is sensory information that stimulates the brain into action and affects both central and peripheral hormone production. The sound of prey, the sight of the scratching post of a competitor, the scent of another cat in oestrus or the scent of danger – all these dramatically affect every aspect of the cat's mind.

TOUCH

The sensation of touch has developed by the time of birth and is really an amalgam of several sensations: pressure (both light and heavy), warmth, cold and pain. Some biologists divide this sensation into even further divisions, but the basic function of touch is to make the cat fully aware of its surroundings. Touch can be comforting and it can also be painful.

When a two-day-old kitten is separated from its mother it will cry and swing its head from side to side until it finds her. Once it has made contact, it stops crying. It finds her because of the warmth she emits. Kittens have a highly developed temperature perception at birth and this continues to develop as they mature. Adult cats are aware of temperature differences as small as 0.9°F (0.5°C) using the heat receptors on their nose leather. It is those heat receptors that tell the kitten in which direction it should crawl to find the security of contact with its mother.

All over the skin there are both warmth and cold receptors, which is why adult cats will seek out the shaft of sunlight to sleep in and will curl up when it is cold. But except for the face, the rest of the cat's body – and that includes the paws – is relatively insensitive to both low and high temperatures. What is painful to us is certainly not to cats. They will stand with their forepaws in hot frying-pans in order to eat the contents of your dinner. They will lie so close to fires that they singe their fur. And at the opposite extreme, they will walk on ice and sleep on snow with no apparent frostbite to their paws or skin. Pet owners often bring in their frying-pan thieves or their burnt-coated heat hogs for me to examine and it constantly amazes me that such injuries can happen without the cat apparently either noticing or caring. It amazes me because it's so difficult to understand that they have different touch sensations. We feel discomfort when our skin temperature reaches 112°F (44°C). Cats don't show signs of discomfort until their skin temperature reaches a dramatically high 126°F (52°C). This relative insensitivity to pain is possibly a consequence of the lack of heat receptors on the body, but also a result of the cat's superior pain-killing endorphin system.

The cat's nose also plays a part in eating, for, as well as scenting,

The nose and paws contain sensitive touch and heat receptors.

it gauges the temperature of the food through the heat receptors that are located there. There are also touch and heat receptors on the tongue that assist the senses of smell and taste. The texture of food is just as important as its taste.

Of all the parts of the cat's body, the paws have the most sensitive and exquisite touch receptors. Using this tactile ability, cats will investigate the size, shape and texture of an object in much the same way as we do with our fingers. After a first gentle tap, a cat will then touch an object more firmly and will finally examine it with both forepaws and with the touch receptors on its nose.

Some investigators say that cats can also sense vibration through special paw receptors. There are certainly pressure-sensitive receptors called Pacinian corpuscles in both the skin and the fatty layer beneath the skin on the cat's paws, as there are on other parts of the body, but whether they can detect vibration is still not known.

Unlike pack-living dogs, cats have not evolved to exist in intimate contact with their own kind. A consequence of this is that contact comfort through such activities as mutual grooming is not as important. Contact comfort is, however, very important to kittens, and as we continue to neotenize cats (to breed them in such a way that they perpetuate juvenile behaviours) the contact-comfort behaviour of the very young occurs more frequently in the mature.

Mother cats groom their kittens by repeatedly licking them, a sensation picked up by the touch receptors that richly supply guard hairs all over the body. When we stroke our pet cats, we stimulate these touch receptors and recreate in our pets the pleasure of being licked as a kitten. Some cats positively beg for this attention, arching their bodies and stiffening their tails as they did when they were kittens. What they are asking us to do is what their mothers did for them. For the first few weeks of the kitten's life it has no sensation that its bladder and bowels need emptying. These functions are stimulated by the mother licking the anogenital region of the kitten. When our pet cats crave contact comfort from us and stiffen their tails, they are asking us to examine the same region.

Although touch receptors are scattered all over the cat's body, they are developed to the most sophisticated degree in the whiskers. Whiskers, or vibrissae, are specially adapted, thick, stiff hairs embedded in bundles of nerves that track back to the brain in the same channel as the nerves from the eyes. Vibrissae are especially well developed on the muzzle and over the eyes, and also occur on the elbows. They seem to have three functions. They protect: if you touch the whiskers over a cat's eyes, it will blink. They 'touch' and in doing so give their owner information – for example, of the size of a hole in a fence. But they are also sensitive to air currents and in that way help cats to 'see in the dark'.

Cats can't see in pitch dark. If a cat that has had its vibrissae removed is placed in a completely black environment, it can't find its way around. But if a mature cat with a good set of whiskers is placed in the same environment, it can negotiate obstacles and avoid them. A possible reason is that solid objects create slight eddies in the air. As an extreme illustration of this, imagine, for example, a new aero-dynamic car being tested in a wind tunnel. All objects cause some alteration in air currents and a cat's whiskers can read these differ-ences and use the information so gleaned either to navigate or to capture prey at night. Cats with perfect whiskers can kill prey by both day and night, but the same cats with damaged whiskers can kill prey only during daylight. At night they misjudge distances or bite the wrong parts of their prey and don't kill cleanly. Photographs of cats carrying mice in their mouths show that their whiskers are drawn forward to feel if their meal is still moving.

Touch affects cats in many ways. One cat licking or nibbling another is sexually stimulating. Tail, cheek and head rubbing are methods of communication with friendly objects or individuals (see Chapter Four for further discussion on this use of touch). And finally, many cats enjoy petting but on their own terms and on certain occasions.

Sometimes when you pet a cat it might suddenly turn and bite your hand. It seems a treacherous thing to do, but usually happens in specific circumstances. Touch is not as important a part of the social vocabulary of cats as it is of dogs. Dogs enjoy contact comfort and can carry it to extremes. Two of my nurses bring their dogs to work each day and one of these, a small boxer bitch, actually sleeps on top of the other, an Italian spinone. Cats, even social felines such as lions, don't often behave in this way. Lions will sleep close to each other, but it is unusual for them to make body contact.

Some cats appear to be in a state of conflict when they are stroked too long or in a rough way. Rough-and-tumbles are exhilarating for dogs but anathema to cats. The conflict is that stroking is pleasurable but also intimidating. The consequence is that the 'fight-or-flight' mechanism is activated. Touch stimulates the brain to stimulate the pituitary to stimulate the adrenal gland. You might notice that if your cat is purring while being stroked, the purr becomes louder.

The cat might flatten back its ears in a menacing way. It might mew and, finally, if it has not got a response from those behaviours or threats, it will bite. The bite itself is usually only a seizure of your hand – not a serious bite – but it is the cat's way of defusing the tension caused by too close and too prolonged touch. It is a classic proof of the fact that cats are not simply dogs in disguise.

SMELL AND TASTE

The kitten has a well-developed sense of smell at birth which, together with the sense of touch, enables it to find its mother and to select its own favourite nipple. The anatomical evidence that smell and taste senses are present from birth is that only the nerve fibres for these senses and for touch are myelinated by the time the kitten is born.

Both smell and taste are 'chemical' senses and it is difficult to examine one without considering the other. Cat-food manufacturers are naturally most interested in them and have carried out consider-able research into the preferences that cats have for certain types of food. (Food preferences are discussed in more detail in Chapter Eight.) Smell and taste are important senses to the cat and frequently domin-ate its mind. Any new object, person or cat, food or even water is smelled and tasted. Smell and taste are obviously vital for eating and drinking, but these senses are also important for sexual behaviour, for aggression and for territorial marking.

The organs of taste are, of course, located on the tongue. The cat's sandpaper-like tongue is covered with backward-facing hooks (papil-lae) that are used to groom its fur and to scrape meat off bones. These papillae have no role to play in taste but other mushroom-shaped papil-lae at the front and sides of the tongue carry tastebuds, as do the four or six cup-shaped papillae at the back of the mouth. In *The Dog's Mind* I mentioned that rather than tasting sweet, salt, bitter and acid as we do, it would be better to describe dogs' tasting as 'pleasant', 'indif-ferent' and 'unpleasant'. This is not so with cats, however. They seem to have more sophisticated tastebuds than do dogs and are certainly capable of tasting salt and bitter and probably acid. Cats are unusual in that they show virtually no significant response to sweet tastes.

This lack of response to sweet is logical in that cats are true carnivores. Dogs are primarily carnivorous but will eat almost any-thing, so it seems logical for them to have rather dull tastebuds. Humans, on the other hand, are true omnivores, so tastebuds for sweet are just as necessary as those for meat tastes.

From an anatomical description we know that cats don't taste sweet because there aren't any of the necessary conduction fibres for sweet in the glossopharyngeal nerve from the tongue to the cerebrum, but up in the brain there are a few units that actually do respond to sucrose. Together with the fact that cats can't taste sweet is the fact that sugars such as the lactose in milk sometimes cause diarrhoea, especially, it seems, in the Siamese breed. High levels of glucose from fruit or sucrose from sugar-cane can also have the same effect. It may be that cats have these few nerve cells which are sensitive to sugar to help them avoid the stuff. In experiments, cats that suffer from diarrhoea because of sugar in their diet have learned to avoid drinking dilute salt solutions which also contain sugar, although they would drink the same dilute salt solution without sugar.

Experiments and theory are, however, different from reality. I see chocoholic cats that will steal a chunk of Cadbury's in a flash. I've met a Ritz-cracker fiend who will mountain-climb open-plan shelves and slash his way into an unopened box of his favourite delicacy. I've cared for a raisin-obsessed cat who carefully separates the nuts that she doesn't eat from the raisins that she craves. Through metabolic selection it might be that sweet-toothed cats are becoming commoner.

In the wild, of course, cats eat only meat, and meat is high in fat and protein. Protein is made up of amino acids, chemical compounds which contain large amounts of sulphur and nitrogen. Compounds with these elements in them are favoured by the cat's tastebuds. The fat in meat is probably not tasted but rather is smelled.

Cats smell life as we do, with their noses, but they also use another scenting device, the vomeronasal organ (or Jacobson's organ), a $\frac{1}{2}$-in-(1–2-cm)-long cigar-shaped sensory apparatus that connects to the mouth through a small nasopalatine tube whose opening is just behind the upper front teeth. During primate evolution we lost the need for this organ and today only a non-functioning trace of it remains buried above our hard palates. The vomeronasal organ in the cat has a rich blood supply and is densely covered in cells that connect by nerves to the amygdala region in the hypothalamus, the brain centre associated with sexual and aggressive behaviour. Its function in association with sexual activity is discussed later in this chapter.

Smell is initially important in allowing the kitten to imprint with its mother, to select the teat it wants and to nurse successfully. If the ability of a kitten to smell is removed, as has been done experimentally, it is virtually unable to nurse. This is why 'cat flu' can be such a dangerous disease in very young kittens, possibly resulting in death. 'Flu' itself may not kill kittens, but through the congestion that develops in the nasal passages the infection interferes temporarily or even permanently with the young animal's ability to scent and so to find food. (Older cats, with body reserves of energy, are not at as great a risk and can be coaxed to eat by being fed foods with strong odours. Gentle heating releases more odours from foods and is often beneficial.)

It's no exaggeration to say that odours can be mind-bending to the cat. Just watch one when it comes across catnip (*Nepeta cataria*, also known as catmint). Smell memories last a lifetime, stored in the long-term memory banks of the brain. Smell depends upon a complicated chemical sensing system involving an equally complex arrangement of smell-detecting cells called olfactory cells. There are at least 200 million of these cells in the cat's nose and they are responsible for making the first response to an odour and then for transmitting that signal through the connecting and quite large olfactory bulbs of the brain.

Scents are always entering a cat's nose as it breathes, but when something interesting comes along it sniffs. The sniff is a dramatic disruption to regular breathing and usually occurs as a series of rapid inspirations. The most sensitive part of the cat's nose, the septal organ, is probably responsible for initiating sniffing behaviour.

The sniffed air passes into the nose and on to the cells (olfactory mucosa) that line the nasal bones. This is a relatively large area covering 3–6 square in (20–40 square cm), almost twice as large in size as that of an equal-sized rabbit and in fact twice as large as we have in our rather puny noses. When the cat breathes out, however, the sniffed air is not expelled but stays put. That's because, unlike us, cats have a structure in the nose called a subethmoid shelf. Air above this shelf, and the scent it carries, are not washed out when the cat breathes out. Regular-breathed air goes through the nasal passages and down to the lungs. Sniffed air, on the other hand, 'rests' in the nasal chambers.

The complex folds of bones in the cat's nose are designed to create airflow patterns that cause odours contained in the air to strike regions of smell receptors. The odour molecules get dissolved and concentrated in nasal mucus which sticks to the receptor cells. Fats produce free odour molecules, which is why cats taste protein but smell fat. One species' fat smells quite different from another's, and for this reason cats develop preferences for specific foods.

Once the odour-laden mucus has adhered to the fine, microscopic hairs on the receptor cells, the chemical smell signal gets converted to an electrical signal and is transferred to the cerebrum, the brain's repository for sensory perception. But the signal is also transferred to the limbic system in the brainstem, the part of the brain responsible for emotion.

A short time ago I met the scientist who designed the recipe for the best-selling rabbit-meat cat food. My experience in practice has been that when cats have been hospitalized, this brand of food, and specifically the rabbit-meat variety, has been dramatically preferred over all other tinned cat foods, including other manufacturers' rabbit-meat foods, and I asked him if he knew why. His explanation was curious. Other manufacturers used farmed rabbits, he said, but the meat for his recipe came from China where the source was wild rabbit. He felt that cats could taste the difference, and when I questioned him further he suggested that because the wild rabbits were chased before they were caught and killed, they tasted like 'the real thing', the type of meat that cats have evolved to eat.

As already mentioned, the vomeronasal organ has a role to play in feline sexual activity, a fact confirmed by recent research at the University of California. It works this way.

Cats indulge in a behaviour that was first described in German and is still known by the German term *flehmen*. There is no equivalent English word for the behaviour, although 'sneering' comes close. Some cat owners describe this behaviour in their cat as a look of profound stupidity, while others read into it utter disgust. What a cat is doing when it exhibits 'flehmen' (or is 'flehming') is simply pumping odour molecules up into its vomeronasal organ. It stretches out its neck, opens its mouth, wrinkles its nose a little and curls back its upper lip in a sort of snarl. By doing so and through curling its tongue, it captures the scent and transfers it, with the help of a recently discovered vasomotor pumping system, into this strange organ.

'Flehming' is primarily, although not totally, a male cat behaviour. Tomcats will 'flehm' when they investigate the genitals of female cats. They will also stop dead in their tracks when they catch what to them must be the delicious fragrance of the urine of a female in season or calling. The Californian research has taken our knowledge of 'flehming' behaviour one step further. It discovered that when male meets female or comes across female oestrus urine, he 'flehms' but she doesn't. However, when there are no other cats present, 64 per cent of females 'flehm' to urine marks. This is less than the 90 per cent of males that did so in the same test chamber, but is far higher than anticipated. And when a drop of urine was applied to the roof of the mouth, both males and females exhibited the behaviour in equal numbers. The conclusion that can be drawn is that both male and female cats have equal abilities to 'flehm' but that females are less interested in approaching or making contact with the stimulus that produces the behaviour. As a final twist the California researchers treated female cats with the male hormone testosterone and observed that under this influence they carried out genital inspections and 'flehmed' oestrus females as much as intact males did.

The role of the vomeronasal organ has also been called into question as a possible answer to the cat's dramatic reaction to catnip, but in fact it has no role to play. Desmond Morris says that the 50 per cent of cats that 'trip out' on catnip are 'junkies'; but the truth is probably a little more prosaic, although there is no doubt that the biochemical pathways activated by smelling catnip are the same as those activated in a human being when smelling marijuana.

All species of cats can react to catnip and to certain other plants such as valerian. The constituent of these plants that causes their strange behaviour is an unsaturated oil called nepatolactone. Kittens never react positively to the substance but 50 per cent of adult cats do, and it seems that there is a genetic predisposition for this to be so. Catnip grows as a weed in the temperate regions of both Europe and North America. You might first discover you have some in your garden when you find it trampled and chewed by your cat. What happens is that your cat first sniffs it, then licks or chews the plant. That's all some cats will do, but others will rub their bodies on it or roll on the ground nearby, rolling from side to side as the female does after mating. Many cats will dig and paw at the plant, but after between five and fifteen minutes they suddenly stop the behaviour and walk away. The eminent German behaviourist Paul Leyhausen notes that the way cats chew catnip with their incisors and premolars is reminiscent of the manner in which they bite into rodents they have killed. The respected American animal behaviourist Benjamin Hart states that the way a cat rubs its chin and the side of its face over catnip or along beside it is virtually identical to the pre- and post-mating behaviours of females. He also says that the manner in which cats bat balls of catnip is the same as that in which kittens play with fluttering leaves and suggests that all of these behaviours, rather than simply being a 'trip', are out of sequence but normal cat behaviours. Experiments that Hart carried out also proved that catnip is smelled by the normal scenting apparatus, not by the vomeronasal organ. Dogs rolling on fox droppings; cats rolling on catnip – no one has or will probably ever have a true answer as to why they do these things, but before I go on to discuss further senses there is one final tasting and scenting ability the cat possesses that dogs don't, although people possibly do. This is its ability to taste water.

Only certain cats react strangely to catnip.

Cats have a remarkable sensitivity to the taste of water. Some people – my wife and youngest daughter among them – also seem to possess this sensitivity, noting differences between the taste of Evian water, Labrador glacial water, Scottish Highland water and so on. Cats have genuine water-taste receptors and it is the presence of these that probably dominate the very few sweet-taste receptors they have. If, for example, the water taste of a liquid is suppressed by adding small amounts of salt, cats will consume sugary drinks. Smell and taste are important senses for eating but also for courtship, scent marking, hunting and even for toilet habits. Smell is not the dominant sense in cats as it is in dogs, but the sensitivity of it is still so grand that we can only imagine its power.

HEARING

To succeed as a hunter the cat developed super-sensitive senses. Just as it is blessed with a superb ability to scent prey, so too does it possess sharp hearing – hearing that has evolved to help it hear the faintest squeaks and rustlings of the rodents it hunts.

Cats hear high-frequency sounds inaudible to the human ear.

Hearing in cats has been studied more than in perhaps any other animal. Almost forty years ago it was already known that cats could hear sounds two octaves higher than we can. Sound consists of vibrations and these reach the ears as pressure waves of air; it is measured according to the number of vibrations or cycles per second. The higher the number, the higher the pitch, although pitch also depends on the size or amplitude of the sound.

Once these vibrations reach the cat's ear, they trigger nerve cells in the hearing apparatus, the cochlea, which send messages to the brain where the sounds are analysed. Human beings hear sounds vibrating up to 20,000 cycles per second (cps); dogs hear sounds up to 40,000 cps; cats hear sounds vibrating at up to at least 55,000 cps and perhaps even up to 65,000 cps. To be technically accurate, cats have the theoretical ability to hear sounds at up to 100,000 cps, sounds that only bats – among other terrestrial mammals – can hear, but in practical terms 55,000–65,000 cps is the realistic upper limit.

To help gather sound the cat's ears are equipped with a dozen special muscles to assist them in rotating through 180° and to cock the ears towards the source of the sound. Each ear catches the tiniest of vibrations and funnels them down the ear canal to the ear drum. In turn the ear drum's vibrations are transmitted through three tiny bones (the hammer, the anvil and the stirrup) which strengthen the vibrations and pass them on to the cochlea and then into the brain for analysis. (A special arrangement of tiny muscles attached to these bones can dampen down vibrations caused by loud noises and help to prevent ear damage.)

Within their range of sound sensitivity cats can discriminate one tenth of a tone. They can discriminate with 75 per cent accuracy between two sounds coming from sources that are only 5° apart – that's 3 in (8 cm) apart at a distance of 1 yd (1 m). They can do this because their brains can calculate that sounds are arriving at slightly different times or with slightly different intensities at each ear. The brain doesn't actually measure the delay but rather simply detects the difference between the two nerve signals it receives. Turning the ears in different directions helps the cat to pick up the faintest of sounds.

The fact that cats can hear over ten octaves and can distinguish between two notes differing by only one tenth of a tone could be the reason why so many writers describe, as does the American author Patricia Noyes, the 'ecstasy of purring' that certain cats emit as they settle into a lap and apparently listen to music. Their exquisite hearing ability also enables cats to tell the sound of one car from another. When I was at university, my silver tabby apartment cat knew the sound of both of my room mates' car engines and on hearing their cars pulling into the parking lot would jump up and go to the door to greet one or the other.

Just as in the case of human beings, cats' ability to hear high notes diminishes with age, although they might be able to compensate by becoming extra sensitive to touch vibrations felt through their feet. Cats readily and easily learn to recognize certain sounds – a knock on the door, the squeak of a fridge opening, the sound of a can opener and, of course, even the names we give them. It's a sort of language. Language recognition can apply in both directions. The story is told that the French writer Colette, never happy in the United

States and able to speak only a little English, was on her way back to her New York hotel one evening, after a typically brash New York party, when she spotted a small black cat sitting on a wall. She spoke to it and it responded. *'Enfin!'* she exclaimed. *'Quelqu'un qui parle français.'*

VISION

Mice and rats don't come in a multitude of colours, each tasting different. And so their predator, the cat, has little need for colour vision. Besides, cats are diurnal animals; they hunt mostly at dawn and dusk, although they are also quite active at night. That's another reason why colour vision isn't important. Twilight and night vision, on the other hand, and a facility to see very slight movement a short, sharp gallop or pounce away, are both advantages for the stealthy hunter, and the domestic cat certainly has these.

Just as with the other senses necessary for good hunting, cats have a highly specialized sense of sight, one that allows them to concentrate and focus on their potential prey while leaving the rest of their visual field in a blur. Their eyes are set well forward on their head, giving them excellent binocular vision; much better than dogs', though not as good as ours. Cats' eyes are dramatically large for the size of their heads, one of the reasons we are so avidly attracted to these animals. Can you imagine what we would think of cats if they had little rat's eyes? The surface of the eye, the cornea, is highly

Cats dramatically constrict or dilate their pupils depending upon light available but also upon their state of mind.

curved and bulges out rather dramatically. This gives a wider angle of view and also allows much more light to get in; about five times as much as gets into our eyes. Inside is a very large lens but the muscles that control it are rather weak and insignificant. The consequence of this anatomical arrangement is that cats are not able to focus well on nearby objects. In fact 30 in (75 cm) is about the closest they can focus and they see best in a range from 6 to 20 ft (2 to 6 m). In dim light the pupil can open its diameter far more than we can open ours – as much as $\frac{1}{2}$ in (1 cm) to allow in the maximum amount of light. This is also one of the most accurate demonstrations of what is going on in a cat's mind. When those pupils are 'wild-eyed' and totally dilated during daylight, you can be sure that something exciting is going to happen.

Light penetrates through the cornea and lens and lands on the retina, the 'film' at the back of the eye where the receptor cells (called rods and cones) are stimulated to send electrical signals to the cerebrum. Just as in our eyes, rods are sensitive to dim light and cones to bright light. But while we have four rods to each cone, cats have twenty-five rods to each cone. When rods are stimulated they have the ability to reinforce each other, and in doing so lots of them trigger a signal in one fibre going to the brain. The consequence is that cats' vision in dim light is quite fuzzy. They can't see fine detail. In daylight, however, the cones are stimulated and each one is connected to a single nerve fibre going to the brain. The result is that daylight vision is much more acute and sharp. The greatest concentration of cones is in the macula in the centre of the field of vision, which is what helps cats to see their prey as clearly as possible, although they probably still don't see as much detail as we do.

The large, curved cornea and the multitude of rods fifteen layers deep allow cats to see so well at night, but one other feature of the eye is responsible for their being able to see in one sixth the amount of light that we need and that is the reflective layer behind the rods and cones, called the tapetum lucidum. This is a mirror-like structure, an image-intensifying apparatus that reflects light back on to the rods in the retina. Cats can't see in pitch dark, but as a consequence of these factors they can make out movements and objects in semi-darkness that are quite invisible to us. This, of course, is the ability that the United States Army tried to harness to help them win the Vietnam War, as I mentioned in the Introduction to this book.

Cats are particularly responsive to movement and scientists have found specific nerve cells in the cat's brain that respond to movement.

Their superb binocular vision (when they are looking straight ahead, there is an binocular overlap of about 98°) enables them to pinpoint the exact position of their prey and to pounce accurately. It works this way.

Something that is seen in the left field of vision enters the left eye, and triggers the optic nerve to send signals to the brain. In species with binocular vision, however, some of these nerves cross over and stimulate the right side of the brain. Fifty per cent of human optic nerves are uncrossed while only 33 per cent of the cat's are un-crossed. The result is that each side of the brain receives *two* sets of signals, one from each eye. The signals differ slightly because of their slightly differing viewpoints. The cat's brain compares these two images and as a result is able to perceive the distance and depth of the object – to see it in three dimensions. (This might be more difficult for Siamese cats to do as they apparently have fewer cross-over fibres in their optic nerves. If this is so, it would mean that the Siamese brain might 'see' two slightly different images and this could be the reason why some Siamese cats with normal-looking eyes squint.)

The question still remains as to whether cats see colour. The retinal receptor cells called cones are responsible for colour vision and meticulous research has shown that most of the cones in the cat's eyes are those that register green. There are, however, a few other cones that register blue and even fewer that are sensitive to very long light waves, beyond red. This means that cats almost certainly see green, they probably see a little blue and they might see light beyond red. With prolonged and arduous training cats can discriminate between colours: red and green, red and blue, red and grey, green and blue, green and grey, blue and grey, blue and yellow and yellow and grey. The fact that the training is so complicated shows that, although cats technically have the ability to differentiate between colours, in practice they are not interested in doing so. They don't care whether a mouse is blue, green or yellow. They are interested only in seeing it, and for that brightness is much more important.

BALANCE AND THE RIGHTING REFLEX

Our world is horizontal but the cat's world is both horizontal and vertical. Cats have a repertoire of jumps, rehearsed jumps, impromptu jumps, vertical and horizontal jumps and the jump of the hunter, the pounce. They jump magnificently and can clear five times their own height. In order to jump a cat needs a superb system of balance and co-ordination, and this it has in its vestibular apparatus, the organ of balance deep in the ears. Its skeleton and muscles are also perfectly adapted for the skills needed by a lithe hunter.

Within the cat's brain, once more in its cerebellum, is a co-ordinating centre that is responsible for receiving movement and balance information from all the senses and for directing further movements. The nerve messages to and from this centre move exceptionally quickly, enabling the cat literally to walk tightropes.

Cats have a reputation for superhuman balance and co-ordination – superhuman in that it is superior to our own, but that doesn't mean that cats never make mistakes. Every year, just as sure as clockwork, on the first warm weekend of spring when windows in houses and apartments are left open for the first time, cats take to the air, not because they have planned to do so but because they have miscalculated their footing. At the local emergency veterinary clinic it is not uncommon to treat two or three in one day.

Flying-cat syndrome is an urban phenomenon, a consequence of the combination of our increasingly keeping cats as indoor pets and our living in high-rise accommodation. And over the years I have observed a pattern in the injuries that cats suffer when they fall, a peculiar pattern with an unusual explanation.

If a cat falls one or two floors, its injuries are usually mild and there is a physical explanation for this based on its musculature and skeleton, both of which are adapted for lightning bursts of speed. In order to run swiftly, the front legs are liberated from the shoulders by not having a bony attachment through a collarbone. The cat's collarbone (or clavicle) is either non-existent or shows on X-ray as an insignificant sliver of bone. Combined with a narrow chest, this means that cats have free movement of the forelimbs and when they walk they place their feet nearly in front of each other, which is why they can walk along the tops of fences with such agility or, as is the case with my Millie, insinuate their way through the china and glass on the mantelpiece without (yet) knocking anything off.

Cats also have a mobile backbone in which each bone is attached to the next in a rather loose manner. This allows them to bend themselves in half and to rotate one half of the back through 180° relative to the other half, a facility that I all too commonly witness when trying to examine a fearful feral cat.

The consequence is that when a cat falls a short distance, two abilities are exercised. The first is to use the front legs as pistons or springs. When the cat lands on its legs, they absorb the shock and prevent more serious injuries to internal organs. But in order to land on its legs the cat has to right itself in the first place and to do so quickly. This need is handled by its superbly refined vestibular apparatus, the organ of balance.

The vestibular apparatus, situated inside the ears, is responsible for balance and orientation and it works in a fascinating way. The apparatus itself consists of a number of gyro-like fluid-filled chambers, each lined with millions of tiny hairs. When these hairs move, signals are sent with amazing rapidity to the cerebrum, to the balance co-ordination centre. The larger chambers of the vestibular apparatus, the utricle and saccule, also have tiny crystals of calcium carbonate in the fluid. With a gravitational effect these settle on whichever hairs are at the bottom and trigger signals to the co-ordination centre on up/down orientation. Meanwhile, in the semicircular canals of the apparatus, the sensitive microscopic hairs project into equally microscopic flaps of tissue which wave and move whenever the fluid inside the canals sloshes around. The three canals are arranged at right angles to each other, and can signal the cat's direction of movement and also its acceleration.

This superbly evolved organ of balance, together with the plasticity of the cat's vertebral attachments, is what gives the animal its fascinating righting reflex, and if your cat doesn't mind you can demonstrate it for yourself over a pillow-covered bed. (I remember when I was ten years old curiously investigating the behaviour myself by dropping Wendy, my tabby, through the bannisters of the stairs. Fortunately the experiment was successful.) To do so, hold your cat by its front and back legs upside down a yard above your bed and then let go. If you have a completely relaxed and passive cat, it might simply fall on its back or side, but if it is alert, it can right itself in that short time and distance. First it will level its head, where its vestibular apparatus is located. Then, with its front legs close to its face but its hind legs still pointing to heaven, it will jack-knife its body through 180° so that the front is facing the ground. With equal speed the hind portion is twisted around as well, and if it's twisted too much the cat will use its tail to counteract the over-balance. It finally lands with its back arched to cushion the impact. This is what happens when a cat falls one or two floors, and its body is able to absorb the shock.

Falls of over two floors can cause injuries. A three-floor fall frequently results in the cat bruising its chin. The front legs absorb the pressure of impact but the head continues on its downward course and hits the ground. Sometimes this causes fractures to the canine teeth and in heavier cats the pressure of impact can be transferred to the roof of the mouth. When this happens I usually see either a tear or a split in the hard palate. At the same time the back legs also have more problems in absorbing the impact and fractures or dislocations can occur.

Falls of four floors can have more serious consequences and the reason is simple. By four floors the falling cat has reached maximum velocity. At this distance and at this speed its legs can no longer absorb the energy of impact. The result is that the energy is transferred inside the body, causing possibly a ruptured diaphragm, torn liver and other serious injuries. Falls of over four floors – of five, six and seven floors – are frequently fatal. But, and this is a fascinating but, falls of *over* seven floors are sometimes not fatal. I've treated cats that have fallen thirteen floors and have only been bruised. Cats have survived falling eighteen stories on to a hard surface, twenty storeys on to shrubs and, in New York City, twenty-eight storeys on to an awning. There is even the verified story of Cognac, an eight-year-old Siamese cat, who fell 1100 ft (335 m) from the wheel cover of a light aeroplane over Long Island and survived. (The pilot was so amazed he flew up to the same height the next week with a stray and this time intentionally dropped it. It ran off into the woods. Bets were then placed and the following week another pilot took off, this time with two cats, and dropped them both, but they both died.)

I had no answer to this flying-cat phenomenon until I had dinner one evening with the director of the Animal Medical Center in New York. Talk, as always, eventually turned to business and the subject of flying cats arose. I explained the frequency of flying cats in London and the unexpected survival of the highest flyers and he responded by telling me that he had experienced the same phenomenon in New York. Curious as to why, had asked an aerodynamics expert to create a computer model of the situation. What they discovered was that if a falling cat falls long enough, its body has a chance to relax and it takes up what amounts to a flying-squirrel position. It spreads out its legs and this has an aerodynamic lifting effect, the result of which is that in aerodynamic terms it partly glides into its landing. Cats are fluid movers with an almost enviable grace, one of the prime reasons they fascinate us so. But it also seems that, even in free fall, their minds work in brilliantly efficient and practical ways.

BODY RHYTHMS

One cat, I am told by his owner, wakes up his human family at 6am sharp each day by going to his water bowl, dipping his paw in it, then trotting to his sleeping human victim who gets moistly batted awake. Others tell me of 6am gifts of pithed frogs or still-squirming mice. Dawn is gift-giving time, but what the cat is really doing is simply following its normal body rhythms. Cats, just like dogs, and much like us, are creatures of habit and their habits are attuned to their biological clocks. But although dogs have the ability to attune their internal clock to ours, cats prefer to live by their own body rhythms.

The question of exactly what is a biological clock still fascinates science, buit there are now a few answers. The master clock is probably located in the hypothalamus in the brain and acts through an adjacent organ called the pineal gland which synchronizes body rhythms through its hormone melatonin. Body rhythms can occur over varying lengths of time. Oestrus cycles follow a seasonal hormonal body rhythm and such activities as hair growth in cats are also seasonal. Hair follicle activity is highest in late summer and lowest in late winter, which is why the fur of a short-haired cat is approximately 0.5 mm longer in winter. Cats also have annual body rhythm productions of the hormones thyroxine, epinephrine and the cortiscosteroids, all of which peak their production during the winter.

The most common body rhythm, and the one that is most interesting is the twenty-four-hour one called circadian rhythm. Circadian rhythm is why ill cats have higher fevers in the evening and seem most ill after the veterinary clinic has closed for the day. It is also the reason why penicillin is most effective when given in the later afternoon. In at least one animal, the hamster, circadian rhythm is under the control of a single gene and it is likely that the same is true of cats. (A hamster with a twenty-two-hour circadian rhythm was noted by an academic and through simple Mendelian breeding it was proved that this unusual body rhythm was the result of a single gene that produced a twenty-hour circadian rhythm. When twenty-hour was mated with twenty-four-hour, the progeny had a twenty-two-hour rhythm.)

As any cat owner knows, cats are most active at dawn and dusk, foraging, investigating, climbing, chasing and generally creating mayhem, especially if they are housebound. Cats sleep more around midday and in the middle of the night, an activity under the control of body rhythms. More specifically, a neuro-transmitter hormone, possibly serotonin, is released in the brain and its release induces sleep. The release of the hormone is in part controlled through the body-rhythm centre in the hypothalamus. It has certainly been possible, as French researchers have shown, to induce sleep in one animal by taking cerebrospinal fluid, the liquid in the centre of the brain, from a sleeping animal and transferring it into the cerebrospinal space of another animal.

The exact function of sleep remains a mystery, although the fact that in a kitten growth hormone is released only when it is sleeping suggests that sleep is necessary for efficient body functions to be carried out. The reason for dreams is a mystery too, but these as well seem to occur in a cyclical fashion, obeying some internal body rhythm. Some scientists see sleep as an occasion when the mind can reorganize and reclassify information and believe that is what is really happening when we – or cats – dream. As with so many other aspects of the cat's mind, this is still an unknown. So are the answers to why pigs are more likely to tail-bite before an electrical storm, or why mice are more active when the barometer is rising, or why we feel invigorated by the air after a storm, or how cats can find their way home when there are no visual signposts to help them and they are in a completely unfamiliar environment. Or can they? Do cats have ESP?

NAVIGATION, HOMING AND ESP

To answer the question of whether cats have extra-sensory perception (ESP) we need to define what we are talking about. My definition follows the ethologist Nikko Tinbergen's suggestion. He stated:

> If one applies the term ESP to perception by process not yet known to us, then extra-sensory perception among living creatures may well occur widely. In fact the echolocation of bats, the function of the lateral line in fishes and the way electric fish find their prey are all based on processes which we did not know about – and which were thus 'extra-sensory' in this sense only twenty-five years ago.

Controlled scientific studies now strongly suggest that cats do have a navigation ability which is 'extra-sensory' in that it cannot be explained through the traditional five senses, although there are good scientific reasons offered for this amazing ability.

Anecdotal evidence has been offered for hundreds of years concerning the cat's ability to anticipate earthquakes or find its way home

over tens or even hundreds of miles. Scientific evidence on sensitivity
to earthquakes began to appear in the 1980s with the publication of
Professor Helmut Tributch's theory that cats, among other animals,
were aware of electrostatic changes in the atmosphere that precede
certain earthquakes. Professor Ben Hart's team at the veterinary
school in Davis, California, later created a baseline rate of randomly
observed unusual animal behaviour and, using this baseline as a
guide, carried out retrospective interviews to investigate animal behaviour prior to five moderate California earthquakes. Just one earth-
quake was preceded by a significant increase in the frequency of
unusual animal behaviour and he concluded that only certain types
of earthquakes can be anticipated by animals, although he didn't
speculate whether these were associated with atmospheric electrostatic changes.

Stories about the cat's directional ability and homing 'instinct' are
just as old but even more common, so common that well over a
hundred years ago crude experiments were carried out to see if the
cat's ability to find its way home was really true. In one incident
George Romanes, a young friend of Charles Darwin, collected a car-
riage load of pet cats from homes in Wimbledon in the western
suburbs of London and took them to the centre of Wimbledon
Common where he released them. The result was chaos and a multitude of disoriented cats, with Romanes concluding that cats were
'exceedingly stupid'.

A little later, Edward Lee Thorndike, a contemporary of Pavlov,
tried what he thought was a more scientific experiment. He starved
thirteen cats, then imprisoned them in puzzle boxes to see if they
could work their way out. Those that did escape did so through the
panic of their behaviour, not because of any flashes of insight or
through an instinctive ability.

But still the stories continued. The behaviourist Michael Fox has
recounted many of these fascinating tales of cats, American, British
and French, finding their way home against all odds. And recently,
when I invited the Russian film director Alexander Zguridi to a
meeting in Monaco to discuss pet cats in the Soviet Union, he replied
with a long letter replete with stories of Russian cats, lost or
abandoned, that found their way home over mountains and rivers.

We want to believe these stories because the constancy of the
companionship of a pet cat is one of its strongest allures, but we can
sometimes get diverted into dead-end explanations. This, I believe,
happened to Michael Fox when he used 'psi-trailing' as an explana-

tion for the cat's apparent homing ability. According to this theory, cats can follow their owners to previously unvisited places.

During the 1960s and 1970s enough reliable accounts were collected of cats negotiating great distances and overcoming natural obstacles, such as rivers and cities, in order to return to their familiar territory that serious researchers turned their minds to the subject. Two of them, Drs Presch and Lindenbaum at Kiel University in Germany, carried out the following experiment. They collected several house cats from their homes, placed them in covered boxes and drove them around the city of Kiel for a while, making the drive as winding, complex and irrational as possible. Once they had completed this manoeuvre, they drove several miles out of town to a field in which they had built a large enclosed maze. The maze was covered so that no sunlight (or starlight, for that matter) could get in. Shades of George Romanes, you must be thinking.

The central area of the maze, into which the cats were released one at a time, eventually lead out to twenty-four exit passages, each one set 15° from the next, like the spokes on a wheel. Cats were allowed to wander at leisure until they chose to find an exit and leave, and when they chose to do so the majority, a statistically significant majority, left the maze by an exit pointing directly towards their home.

The ethologist Desmond Morris attended the scientific meeting at which the Germans presented their findings and was satisfied that the experiment was rigorously conducted but was still sceptical. He says, however, that his own personal doubts about the scientific validity of cats having a homing or navigational ability were removed when further studies were carried out in the USA. The same type of maze-testing was used, but this time the cats were deeply sedated before their car journey, falling into a deep sleep. Upon arrival at the testing station they were allowed to wake up fully and then were tested. As with the German cats, a significant majority exited in the direction of their homes.

In these tests older cats performed better than younger animals and their homing ability tended to drop off with distances greater than $7\frac{1}{2}$ miles (12 km) from home, but the conclusion was that cats have a probable sensitivity, as birds do, to the earth's magnetic field which enables them to find their way home. When magnets were attached to the American cats, their homing ability was disrupted.

Now it may well be that cats really are in touch with the universe at a different level, that their minds are tuned into frequencies of which we have no understanding or even imagination. The scientist in me argues against it. There are traces of magnet sensitive iron particles in most animal tissue, although we don't really know why. There is an ever-present magnetic force at work, but it is invisible and we aren't aware of its presence unless we start playing with magnets and magnetic compasses. Extra-sensory perception is a sensory ability for which there is no scientific answer today but for which, almost undoubtedly, there will be tomorrow.

Chapter Four

Communication

For the past hour, while writing this, I've been an unseen observer of two cats ritually communicating with each other. Through my window I can see the black-and-white barn cat from next door and a predominantly black cat crouched staring at each other. Neither has moved but, although nothing much appears to be happening, through their very stillness they are trying to manipulate each other.

Non-verbal communication – and that is what is going on right now between the cats I'm watching – consists of inherited behaviours but also of learned components. These cats inherited the quiet body language they are now using on each other but have learned to be resistant to the 'sales tactics' of the opposition. That's why the confrontation has gone on for so long and has now turned into a ritual stare.

In this simplest of ways, these cats are expressing their attitudes and emotions. Their feelings and intentions are coded in subtle body language, in posture, even in the proximity of one cat to another, and although we might have difficulty understanding what they are communicating they certainly don't. The recipient of the message can instantly decode the communique and knows what is being said. In the confrontation that has now been taking place so silently and quietly for so long, neither cat has been sufficiently impressed or intimidated by the other to alter her message (both appear to be females).

Compared to dogs, cats are far less sociable. The defence of a personal or a hunting territory is much more important than social relationships with other felines. Cats can and do survive on their own and their security is not dependent on group activities as it is in the case of most species of livestock or even dogs. In these other species well-defined dominant-subordinate relationships developed. And in the process friendly or 'distance-reducing' communication evolved. The dog's wagging tail or rolling over 'to be tickled' are 'distance-reducing' signals.

These 'distance-reducing' signals are poorly defined in cats because their social order is also poorly defined. That of the domestic cat consists simply of a top-ranking cat, usually a tom, then a large middling group of equals, two of which, as I have described, are now confronting each other outside my house, and finally a few low-ranking pariah cats. Although 'distance-reducing' signals are poorly defined, that is not so with 'distance-increasing, go-away' signals. Through the use of scent and marking, of body posture and of voice, cats have a wide range of methods of letting other members of their own species, and also members of different species, know what is going on in their minds.

Communication signals evolved from previous behaviours. The original function of purring, for example, was to enable a kitten to signal to its mother that all was well. But, of course, a kitten couldn't use its voice to signal as its mouth was busy suckling, so the purr, a sound that doesn't come from the voicebox, evolved. Later on in life the purr communicates different meanings. The mother purrs as she approaches the nest to reassure her young. She purrs as her kits suckle and that enhances their mutual comfort and feeling of security.

Later on, as the kittens mature, they will purr when they approach adult cats or us when they want to play. That was the simple way in which my cat Millie ('Ratbag' to her closest friends) ingratiated herself instantly with our entire family, including the golden retrievers. Purring can also be used by adult cats as a 'distance-reducing' signal, however. A dominant cat in a friendly or playful mood might purr when approaching a young or inferior one. But also, paradoxically, distressed cats will purr. When treating cats I frequently have difficulty listening to their heartbeats because my stethoscope picks up the purr rather than the valve sounds. Cats emotionally traumatized by an hour in a cat basket or physically traumatized by falling from a window or being hit by a car will purr. So too will seriously ill and debilitated or even terminally ill patients. In these circumstances the purr has yet another meaning, signalling, as the eminent behaviourist Paul Leyhausen notes, that the cat is saying, 'I am only small, helpless, inoffensive and innocuous;' or, as I believe, that the cat is reducing its state of arousal by employing its most primitive signal of contentment.

MARKING SIGNALS

Communication through marking has also evolved from previous behaviours. Sharpening claws is necessary; so why not employ the scratching posts as visual markers? Discharging body waste is also necessary; then why not use the discharges to inform about territory, state of sexual readiness, mood and status?

Scent marking is exquisitely developed in cats and communicates far more than we understand about the state of the cat's mind. For example, we know that wolves and dogs can discriminate between the odours of urine from different animals and consequently can probably recognize individuals this way. We don't know whether cats can identify each other through scent marks, but it's worth remembering that we can only vaguely imagine the world of scent as it appears to cats. It's worth remembering too that it is not necessarily the most abundant chemicals in the body's discharges or secretions that are most important in communication. Cats certainly are attracted to specific scent marks. I treat one nineteen-year-old who, after treatment, usually walks around in the examining room while I talk to her owner. Invariably she finds the same spot on the floor by the filing cabinet, sniffs and then head and body rolls on it. No matter how fastidiously the spot has been cleaned, she can scent that a dog has urinated there and is marking the sight with her cheek glands.

Cats have more scent-marking equipment than dogs. Their anal glands are similar, although cats' don't contain the chemical trimethylamine as do dogs'. In addition cats' anal sacs are lined with cells that produce secretions rich in fats. Their exact function is unknown, but the anal sacs are emptied when a cat is frightened. The red fox has over a dozen identified substances in its anal-sac secretions and probably many more, each with its own function. Cats probably have a similar range of chemicals producing a whole vocabulary of signals about individual identity, age, sex, rank and status, sexual receptivity and even the emotional state of the marker. The decomposition of anal-gland marks might also communicate how recently the 'author' was at the sight of the mark. We know that anal-gland scent is important because of the way that strange cats will circle each other trying to smell the perianal area. (The confrontation still going on outside my house as I write hasn't reached that stage as the protagonists haven't got close enough to each other.) Cats also have glands around the anus (known as perianal glands) but, once more, although these are pheromone-producing glands, their function is unknown.

Unlike dogs, cats have facial glands around the eyes, on the chin and below the ears. Secretions from these glands tell tomcats of the hormonal state of females, but while female cat urine stimulates 'flehming' in tomcats, cheek-gland secretions do not. Experimenters allowed cats to cheek-rub on pegs and then compared the interest of tomcats to these pegs and clean pegs. As the hormonal condition of the females increased through their oestrous cycle, the interest of the toms increased in phase to the cheek-rubbed pegs. Saliva, incidently, didn't provoke an increased interest, but cats do use saliva for scent marking.

Cats will, of course, leave their facial-gland scent mark on objects they wish to identify as being 'theirs' – us, for example. There is a visual aspect to cheek-rubbing too in that it occurs much more frequently when we are around than it does when we are not.

Although our bodies are covered in glands that produce a watery sweat, cats have these only on their paws. These secrete when a cat is hot or frightened. (Cats lose body heat by panting and through the evaporating of saliva from grooming the hair. Cats lose almost as much body fluid each day through saliva used in grooming as they do through their urine.) The sweat glands help to mark trails by leaving their distinctive odour wherever the cat walks, although this can be disadvantageous too as the sensible rodent will thus pick up information on the cat's whereabouts.

Between the toes exist some small interdigital glands. These are activated when a cat scratches, as are the sweat glands on the pads. Some of the large cats will scratch trees smooth and use these scratching posts as visible as well as olfactory markers of their territory. Domestic cats too will use scratching posts as markers. The behaviour starts early in life and often occurs just after sleeping and close to the sleeping area. Some of the large cats, leopards for example, will urine-spray their marking tree and then stand on their hind legs and scratch it, leaving a very impressive visual and scent signal. Domestic cats fortunately do not and are content to simply destroy upholstery and curtains. Scratching is *not* just a way that a cat sharpens its nails. The scratching post is a visible territory marker. It reinforces in the cat's mind that this is its territory and tells others of its presence. Scratching is an inherited behaviour but it is also learned from the queen. Mothers train their kittens through example and this is why the intensity of the behaviour varies from cat to cat, although there is no difference in the frequency or intensity of the behaviour between the sexes.

Because the scratching post is like a newspaper to be read by other cats, the same post (or sofa, or curtain) is consistently used. (Millie started out trying to use my elder retriever's leg, a behaviour the dog found to be curiously amusing!) Just as leopards do, cats like to stand when they scratch so a purpose-made post should be taller than the cat and between 4 and 6 in (10 and 15 cm) wide. Generally speaking, cats prefer a loose, longitudinal weave (like bark), although there is no universally accepted scratch-attractive material. As they scratch they strip off their old worn claws, revealing glistening new weapons beneath. They exercise and strengthen the muscles used to extend their claws, but they also squeeze out scent from the eccrine watery sweat glands on their paws and the apocrine and sebaceous oily scent glands between their pads, leaving a cocktail of scent, a virtually individual signature of their presence.

Scratching leaves a visible territory marker as well as sharpening the claws.

The final glandular secretion used in communication comes from the dorsal tail gland. This large sebaceous and apocrine gland, sited at the root of the tail, wasn't anatomically described until 1940. It is larger in males than in females and, once again, its exact function is unknown. Even its presence remains undetectable except in some

intact males where, very rarely, the gland becomes over-active, causing hair loss at the site, a condition that cat breeders call 'stud tail'.

Because they are produced daily in abundance, urine and faeces
are the cat's most obvious scent and visual methods of communication. Both of these body discharges give information on who is where,
when he or she was there, whether she is ready for mating, what
rank he has and even where food has been stored.

Faeces is used to indicate rank. Only the dominant territorial cat
does not bury its own faeces. Although lions, for example, apparently
defecate at random, dominant feral domestic cats leave their faeces
along trails or even on top of conspicuous objects. Some even mark
food caches with it. The vast majority of 'middling' cats are content
to leave their faeces in latrine sites, usually provided by us in the
form of litter trays. They also bury their solid wastes, another reason
for their acceptance as pets. By doing so they are reducing their
odour display, the behaviour of the subordinate. This isn't really
surprising. In the cat's mind we are profoundly dominant creatures.
We are gigantic in size. We feed them. We handle them. In these
circumstances, as the dominant 'cat' in the territory, only we would
be allowed to leave our faeces unburied. Our pet cats, on the other
hand, all bury theirs.

Urine marking is the most frequently used method of communicating by scent. Cats of either sex, but especially males, will spray their
urine on particular objects such as shrubs, walls, posts, table legs,
stones, curtains and trees. Urine spraying is not used for threat but
rather is a social function, a method of leaving a feline calling card.
Urine marks are used to spread information about who was where
and when. The signal value of urine is lost within twenty-four hours,
which is probably why tomcats seem to make the rounds of their
ranges daily.

The urine mark represents the 'author' in his absence and in that
sense it has a specific territorial function, but it also surrounds the
cat with the familiar and can simply help it to define its own range.
Smelling a scent mark erodes an intruder's confidence and increases
the likelihood of the intruder fleeing if it is seen − something that did
not happen, incidentally, and prevent the feline confrontation that is
still going on outside my house.

Field studies of feral domestic cats suggest that urine marks are not
used to help cats orientate themselves. It seems that they know
where they are going. These marks do help non-residents to navigate
through territories, however, as the intruders can avoid the most

heavily marked areas. Scenting another cat's urine doesn't seem to frighten the intruder; it is more as if it is reading a scented newspaper, picking up the facts for the day.

Urine marks, and to a lesser extent unburied faeces, help the intruder to assess the status of the dominant territorial cat. Marking consists of backing up, positioning, trembling of the vertical tail and then spraying. The sequence is the same regardless of how much urine remains in the bladder. Some cats will continue to mark long after they have totally emptied their bladders, and in studies of feral cats on Dassun Island some tomcats were seen to spray on average at least once per minute during five hours of observation. Females never sprayed more than once every ten minutes. In another study in rural Sweden, toms sprayed around once every three minutes and non-breeding males around once every six minutes.

Paul Leyhausen suggested that these scent posts act like traffic lights: old scent marks mean 'proceed with caution'; new ones mean 'stop'. Recent field observations don't support his theory, however. Farm cat colonies frequently have overlapping hunting territories, and scenting urine marks or seeing faecal marks do not make an intruder avoid the area. Markers will place most of their marks closest to their home barns, but when they do meet intruders their marking behaviour distinctly changes. When feral farm cats spray during an aggressive confrontation with another cat, 60 per cent of the time they will rub their cheeks in their sprayed urine. This curiously unpleasant behaviour is also carried out 20 per cent of the time when there is no aggression involved. Because dominant cats cheek-rub subordinate ones, it may be another method of urine marking. Whatever the reason, it should make us wonder exactly what a cat is doing when it rubs its cheek against its owner's leg, and what it was doing *before* it so sensuously rubbed.

Urine marking is vastly important in feline communication. If this method of manipulating the mind of another cat did not exist, a fight would more readily occur each time two strangers met. As it is, all but the strongest of intruders know that it is hopeless to challenge the incumbent. Cats in a community are able to differentiate between the scent of urine sprayed by an outside cat and that sprayed by one belonging to the group. They will linger over the outsider's spray, carefully analysing it. This can stimulate the resident cats to spray, an unpleasant fact of which so many cat owners are aware. Spraying can be triggered by other changes in the environment too: a new member of the family, a change of owners, a new home, even new furniture. What we consider the unpleasant smell of sprayed tomcat urine is not in the urine itself but rather in a viscous fatty material selectively voided as a 'scent' when marking. Castration eliminates that scent, although it doesn't necessarily eliminate the marking behaviour itself. The scent of tomcat urine should be mildly intimidating to other toms, and one method of 'intimidating' the neighbourhood tom from spraying in your (castrated) tom's garden is to lay down a scent that the intruder will find intimidating. Several commercial products are available to do this but I have found that mothballs, safely placed out of the reach of children and dogs, are the cheapest and most effective remedy.

The urine of cats in season has a special attraction to males in particular but also to females which is why they will 'flehm' in their gape-jawed manner when scenting it. Cats, of course, don't think out their marking strategy but scent marks have a potent effect on their minds. Familiar scents or visual marks have a calming effect and make them feel more assured. Unfamiliar scents and visual marks arouse the 'fight-or-flight' system, and indeed the body's hormonal system is the basis from which these methods of communication evolved. The original hormonally driven emptying of bowels and bladder as a result of severe fright has evolved into selective use of the discharges in communication. But there are further equally good methods of trying to manipulate the minds of other cats and these use body language.

BODY LANGUAGE

If I were to describe what is still going on between the two cats outside in terms of human behaviour, I would say that they are both indulging in 'whole-body lying'. I would use this term because we express our emotions in our body language. In fact, with us, non-verbal signals have a greater impact than do verbal messages, although speaking is much more important for communicating detail. Our greeting displays of smiling, jabbering away and touching all reinforce a feeling of friendliness and a lack of hostility. Greeting displays assure a bond of friendship or re-establish old relationships.

Body contact does the same. Desmond Morris states that the pat on the shoulder or the pat on your pet is primarily a parental bonding device. He notes that the pat is a kind of miniature embrace, performed by one hand alone that signifies in a parental way that the 'patter' is in control. The full embrace is used by adults only for intense emotional moments. It is the highest intensity of the expression of the bond between two people.

Because we express so much with our body posture, one of the ways to deceive observers about how we really feel is to send as few body signals as possible. Good poker players know this and try to control giving away their hands by showing too much excitement or despondency. In human terms this type of cover-up of emotions is untrue or dishonest and that's why many people would interpret the behaviour of the cats I'm watching while I write as 'whole-body lying'. We think it deceitful. (Culturally the Japanese learn as children that in many situations it is not polite to show emotion in public and this is a reason why one of the cultural stereotypes of that nation is that of inscrutability.)

What is really going on between the cats outside is a power struggle, and if I were close enough I might be able to detect who is actually winning. Although cats can control most of their body postures, there are some behaviours over which they have no control – for instance, the dilation and constriction of the pupils. Narrowed pupils are a sign of tension and threatening aggression while dilated pupils express surprise, fear and defence. By seeing the pupils I would know who is the aggressor and who the defender.

Body postures and facial expressions don't simply signal one emotion but rather suggest the constant shifts in the cat's mind. It's pointless to look at only the position of the ears, for example, while ignoring that of the tail, the angle of the whole body, the arch of the back and many other body postures. The component parts of the body posture associated with fear or aggression can both occur at the same time. A cat might have dilated pupils, suggesting fear, and at the same time growl or swipe with its paw in an aggressive way. It is the ability to express several emotions at once that gives the cat such a rich repertoire of body language.

As I have mentioned previously, because of the relative lack of importance of social structure in the cat's life it has a richer vocabulary of 'distance-increasing' than of 'distance-reducing' behaviours. Offensively a threat is implied by a direct, constricted-pupil stare with the body poised so that the cat can suddenly rush forward and strike. The whiskers are forward, as is the head. The tail is often held straight out with only the tip turned sharply down. The tip of the tail may wag and the hair along the cat's back stands up. The ears are up and turned out so that the opponent sees the backs of them. This is the position the two statues outside my window have assumed, except that they are lying down.

Defensive body displays involve crouching down so that the body is parallel to the floor. The pupils are dilated and the ears laid back beside the head. The hair stands on end all over the cat's body, not just on its back, and if it is cornered it might roll over to prepare a counter-attack with teeth and all four feet. This is one of the dramatic differences between dog and cat body language. A dog rolling over indicates complete abject submission. A cat rolling over is exposing the attacker to all possible weapons and is about to counter-attack. (Relaxed cats roll over too, and stretch out their legs, yawning and exercising their claws as a greeting ritual for their closest intimates. Their ambivalence in this position reveals itself when people start stroking their bellies. After the requisite number of strokes, many if not most cats will swat the stroker to indicate that they have had enough.)

The most extreme example of a feline expression of fear can be witnessed in the 'Halloween cat', the cartoon image of the cat that has just seen a dog. The body is arched to its highest presentation, the tail is vertical, all hair on the body stands on end, the pupils are dilated and the ears are laid back. To this display is added the hiss or spit.

The first physical sensation a kitten experiences is the lick of its mother, and pleasure in this sensation continues throughout life. Petting a cat offers the same tactile sensation to the recipient as did the tongue of its mother when it was being groomed. Mutual licking continues in adult cats but is restricted to a small group of intimates that often includes us. I see worried cats lick each other after I have examined and treated them at the clinic. It appears to be a way of defusing the tension they have recently felt. Otherwise licking is a voluntary behaviour carried out for self-grooming, for grooming a fellow cat or in a seemingly almost affectionate way on their human companions.

The ears and tails are among the most expressive parts of the cat's body. Very often the first sign of anger a cat gives is a rhythmic horizontal lashing of the tail. It begins in a gentle way but becomes more pronounced as provocation continues. If the tail is down, a cat is relaxed. If it is held high, the cat is active, frustrated, greeting another cat or person (or, in the case of Millie, the dogs) or is investigating something. The high-tail greeting is a vestige of the kitten's original tail-high presentation of the anal region for its mother to clean. If the tail is arched down, the cat is in an aggressive state of mind. Dogs wag their tails when happy and alert. Cats wag theirs when in a state of conflict. They use them for balance but also to let others know that they are worried about something.

When a cat's ears are held forward, it is relaxed, exploring or greeting. Ears down mean aggression, a logical position as they are less in the way of tooth and claw if they are plastered to the head. If the ears are back and down, this indicates fear but also aggression. When the head is down a cat is aggressive, but when it is higher it feels a mixture of fear and aggression. Because ears are such good indicators of what is going on in the cat's mind, some species – for instance, the caracal lynx – have developed special tufting to accentuate them. The Abyssinian has small, dark, hairy points to its ears but the winner is the Maine Coon, such as Millie. This breed is equipped with luxurious 'ear furnishing', something that breeders adore but that originally developed in the wild as a method of the cats' expressing their feelings and state of mind.

The position and spread of the whiskers also contribute to body language. If the whiskers are pointed forward and fanned out, the cat is attentive, tense and ready to act; when sideways and less spread out, the cat is relaxed and calm; and when bunched together and flattened to the side of the face, the cat is fearful or apprehensive. My cat's whiskers all droop down in a limp and morose 'Salvador Dali' expression, but she can still move them through all these stages.

Facial expression is shown by ear and whisker position. The pupils dilate when a cat is stimulated.

When a cat has crouched passively, that display may effectively cut off an attack or appease a potential aggressor. However, as I have mentioned, rolling over does not indicate submission but rather it reveals all weapons, solicits play or, in a sexual context, is the female's courtship display. During mating the male will bite the female's neck but dominant male cats will also do this with lower-ranking males. The dominant cat mounts the other, treads and bites the scruff. As it does so the lower-ranking male assumes the passive crouched position. This isn't simply a homosexual behaviour but is a method the dominant cat uses to assert rank and authority.

When two cats meet they try to investigate each other's scent glands. One cat takes the initiative and sniffs the anal or temporal or mouth region of the other. Noses might touch, and if the cats know each other head rubbing might occur. Actual fighting between males is often ritualized into bites to the neck and claw rakes directed towards the shoulders. This is why tomcats develop such thick skin in those regions, although the thickened skin is also probably a secondary sex characteristic.

The thicker cheeks of the tomcat give him a fuller face – better to display with and to intimidate his rivals, but all cats use the cheek ruffs for display. When a cat is excited or fearful, the cheek muscles pull the ruff downward and towards the throat, sometimes in a pulsing rhythm. This is easier to see in cats such as lynxes with prominent cheek ruffs, but it occurs in domestic cats too.

A lion will face his adversaries head on in a display of intimidation because that way he can show off his intimidating mane. (His mane is a secondary sex characteristic. Castrate a young lion and his mane won't develop.) Domestic cats can't put on an equivalent display and instead turn sideways and arch their backs, fluttering out the hair and tail to intimidate a rival. My Maine Coon, Millie, has a typically luxuriant tail but this evolved naturally when the breed was multiplying without human intervention, to give intruders the illusion that the displayer was bigger than he or she really was.

Cats are more dextrous than dogs are with paws and claws and use them to investigate and play but also to intimidate. When I recently went on a house visit to vaccinate six neutered cats, the dominant female boxed all the others around their faces after I finished vaccinating her: something she was in the process of doing when I arrived. A brisk slap with a front paw expresses anger or impatience and is used in a disciplinary sense. It is a throwback to the disciplinary maternal nose taps on kittens and is carried out with sheathed claws. If a cat is angrier, it will flatten back its ears slightly and box again, but perhaps with a little claw protruding. When a cat is fully annoyed or frightened, the sheathed box becomes an unsheathed slash.

Perhaps the most endearing use of the paws is the gentle and very deliberate placing of a velvety paw on the owner's nose. Cats will do this when they are held or even when their owners are sleeping. One hospice in England employs a resident cat (naturally called 'Hospuss') who wins the affection of the resident cat lovers by performing this behaviour upon their sleeping proboscises.

Infantile body language can persist into adulthood, especially in 'neotenized' cats – individuals or breeds in which we have intentionally perpetuated juvenile behaviour. When asking for milk, a kitten passes round and round its mother, rubbing its body against hers. Its body is slightly arched and the tail straight. It stretches out its head and tries to rub under its mother's chin with a movement beginning with the nose and ending with the area between the ears. Sometimes it purrs at the same time. This is food- or attention-seeking behaviour.

The same behaviour can be seen in adults, only now it is directed at us. But our pet cats have a problem because we are so tall. How can they rub their owner's face when it is so far away? In most instances they will be content to rub an outstretched hand, but their natural inclination to face-rub can produce a stiff-legged greeting hop in which the front legs leave the ground. I've seen dozens of stray cats perform this behaviour when their 'cat-lady' arrives with fresh sardines. In these circumstances she is greeted as a surrogate 'mother'.

One of the pleasures of sharing your home with cats is to watch the fluid grace of their movement. The enjoyment increases when we come to understand what they are saying and doing with their body language. And if we understand their spoken language, the relationship we have with these graceful and beautiful animals improves even more.

VOICE

Cats give information with their voices: they welcome us home, they demand food or attention, they complain, they panic, they protest, they show anger or indignation, they threaten and carry out courtship. They do all these things using different sounds. Cats have a rich vocabulary. They even use their voices silently in the 'silent miaow'.

Scientists have distinguished at least sixteen different cat sounds and cats probably distinguish countless more. Some individuals and breeds, especially the Siamese and their relatives, are more vocal than others.

According to the behaviourist Michael Fox, cat language consists of three general sound categories: murmurs, vowels and high-intensity sounds. Murmurs include purring and the soft sounds used for greetings, for calling attention and for calling for approval. These sounds are made with the mouth shut. Vowel sounds, according to Fox, are used only in specific contexts. The 'miaow', '*mee*-ow', 'me-ow', 'mew' and others are used to demand, to complain or to express bewilderment. These sounds are completed by the closing of the mouth and are used when cats 'talk' to their owners. Most cats quickly build up a rich vocabulary that alert owners soon come to understand, with different vowel sounds meaning 'out', 'food', 'food *now*', 'filthy litter tray!', 'please', 'help', 'no' and so on. The way a cat pronounces its vowels gives its voice a unique identity, certainly unique enough for us to differentiate one cat's vowel sounds from another's. High-intensity sounds are reserved for communicating with other cats. The mouth remains open but tense and, by changing its shape, creates different sounds. This produces the growl, the angry wail, the snarl, hiss and spit. It brings forth the shriek of pain or fear and the high-pitched mating cry of the females.

Paul Leyhausen categorizes sounds in a different way. He says that cats produce vocal sounds in their voiceboxes and non-vocal sounds elsewhere. Purring, hissing, spitting and tooth-chattering are all non-vocal sounds, while miaowing, growling and gurgling are all vocal sounds.

I have already described why cats purr, although how they do so is still a mystery. An old explanation is that the sound is made by the false vocal cords, two folds of membrane behind the true vocal cords in the larynx (or voicebox). Certainly when I want to obliterate the purring sound in order to listen to a cat's heart I can do so by gently squeezing the bottom of the larynx. Anatomists argue that the purr cannot emanate totally from there and suggest that turbulence in the main vein bringing blood back to the heart creates vibrations that are transferred up the windpipe to give the impression that the purr is created in the larynx. A third explanation is that out-of-phase contractions of the muscles of the larynx and diaphragm create the purr. However it is created, it undoubtedly relaxes both the cat and any humans who hear it too.

As well as their clearly delineated sounds, cats produce mixed sounds. The soft, bird-like greeting chirp of some cats sounds like a cross between a purr and a miaow. And the curious, tooth-rattling stutter of the indoor cat frustrated to see an inaccessible bird through a window is another sound that is difficult to classify.

Kittens are not born with a full vocabulary. They can purr, growl, spit, hiss and make distress calls, but by twelve weeks of age they have developed a full adult vocabulary. How well they continue to develop this method of communication then depends upon the other factors that control their minds, such as the social circumstances in which they find themselves.

My dogs and even my family were amazed at the hissing and spitting ability of our newly arrived nine-week-old kitten. I had made sure that Millie's breeder had raised her in the presence of her Gordon setter, but my dogs were strangers and they initially received the full treatment. Hissing is a common sound in many species of mammal.

Desmond Morris has suggested that because predators have a great respect for venomous snakes (which hiss and spit) and because they have an inbuilt reaction to avoid snakes, cats added hissing and spitting to their verbal repertoire to defend against predators. Morris goes on to suggest that its natural colourings would also give a snake-like appearance to a curled up tabby cat and camouflage it from overhead predators.

When a cat hisses it opens its mouth about half-way, draws back the upper lip, arches the tongue and then expels a jet of air so abruptly through the arched tongue that if you are close enough, as I frequently am, you can feel it. I can hear it, see it and feel it. Spitting is equally dramatic and in adults is often accompanied by a dramatic hitting of the ground with a forepaw. The author of the behaviour often leans forward to spit and thump. More often than not, this is all bluff, but the purpose is to stun the supposed attacker visually and give the cat a chance to escape. (My dogs were certainly surprised by the noise and sight of Millie's behaviour, but within days she was using their tails for target practice and their noses for boxing matches.)

Finally, the silent miaow. It is exactly as it sounds: the mouth opens, but nothing happens. Paul Gallico was so enchanted by it he wrote a whole book about the silent sound, suggesting that it was the cat's way of getting a human disciplinarian (often the man of the family) to break his own rules such as 'no food at the dinner table'. We certainly are putty in the paws of the silent miaower and it is flattering and delightful to be the recipient of the silent miaow. What it means is known only to the cat.

The question remains concerning exactly what cats understand when they hear cat noises. Can they create images in their minds from the sounds they hear? Primates certainly can. Vervet monkeys in Africa, for example, employ two different alarm calls. When a monkey emits one alarm sound, other members of the troop look to the ground (for snakes) and might climb up trees. But when they hear another type of alarm sound, they look upwards (for eagles) and head for the bush. Paul Leyhausen argues that cats can create images in their mind and cites as an example the different gurgling noises his cat made when bringing mice and rats back to her four-to-five-week-old kittens.

Leyhausen was able to differentiate what he described as 'calling mouse' from 'calling rat'. The 'calling-mouse' sound was a gentle, high-pitched gurgle, but the 'calling-rat' sound was closer to a scream. Leyhausen explains that mice – even live ones – are harmless to kittens, but a live rat is possibly dangerous. He notes that 'calling mouse' and 'calling rat' are two variations of the same sound. His own cat called 'mouse' only when she had a mouse and 'rat' only when she had a rat, even if she had only a piece of rat smaller than a mouse. Her kittens responded in two ways to the two sounds, coming running with no fear to the 'mouse' sound but approaching the prey much more cautiously when mother called 'rat'. Leyhausen concluded that they understood the difference in meaning of the two sounds.

Cats have richly developed methods of communication and through scent, body language and sound are well equipped to learn about the world they live in. And as we are an integral part of that world, may I suggest that we add a personal sound recognition to our cats' minds, a sound made only by us. To do this we must first train them to come to our sound. My family and I did this with our cat simply by saying, 'Millie, Millie, Millie,' each time we prepared and gave her her food. Within days Millie was coming to us when we were in the kitchen and called her name.

This is the first and most important step. The next is to train your cat to answer you. Naturally talkative cats will do so without training and will develop a consistent vocal response to your call. More taciturn felines need to be encouraged to reply and the simplest way of doing this is to withhold food until you get a response. When your cat arrives, hold its plate of food over its head and continue talking to it. The cat might try standing on its hind legs but if you persevere and have patience it will eventually 'talk'. This might sound like a cruel and pointless procedure, a needless whim, but remember: if your cat is ever lost and has been taught to respond to your call, you will be forever grateful that it has learned to use its mind in this way.

And, finally, that confrontation outside my window? Eventually, with an insouciance verging on disdain, the interloper, painfully slowly, almost in slow motion, turned her head, got up and simply walked away.

PART TWO

The Psychology of the Cat's Mind

Chapter Five

Early Learning: The Influence of Parents, Littermates and Humans

Kittens must learn to behave like kittens before they learn to behave like cats. And although behaviourists have historically stated that *all* early experience is important and necessary for the development of the adult mind, that traditional view has now been replaced with the realization that certain behaviours must be learned for kittenhood only. Then, as the kitten matures into an adult, the blackboard is erased and new behaviours learned. Suckling is the most dramatic example of a behaviour that is necessary for a kitten's survival but unnecessary for an adult's. The more realistic view that is widely held today is that not necessarily all early experiences exert long-term effects on behaviour, simply because an adult cat is quite a different animal from a kitten.

I'm not saying that early experience is unimportant. On the contrary, it is the most influential experience that the cat's mind will ever be exposed to, so influential that, by the time we acquire kittens at around ten weeks of age, their minds are already dramatically and in some ways irreversibly formed. Whereas with pups we still have an opportunity to undo any bad habits and to alter misconceptions that may have been acquired, with kittens this is not so. Proper socialization is almost totally the responsibility of the breeder, simply because the end of the socialization period in kittens occurs much earlier than it does in pups.

Konrad Lorenz was influential in the identification of the concept of 'critical periods' in the emotional development of young animals. This concept stated that there are certain short periods, early in the life of an animal, in which the experiences it undergoes will have long-term effects on the individual's development. For example, if a kitten is not exposed to human contact during the 'critical period' for socialization with humans, it will always be timid in the presence of humans. In the 1990s behaviourists now prefer to use the term 'sensitive period', feeling that the older term implies too sharply defined stages. The sensitive period for socialization with humans is roughly two to seven weeks, but it doesn't abruptly begin and end at those ages. Some kittens over seven weeks of age can still socialize with humans, but they find it much more difficult to do so. The sensitive periods in the development of the cat's mind begin even before birth and can be divided into:

1. The prenatal period – conception to birth
2. The neonatal period – birth to two weeks
3. The socialization period – two to seven weeks

THE PRENATAL PERIOD

If a mother is severely under-nourished when she is pregnant, her kittens will have poorer learning ability, will be more antisocial towards other cats and will be more emotional, showing abnormal levels of fear and aggression, even if the mother is well nourished from birth right through weaning. When mothers have been fed a low-protein diet during pregnancy, their kittens perform poorer in balance tests. Poorly fed mothers produce kittens that are slower to learn to crawl, suck, walk, run, play and climb. The kittens' eyes open later and they don't control their posture until later than young from mothers that were well fed during pregnancy.

Kittens of under-nourished mothers show growth abnormalities too, even when they themselves are well nourished, although these abnormalities are often not apparent until after the kittens are weaned. And perhaps most dramatic of all, the kittens of mal-nourished mothers go on to become poorer mothers themselves, pro-ducing kittens that have learning deficits, emotional abnormalities and delays in physical development, although not in as severe a form as they themselves experienced.

Research on rats has shown that if the mother is stressed during pregnancy, her rat pups will grow up to be more fearful, or that if she is stressed during the third term of pregnancy, her pups will show reduced learning ability and grow up to become more emotional. The evidence is overwhelming that proper nutrition, good exercise, warmth and security during pregnancy are all necessary for the kitten's mind to develop to its optimum. It is equally important to protect the mother from illness, parasites and unnecessary drugs, chemicals and X-rays.

While it is still in the womb, the kitten's sensory abilities are already developing. I can feel if a cat is pregnant by palpating her abdomen at around three weeks from conception. The developing kittens can probably feel me doing it, as touch sensitivity develops around day 24 of a typical sixty-three-day conception-to-birth period. Even a kitten's magnificent righting reflex develops while it is still in the womb, by day 54. By the time of birth the kitten is ready to right itself and home in on its mother to find a teat and suckle.

THE NEONATAL PERIOD

The normal gestation period in domestic cats is sixty-three to sixty-six days (three to seven days longer than in their wild ancestor, the North African wild cat) and kittens are born weighing on average just over $3\frac{1}{2}$ oz (100 g) which is about 3 per cent of their adult weight. Their brains, however, are already 20 per cent of their adult weight. There is a seasonal distribution of births, with the greatest numbers of litters being born in late spring and summer and the least numbers in late autumn and early winter.

As most owners of breeding cats know, *she* decides where to kitten, rather than us. We might prepare a warm, clean box, but she might prefer a cupboard or even an open drawer. Birth itself involves a lot of licking, first self-licking the belly and genital area, then licking the foetal fluids from her fur and from the floor and finally licking the kittens. It appears that she responds to the fluids of birth first and then to the kittens.

During birthing she will be restless and might lie down, sit up, lick her vulva, squat, circle, lie down once more, roll over, lick a kitten or repeat any of these behaviours, but in no special sequence. When her uterus (womb) contracts, she usually flexes her hind legs. Very sociable cats don't seem to mind their owners being present, but timid cats do. And, as might be expected, Siamese cats are more vocal during parturition than are other breeds.

The restless behaviour of the mother does serve a purpose as it stretches the umbilical cords of newly born kittens, and once the attached placenta is delivered she will turn around and eat it as she would eat prey, chewing off part of the umbilical cord too. This provides her with a little nourishment but also with the hormone oxytocin, which is necessary for her to let down her milk. Only very occasionally will she continue eating the cord and then eat the attached kitten. This type of population control, normal in rodents such as hamsters and mice, is rarely practised by cats.

The interval between births is usually quite short but can be up to an hour and during this time the mother appears quite oblivious to the new-born kittens other than licking them. She might stand on them when she gets up and pays little attention to their cries. But once the last kitten has been delivered, she lies down with an encircling motion, positioning her legs so that they form a semi-circle around her young. And for the next forty-eight hours she will rarely leave them, if at all.

The kittens probably find their mother through the saliva trail she has laid down in licking them and licking her nipples. Although blind and deaf at birth, they use smell, touch and warmth to find food. Suckling itself is actually initiated by the mother. She cleverly guides the kittens to her nipples.

In the 1970s, Jay Rosenblatt carried out a series of experiments to observe this behaviour. He saw that, regardless of litter size, by the third day of life 80 per cent of kittens had a preferred single nipple position and would suckle only from that. If one of the other 20 per cent took that nipple, it would be relinquished when the rightful 'owner' nuzzled in. Kittens would readily abandon the 'wrong' nipple but held on tenaciously to the 'right' one. This type of teat preference isn't restricted to kittens. As a veterinary student I, along with my colleagues, once labelled a litter of piglets with the numbers 1 to 8, then thrilled onlookers by releasing them on to the sow and convincing the viewers that the piglets knew how to count. They lined up sequentially 1 to 8, but we already knew their individual teat preferences and had numbered them accordingly!

Kittens rapidly develop a preference for a specific teat.

Kittens locate a teat by pulling themselves forward while swinging their heads from side to side. When a nipple is encountered, they pull their heads back, then lunge forward open-mouthed. The biggest kitten is not necessarily the one who chooses or gets the best-producing gland, and after several days they can use the position of their littermates to find 'their' nipple. Soon after birth kittens will suckle for eight hours a day, but this length of time diminishes as they grow older.

Nursing itself is divided into three stages. During the first stage, from birth until two weeks, nursing is initiated by the mother. From two to five weeks both the mother and her kittens initiate nursing, and after five weeks nursing is mostly initiated by the kittens. Kittens will knead with their forepaws and purr when they suckle, both behaviours that stimulate milk release. Purring is like a dinner gong. One kitten purring is a feeding summons that signals to the others that Mum is back and they all come running for a meal (and for contact comfort). An unstudied phenomenon is that of group care and feeding of new-born kittens by several lactating mothers. Natural colonies of domestic cats are strikingly similar to prides of lions, consisting of several mature and immature females and possibly some immature males. Lactating females will often share nursing responsibilities, one acting as wet nurse for all the kittens while the other hunts. The roles are often reversed, allowing any females to leave to hunt while another provides all the young with nourishment. Litters from different females can share the same nest and become mixed, with females giving maternal care to young that are not their own, even severing umbilical cords. No one knows how this affects the developing minds of the kittens, but it is a common enough behaviour apparently to have no adverse effect and should in fact enhance sociability with other cats. Male cats, incidentally, usually play no direct part in the rearing of offspring. They don't provide food for either the mother or her kittens and can, in fact, sometimes cannibalize their young, although this is a rare occurrence.

Mothers do not build nests for their kittens but they do look for shelter and protection from predators (including male cats) and can be quite aggressive to both strange and familiar cats. Often, within a few days of birth, a mother will move all her kittens elsewhere. She does so either because her birthing den is soiled or because she wants to protect her kittens from the predators who can scent the presence of kittens. Her desire to change nests is strongest two days after birth and then again around four weeks later.

Kittens cry when lost or removed from close contact with their mother, but even by four days of age they do have some ability to return to the nest site. It is still up to the mother, however, to retrieve them. Mothers seems to understand a certain cry that indicates distress, much as human mothers can instinctively distinguish between the different cries of human infants. Kittens use their distress cry when they are hungry, trapped, isolated, restricted or cold. The mother responds to this call with her own 'chirping' approaching call. (One behaviourist calls this sound a 'chirp'; another calls it a 'brrp'; and a third calls it a 'mhrn'!)

Mothers carry their kittens by the nape of the neck.

During the neonatal period the mother nuzzles and licks her kittens to stimulate them and licks their anogenital regions to stimulate urination and defecation. The average litter size is four kittens and as the mother has at least six active nipples there is no need for a 'musical-chairs' routine each time they suckle. With larger litters, however, the young kittens show proportionally more competitive scrambling and pushing among themselves when searching for a teat. Mothers show individual differences in their behaviours with their kittens – for example, in the way they respond to their kittens' cries or nuzzling.

Kittens that are separated from their mothers during the neonatal period will subsequently develop emotional, behavioural and physical abnormalities. They become unusually fearful and aggressive towards other cats and people, they wander and move about aimlessly and are poorer learners. Some of them even grow to develop asthma-like respiratory disorders more frequently than do kittens that are not separated from their mothers during this period.

By two weeks of age a kitten can orient towards sound and its eyes have opened. The actual time of eye opening depends upon many factors. Millie's breeder was proud of the fact that she and other members of her litter had their eyes open four days after birth. Most kittens don't open their eyes until seven to ten days of age and some don't open them until they are fourteen days old. The number of siblings and the growth rate of kittens have no bearing on when the eyes open. Rather, it depends upon the kitten's sex, the age of its mother, the amount of light it is exposed to and who its father is. Dark-reared kittens open their eyes faster than kittens reared in normal light. Kittens of young mothers open their eyes faster than kittens of older mothers. Female kittens open their eyes faster than male kittens. But, most important, fathers pass on the genetic potential for kittens to open their eyes early. This is the strongest factor in determining when the eyes first open. And, once they are open and focusing, the kitten enters the most sensitive period of its life, the socialization period.

THE SOCIALIZATION PERIOD

The socialization period is the time in a young animal's life during which it forms relationships with others of its own species or, in the case of domesticated animals, with other species such as humans and livestock. This sensitive period in the young dog's life begins at around four weeks of age and continues for eight weeks until it is around twelve weeks old. In kittens, on the other hand, the socialization period starts earlier, at two weeks, and is shorter; it lasts only five weeks and finishes by the time the kitten is about seven weeks old. The short duration of this sensitive period was outlined only recently by Eileen Karsh at Temple University in Philadelphia.

Using domestic (British) shorthaired cats born and reared in the Feline Behaviour Laboratory at Temple, Karsh randomly assigned kittens from various litters into different groups. One group was stroked and petted for fifteen minutes a day from the age of three to fourteen weeks. Another group was similarly handled from seven to fourteen weeks and the final group wasn't handled at all. Then she observed the behaviour of the kittens by recording friendly gestures such as head and flank rubs, purrs and chirps, and the time they took to greet the observer in designated periods of time. She noted that the late-handled kittens, those handled from seven to fourteen weeks, behaved more like the non-handled controls.

In her next experiment, a group of kittens was handled starting earlier, at the end of the first week, and for longer – forty minutes on each occasion – because she had seen that longer handling increased attachment. Another group was handled in a similar fashion between the ages of three and fourteen weeks. The early-handled kittens behaved no differently from the second group and she concluded that socialization starts later than one week of age.

Early handling ensures socialization to humans.

In her third group of experiments kittens were handled for forty minutes a day for exactly four weeks, from the ages of one to five, two to six, three to seven and four to eight weeks. These experiments showed that kittens handled from two to six and three to seven weeks had higher attachment scores than the other groups.

Karsh's work has shown that this sensitive socialization period finishes earlier than we had previously appreciated but it has revealed more. She has shown the importance of the amount of handling. Forty minutes a day produces kittens more attached to their handlers than fifteen minutes a day. Kittens handled longer approached people significantly faster and stayed longer. She also observed that kittens handled by one handler would allow themselves to be held by that person considerably longer than they would allow someone else to hold them. Even more important, she observed that if a mother cat has been socialized to humans, her calm presence can reduce her kitten's anxiety and enhance its exploration of the environment. Shy mothers can induce their kittens to be shy. Calm mothers can facilitate the relationship between their kittens and us. Some writers have felt that the act of feeding is the most important in establishing the cross-species relationship between cats and humans. Karsh has shown that petting, playing and talking are more important to the relationship.

Karsh isn't the only behaviourist to observe the importance of handling, only the most recent. Thirty years ago scientists observed that when Siamese cats were handled early in life during the socialization period, they emerged from the nest box earlier and even developed the characteristic adult coat coloration earlier. Early-handled kittens approached strange toys and humans more readily but were slower to learn to avoid an unpleasant experience, probably because of the general reduction in fearfulness that developed as a consequence of this early handling.

Others have shown that, just as malnourished mothers produce kittens with retarded social abilities, malnourishment during kittenhood has equally devastating effects. Even when kittens were malnourished up to six weeks but fed all they wanted from then on, although they eventually achieved normal size, they suffered more accidents during free play and performed poorly in several behavioural tests. Males were more aggressive than were controls and females did less climbing and random running.

During the early part of the socialization period, kittens' sensory abilities mature. By three weeks of age their sense of smell is well developed and they see well enough to locate their mother by sight rather than scent. They can also, at least to some extent, control their temperature and leave the nest to deposit their faeces elsewhere. By four weeks their hearing is well developed, their sense of smell fully mature, as is their righting reflex, and they start actively to play with littermates. Their teeth have erupted and they can walk reasonably well. By five weeks of age the fluid in their eyes has become crystal-clear, allowing mature vision. They can right themselves in the air to land on their feet. They can run, avoid obstacles, place their paws where they want them, follow prey with their eyes and, in fact, stalk and pounce as proper predators. They can also groom themselves and have started grooming their littermates.

One of the reasons for cats' great popularity as pets is their fastidious cleanliness. Adult cats commonly spend 30 per cent of their waking hours grooming themselves or grooming others in their social group. And although it seems to be a simple behaviour, it serves many functions other than just tidying the fur. As I've mentioned previously, cats daily lose as much body fluid through the saliva in grooming as they lose in their urine. Evaporated saliva accounts for one third of all daily body water loss.

Kittens are superbly equipped to groom themselves and to groom members of their social group, which often includes us. Their barbed tongues and forepaws are the principal tools of grooming, but teeth and claws are also used to dislodge tougher debris.

Grooming is a natural 'pre-wired' activity.

Face washing always follows a stereotyped pattern. The kitten applies saliva to the inside aspect of the paw, then rubs the paw back to front over its nose using a circular upward motion. More saliva is applied to the paw and the action is then repeated, but this time the semi-circle is extended a little further to behind the ear. The next motion is extended even further, down over the back of the ear, and eventually the semi-circle includes the forehead and the eye. Once a kitten has washed one side of its face it switches paws and washes the other side.

Other parts of the body are not washed in such a stereotyped way. Using long strokes of the tongue, a kitten will lick its front legs and shoulders, flanks, anogenital region, hind legs and tail, but in no particular order and not all areas necessarily at the same time. In doing so it removes loose hair from its coat and clears away any debris. If thorns or burrs are caught in the fur, the kitten uses its teeth and claws to dislodge them. This daily cleansing also eliminates some skin parasites. I have only ever seen ticks on debilitated cats, because any other cat will rid its body of them through daily grooming. A cat can also, to a lesser extent, control lice and fleas, but the sensible parasite simply moves away from the approaching serrated-edged steamroller of a tongue. Many fleas are thus removed from the coat and swallowed in the process. This is the most common way in which domestic cats acquire tapeworms as the egg of the most common tapeworm resides in the abdomen of the flea. Because cats are such efficient groomers, if your cat has fleas you should consider that it may also have a tapeworm as a consequence of its efficient grooming ability.

Grooming serves more purposes than simple cleanliness, parasite control and fur smoothing. Each time a kitten licks its fur it stimulates the sebaceous glands attached to the hair roots. These secretions are necessary to keep the fur water-proofed. The kitten cools itself down through the evaporation of saliva, much as we do through sweating all over, which is why cats groom more in warm weather than in cold. It has even been suggested that, on warm sunny days, cats can ingest vitamin D from the skin through grooming.

There are less obvious reasons for grooming too. Cats will often groom themselves after handling. They may actually be 'tasting' the handler, though it is more likely that they are masking your scent. But perhaps the most interesting function of grooming is to reduce anxiety and conflict, and this is also the basic reason why pet cats enjoy being petted.

When cats are puzzled or frightened or indecisive, they often start grooming themselves. Psychologists call this a displacement activity. Physiologically it may mean that fear or worry causes cats' body temperature to rise much as ours does in similar situations. In these circumstances we blush and sweat in order to lose heat, and cats groom to lose extra heat through the resulting saliva loss. It may also be that grooming in these circumstances is more like my scratching my head when I'm indecisive. Whatever the reason, it's a comfort behaviour that relieves tension. A modification of this is the quick tongue flick. Agitated, perplexed, curious or anxious cats will flick their tongues over their noses, much as we scratch our arms or behind our ears. Excessive grooming can indicate that a cat is emotionally stressed, especially in Siamese and Abyssinians, and it can become exaggerated into hair pulling.

As well as grooming themselves, kittens at around five weeks of age will also start to groom their littermates and this mutual grooming will continue into adulthood among cats that have formed close social bonds. Social bonds are reinforced through licking and as kittens grow they now start to lick their mother. Mutual grooming between long-term associates continues throughout life and is one of the social activities that binds cats together. One cat licking behind another's ears is a practical solution to 'getting to the parts other tongues cannot reach' as well as a means of communicating intimate feelings. This is the basis for cats' enjoyment of being petted. Comfort giving originally comes from the mother licking the kitten. Now it can come from a littermate's lick and eventually it comes from our stroking. And if we really want to be efficient cat substitutes, we now know that we should really be doing.

During the following two weeks kittens develop an adult-like sleeping pattern, adult-like responses to social stimuli, adult-like motor abilities such as weaving when they run and adult-like temperature control. By seven weeks of age they have all the gaits of the adult although they won't be able to perform such delicate tasks as turning on a thin plank until they are ten weeks old. By the time kittens are four weeks of age, if under free living conditions, mothers start bringing live prey to them, and by five weeks of age kittens may start to kill mice.

Although weaning finishes by seven weeks, many kittens will continue to suckle intermittently, some for several more months, regardless of any milk flow. It is simply a comfort behaviour. Kittens raised during this period with their mother, siblings and with us are exposed to a rich environment of suitable stimuli. This is the most important reason why kittens should not be adopted early, certainly not before eight weeks of age. Early-adopted kittens can grow to be hyperactive and can develop the common behavioural problems of wool-chewing and sucking. And in the absence of any other suitable subjects, early-weaned kittens find that we are the most suitable suckable objects.

The behaviour of kittens during the socialization period might answer a few queries regarding adult behaviour. In the 1970s it was discovered that when kittens first explore around their nest, they give a call made up of pure ultrasonic components separated by low-intensity, low-frequency components which are within the range of human hearing. Although we can't hear the ultrasonic cry, their mothers can and respond to it. Is this the origin of the 'silent miaow'?

Another question relates to the size of kittens when they are weaned. Does small size at weaning put a cat at any disadvantage? The answer is that, in free-ranging cats, the smaller and lighter are more likely to be low ranking and less likely to reproduce.

A final query concerns why all-female litters of kittens are so rare, yet all-male litters are not uncommon. The answer lies in play behaviour. Briefly, females raised with male cats during the socialization period develop a full range of play behaviours, including how to play like males (and male kittens play with objects more than female kittens do). For example, females from mixed-sex litters show significantly higher frequencies of object play than do females from all-female litters. The object play of male kittens is not affected by the number of female littermates. We already know that siblings play an important role in social development, but it also appears that females raised in the absence of male siblings never develop a full range of social play activities. It seems that male kittens are necessary in a litter for proper social development of the females, yet the opposite is not the case. And natural selection assists by rarely producing all female litters. The biological reason for this might be found back in the womb. Female foetuses can be partially masculinized in the womb through exposure to the male sex hormone testosterone, produced by male kittens before they are born. This might have a long-term effect on the behaviour of the females.

With the evidence that is now available it is a virtually irrefutable fact that the social behaviour of pet cats depends almost totally on how they are treated by their breeders rather than on how we treat them once we adopt them. Early handling of at least forty minutes a day affects the development and functioning of the brain, the senses and the hormonal biofeedback systems involving the pituitary and adrenal glands. Handled kittens develop larger brains with more connections between nerve cells. They are less emotional, more exploratory, more playful and better at learning. Orphaned kittens or even kittens from single-kitten litters grow up to be more unsure of themselves and more fearful. They don't develop normal feline social graces. Too much handling too early and lack of contact with other cats produces a cat that is fearful of other cats and that will often refuse to breed. In the best of environments kittens should be exposed to as wide a range of stimuli as possible during the socialization period – to dogs, other cats, loud noises, car rides, to anything they might experience later when they move to their new homes. This puts the burden of creating cats that are good companions directly on the shoulders of breeders. Behavioural skills that are missing by eight weeks of age are probably lost forever.

LEARNING BY OBSERVATION

Kittens are better at learning by observation than puppies are and they learn faster if they watch their mothers than if they watch other cats. For example, kittens that watched their mother press a bar to obtain food learned to copy her faster than kittens that watched a strange female cat do the same thing. Kittens given the opportunity to learn by simple trial and error to press the bar for a good reward never learned to do so.

Experiments in learning by observing, or 'operant conditioning' as behaviourists call it, were performed with cats sixteen years before Pavlov carried out his more famous conditioning experiments on dogs in 1927. In those first studies, cats learned how to operate in their environment to escape from puzzle boxes. They also learned how to pull strings to which food was attached, selecting the meat-attached string from several others. Cats won't perform simply to be reunited with the experimenter as dogs will, but rather perform for food rewards. They will, however, work harder for a food reward if the experimenter is the person who normally feeds them in their home cages. Even more rewarding to kittens is freedom to explore. They learn faster when the reward is freedom to explore a room than they do when food is the reward.

Although at one time we thought that only primates could learn sets of skills, we now know that cats can 'learn to learn'. Kittens learn best from their mothers, which is why a mother which is successful at catching birds is more likely to produce a kitten of similar talents than a mother which is not. Kittens are also good at avoidance learning. If something distasteful happens, they learn to avoid the circumstances that lead to the unpleasant experience. That's why squirting a cat with a water pistol when it scratches a table leg is an effective method of 'teaching'. Physical punishment, however, is of little value in training cats. At best it will only stop a behaviour when the owner is present and at worst it will lead to the cat simply avoiding the owner.

Kittens' socialization period and the seven weeks afterwards is the most active period of play in their life, and although why they play is not exactly known it is undoubtedly important to their physical and psychological development (and equally to our enjoyment in sharing our homes with them). Watching kittens play is a delight. Studying play is another matter.

PLAY

Kittens start to play with each other as soon as their senses are sufficiently developed, usually by three weeks of age. This 'social play' helps with motor co-ordination and provides information about siblings. At around the time of weaning, another form of play, 'object play', becomes equally important. This teaches kittens about their environment. Both types of play help to rehearse kittens for adulthood, but both might also be ends in themselves, carried out for the sheer pleasure of the activity.

Play is any type of activity that *appears* to be purposeless. At three weeks of age kittens start to make mock-aggressive rushes at each other and play rough-and-tumble and helter-skelter. At four weeks they start wrestling with each other, clasping with the forepaws and kicking furiously with the hind ones. By five weeks of age the pounce, especially the stiff-legged sideways pounce, has been perfected. And by six weeks they can leap and chase each other with delightful dexterity. At around the same time, three hunting manoeuvres enter into play, the 'mouse pounce', the 'bird swat' and the 'fish scoop'. (Research in the Netherlands showed that kittens allowed to hunt fish without mother to instruct them became successful anglers by seven weeks of age, using the flipping action of the 'fish scoop' to throw the fish out of the water.) All of these play activities are easily stimulated by us. Small, fluffy toys or even rustling leaves elicit the 'mouse pounce'; a piece of dangled string or seeing a fly provokes the 'bird swat'; and table-tennis balls or even feathers will induce a kitten to 'fish scoop'. Kittens are silliest (and most enchanting) when they 'hallucinate' or play with non-existent things, leaping at the wall or batting at invisible objects.

Certain activities are used in both social play and object play. These activities include the following, all of which, incidentally, Millie can carry out with effortless ease. For social play she uses my retrievers instead of her littermates.

Social play
Facing-off
Sparring
Licking

Hugging
Belly-upping

Object play
Scooping
Tossing
Poking or batting

Grasping
Mouthing or biting

Social and object play
Horizontally leaping
Vertically leaping
Side-stepping

Tail-chasing
Pouncing

Social Play

In social play, although two behaviours might be alternated, they are
rarely duplicated. Social play with siblings and other cats is at its
maximum when the mother is reducing the time she spends with her
litter. Mother cats become less tolerant of their kittens around the
sixth week of their lives and at that time kittens increase their social
play with other cats. Other adults rarely reject social play behaviour
from kittens and almost never reply in an aggressive manner. A
mother, however, will swat and growl at her kittens if the playful
antics of her litter annoy her.

This transfer of social activity from the mother to siblings has a
neat logic to it, for when her kittens have reached this age the
mother has to absent herself more frequently to go searching for
food. Social play might have evolved, in part, to keep the kittens
together until the mother's return.

Analysis of social play in adult cats shows that most play sequences
(87 per cent of them) consist of a pounce then a chase. Kittens prefer
belly-upping and stand-offs. Female-to-female activity accounts for 85
per cent of adult social play, while male-female accounts for 10 per
cent and male-male only 5 per cent.

Social play declines after fourteen weeks of age and this coincides
with the kittens' increasing independence of their mother, increasing
sexual behaviour and the dispersal of their littermates. Generally
speaking, females become less tolerant of close contact with males,
during play or otherwise. Social play that once ended amicably now
often ends with a growl and a hiss.

Object Play

Object play begins at around three weeks of age when kittens first tentatively paw at moveable objects. Soon they are patting, poking, batting and leaping on anything available. Millie pounced on my retrievers' tails, batted their noses, climbed their ears and chewed their legs. (They didn't much like the ear climbing but rather benignly accepted everything else. They even tried to join in, doing play bows, but at the sight of reciprocal action Millie darted away.)

Favourite toys seem to be prey-like in their physical properties and there are undoubtedly similarities between the behaviours used in object play and those that will eventually be needed to capture prey. Very detailed experiments have shown, however, that the amount and the quality of object play a kitten carries on has little significant effect on that animal's predatory abilities later in life. What, then, is the significance of all this activity?

As I have mentioned, as kittens grow older and become more mobile, they are more likely to wander from the nest. Social play might tend to keep them together in one place. But equally, play teaches kittens about their abilities, about the abilities of others and about their environment. Play postures mimic the postures of both offence and defence. Play can mimic aggression. It improves physical fitness, co-ordination and balance. And although the hissing kitten with its back arched, in confrontation with a littermate, looks like serious business, somehow the two of them know in their minds that this is only play. The threats, the scuffles, the punches are all given with just that little less vigour than in a real fight. We can't see it but they understand and signal their intent to each other in the subtlest of ways.

Although play activity declines from about five months of age, it doesn't disappear completely. Play can be elicited from cats of any age as long as you are willing to try to play with them. If you keep two or more littermates, they will often interact socially in a very playful manner. This could simply be a retention of juvenile behaviour or it could be a natural way in which cats in groups interact with each other. If there is only one cat in the household, however, it is up to us to keep it playful and active.

One major question still remains. If all of this play activity does not create a more successful hunter, how do kittens learn to capture and manipulate prey? The answer is that they learn in many different ways.

PREY KILLING

Minnie, a cat of indeterminate parentage, is alleged to have killed 12,480 rats in a six-year period at White City Stadium in London. Aside from wondering why so many rats chose to end their days at White City, you would no doubt ask how Minnie ever learnt to kill six a day, and whether she ate them.

The ability to kill prey has developed by the time a kitten is five weeks old but does not appear to be related to how much play the kitten indulges in. It is, however, directly related to what its mother teaches it. Good teachers pass on their own social techniques. Prey killing depends upon whether the kitten was allowed to go hunting with its mother and whether she brought back injured prey for it to despatch. It does *not* depend upon hunger, although the swiftness of killing does.

A kitten can also learn to kill without its mother's help. Kittens raised in the absence of their mothers can become proficient rodent killers, but they do so more quickly if they have seen another cat kill a rat. Kittens that have never had an opportunity to play with objects can become proficient rodent killers too.

Under natural conditions, mother cats 'teach' their kittens to kill. They bring live rodents back from the hunt and allow their kittens to 'play' with them. Paul Leyhausen describes three different ways in which kittens manipulate prey. There is 'restrained play', during which the kitten is apprehensive or fearful of the prey; 'overflow play', in which the kitten chases, catches and throws the rodent; and 'relief play', in which the kitten leaps around and over the dead body.

Some behaviourists have argued that play and predation are simply graded aspects of the same behaviour, claiming that play behaviour is fundamentally no different from predatory behaviour. But if play is a means to an end and that end is predatory behaviour, why do adult cats still play and, even more important, why do they continue to play with live prey?

Several facts are known about how cats play with prey. They will often play with prey when they are in conflict about what to do. Unfamiliar prey, for example, will stimulate prey manipulation rather than a simple death bite. Cats will play less with prey when they are hungry or dealing with small prey, although the old story that a hungry cat will catch more rats and mice is not exactly true. A well-fed and healthy cat is more likely to catch prey. Hunger motivates an experienced cat but has little effect on an inexperienced one; however, cats play more with prey when their stomachs are full, when they are given easy prey or are very hungry but confronted with large and difficult prey. And as a curiosity, cats given the anti-anxiety drug Valium (diazepam) will play with prey that they normally immediately kill.

For a kitten to learn to kill prey it must first learn to identify it, something its mother teaches it. Mothers which kill a certain strain of rat can teach their kittens to kill only that strain of rat. When presented with a rat of a different strain, the kittens do not kill. Kittens must also assess the prey, orient themselves to it and time their first moves. Now, there is no unequivocal evidence that play activity has any long-term benefits in teaching kittens how to do these things, but it seems only logical that play activity assists in co-ordination and use of the reflexes. Yet we already know that cats denied any play can still become good hunters, so if play is not fundamental to predatory activity, what other purposes does it serve? The answer is, as mentioned at the beginning of this chapter, that a kitten is not simply a miniature version of an adult. Kittens have special characteristics and needs that are different from adult characteristics and needs. This means that some early behaviours, including the fascinating, mesmerizing range of play activities that kittens enjoy, can develop to help kittens become adept as kittens as well as to act as scaffolding on which to build adult behaviour. Normal adult behaviours (such as prey killing) can be reached by several different routes of development and differences in behaviour in kittens will not predict similar differences in their adult behaviour. Play is a delightful way that kittens learn about life, but it is not the only way.

Chapter Six

Later Learning: Rank and Territory

CAT SOCIETY

Until 1965 when Paul Leyhausen wrote his book, *Cat Behaviour: The Predatory and Social Behaviour of Domestic and Wild Cats,* the image of the cat was that of the loner, the solitary hunter without a group culture. 'I am the cat who walks by himself . . . ,' wrote Rudyard Kipling in his *Just So Stories,* and that delightfully eloquent statement alluding to the cat's solitary existence still exemplifies our attitude towards the social behaviour of the animal.

Yet in the last decade there has been an explosion of over a hundred scientific treatises on the cat's social and territorial behaviour, and what is now apparent is that there are possibly more variations in feline society than in that of any other studied species. Cats have an elastic ability to vary the way they live. Today they live in habitats as diverse as remote intemperate sub-Antarctic islands and polluted industrial city centres. As Rudyard Kipling noted, many are lone hunters, each with an individual home range of over 250 acres (100 hectares), but others have developed a social structure that permits 2000 individuals to live commensally in a similar-sized area. Some are dependent upon us for survival; others maintain stable populations without or, indeed, in spite of our interference. Cats are solitary hunters, but embellishing their hunting activity is a complex net of relationships we are only now discovering. Females have dramatically different social behaviours and societies from males. Cats living in groups act and think differently from cats living alone. Cats with restricted home ranges, such as indoor house cats, live by different social rules from cats that have access to larger territories.

With the substantial scientific evidence that is now available only one fact can be stated with certainty about the social behaviour of

cats and that is that in no case has the social structure of one group
been exactly like that of another. In some circumstances females will
tolerate each other or even mutually co-operate by feeding and grooming each other's kittens. In others they are strictly territorial, fiercely
protecting their dens and feeding territory from other females who
hazard into them. Some females tolerate dominant males on their
territory and others don't. They may live widely spaced, or live and
sleep crowded together. They may share their homes with other
females or viciously and tenaciously defend them from others of their
own sex.

Males may share both territories and females, but a dominant
male is equally likely to terrorize any other male that tries to mate
with a female within what he considers to be his domain. Young cats
may be tolerated and permitted to take great liberties with males and
females alike, playing outrageously with them, but in certain situations they are beaten and chased by all but their mothers. After
weaning, females may be permitted to stay but male kittens chased
away, or both may be permitted to stay or both chased away.

These differences in behaviour are a result of environmental pressures and the most important is the size and proximity of the local
source of food. The greater the source of food, be it ground-nesting
birds, a rubbish skip or a cupboard full of tinned cat food, the greater

Cats are solitary hunters.

the likelihood that cats will live in social groups. But in addition to environmental pressures, our unintentional selective breeding of cats has probably been responsible for making them more sociable in groups, and at least one scientific investigator has recently found that to some extent genetic differences between small populations of felines are also responsible for their social diversity.

POPULATION DENSITY

The European wild cat lives a solitary life and so do many feral and house cats. Where the wild cat still exists in Scotland and Czechoslovakia, there are around three individuals per 250 acres (100 hectares). In New Zealand, on the grassy slopes, woods and river valley area of Orongorongo, where domestic cats have become feral, their population density is around one to two per 250 acres. In rural open land near Schiermonnikoog in the Netherlands, they live at a similar population density, while in the flat Sacramento Valley of California and in the hedgerowed farmland of England's Devonshire, their population density is between six and twelve cats per 250 acres. Similar densities have been noted in Australia and on isolated islands. In Australia 90 per cent of all the adults sighted were on their own and when feral cats were studied on sub-Antarctic Marrion Island a similar 90 per cent of sightings were of single cats. The home ranges of these solitary cats overlapped less than chance would suggest and this implies that the cats had actively spaced themselves out. They had staked territories where they hunted rabbits, rodents and birds.

When food is clumped as a central source the dynamic of social behaviour is capable of great change. In Portsmouth, England, dockyard cats live on rubbish from skips and on hand-outs. Here they tolerate a population density of 200 per 250 acres (100 hectares). In the public gardens of Belvedere Tarpeo in Rome, where cats are completely dependent upon 'cat lovers' for their food, they live at a population density of up to 2000 per 250 acres, and in the Japanese fishing village of Ainoshima where the food source is waste from the local fisheries there are 2350 cats in an area of equal size!

Group living does not mean travelling or spending long periods of time with each other but rather involves a tolerance of each other. But when these groups have been closely observed, the researchers noted that there are also active social behaviours – mutual grooming, licking and body rubbing – which are carried out for social satisfaction.

Cats scavenge communally at major food sources.

From the studies that have been published some broad conclusions can be drawn. The density of a feral cat population is directly related to the quantity and availability of food. When the only food available is prey that must be captured, cats live at a population density of less than five per 250 acres (100 hectares) and are solitary animals, with the exception of mothers with kittens and during the breeding season. When the food source is a combination of prey and hand-outs, either rubbish or other food intentionally left for cats, the population density increases to between six and fifty cats per 250 acres. This is the density of feral cats on a typical European or American farm. Finally, when there is an intense food source such as that provided by 'cata-holics' in the piazzas of Venice, the parks of Paris or the gardens of London, or a naturally abundant resource such as rubbish dumps and waste skips, the population density increases up to in excess of 2000 cats per 250 acres.

Male and female distribution

The home range of the feral female cat is based upon the abundance of food, its distribution and the availability of shelter. Male cats have home ranges that are on average three and a half times larger than those of females. Feeding a larger body can account for a slightly larger hunting territory, but males are rarely more than one and a half times larger than females. To account for the larger male territory strictly by body weight a male would need to be almost five times bigger than a female, a distinct indication that food alone is not the reason for the male cat's need for more elbow room. The accepted assumption is that the density and distribution of female cats, as well as the abundance of food and the availability of shelter, are factors that contribute to the size of the male cat's territory.

Not all male cats are equal, however. One Swedish observer has classified feral males as 'breeders, challengers, outcasts and novices'. The breeders have the largest territories and significantly increase their ranges during the mating season. Among the farm cats in this study there was a 'central' breeder who monopolized matings at the given farm and several increasingly aggressive two-to-three-year-old challengers who refused to leave the territory. Outcasts were mostly young males forced to emigrate from the farm territory. These males avoided contact with any other cats. Novices were yearling males allowed to remain temporarily with their mothers but subject to increasing attacks from breeders and challengers.

The territories of feral males conform to their social status. During the mating season there is considerable overlap of territories between dominant males, but the ranges of subordinate males remain the same and are covered by dominant males year round. During the non-mating season food is the most important resource, yet young adult males are subjected to continual harassment and are eventually forced out of their homes by older males. (Male house cats retreat indoors for protection.) Dominant males try to keep all other males off their territory by frequently roaming. Staying at home is the best tactic of the subordinate male.

When the source of food is sparse feral female cats will live and hunt individually, but when food is clumped their social organization radically changes and the population density increases. Other than on Marrion Island, where feral cats sleep together, possibly for warmth, group living seems to be a phenomenon of the female cat's association with food sources provided by humans. But this matriarchal society is so dramatically similar to the natural social organization of lions which hunt large herbivores – meals for many – that I feel it is a natural manifestation of cat culture which has been permitted to flourish only in the man-made circumstances of surplus food.

In the social organization of the lion pride, several adult females together with their still-juvenile young form the nucleus of a community that occupies and defends a piece of land. Two or more males accompany the pride, patrolling the territory and defending it and the females from any intruding males. Other unrelated females are driven away by the pride females and the continuity of the pride is guaranteed solely by admitting daughters, before they reach adulthood, to fill gaps left by deaths. All other young females and all growing males are expelled and must leave the pride territory at about three years of age. These lions become 'nomads' and in fact make up the majority, leading vagrant lives on the periphery of pride lands. They are less successful at breeding and at rearing cubs.

Competition from males to displace the pride males is intense and in the Serengeti plains of Tanzania a pride male group only rarely succeeds in keeping the pride for more than three years. In Uganda, on the other hand, males stay with their pride for six or more years – all of their reproductive life.

A similar social organization is seen with feral female cats clumped around a grand food source. A cat colony is often a female colony consisting of several related females and their sub-adult young. Overseeing the colony is the breeding tom which defends the territory from other males, while the females chase off any other females who chance too close. New members for the colony are recruited from sub-adult female descendants; male kittens, upon reaching adulthood, are expelled, to become nomads or challengers. The colony is matriarchal in that it depends on female recruits from within. The female line always continues, although the male line is abruptly changed whenever a dominant male is successfully challenged. (The male challengers, and outcasts or nomads, should not be thought of as simply surplus to requirements, for out on the periphery of the cat colony or lion pride there is a constant dynamic in action – what Paul Leyhausen has called the 'tomcat brotherhood'. Here, a large number of fairly evenly matched cats vie with each other through physical combat and mental agility for the right to challenge the colony or pride male.)

There is no published evidence that groups of females living together actively defend their food source, but they do prevent 'strange' females from joining their group. Male cats, however, are allowed to move between groups of females. This could be because they have greater physical strength, because of sexual relationships or simply because a male does not pose as much of a competitive threat as does another female. As well as competing for food, a strange female would also be competing for den sites and, more important, for the services of the breeding male. Her successful reproduction would be a serious threat to the existing female line.

Within female groups, relationships are reasonably amicable and much more social than would be expected if the members stayed together only because of the convenience of a nearby food supply. Individuals will rest together, will greet each other and sometimes groom each other. Colony cats will actively seek each other out, and each has its own particular favourite other cat or cats. When they sleep together, half of the time they are in physical contact with one or more other cats. When there are adult males in a colony, they will touch other individuals only half as often as will other females. The relationships between colony members differ in quality and range from affectionate to aggressive. In one study of 1547 interactions between colony members 64 per cent of interactions involved licking, 29 per cent involved rubbing and 7 per cent involved aggression. Kittens initiated contacts with adults, females with males and females with other females, but males seldom initiated any contacts.

From observing the social behaviour of feral cats we know that it is unwarranted to claim, as some have, that cat sociability is an artificial creation of cat fanciers. In fact, with good justification, we can say that sociability is a profound component of the cat's mind and exists in all groups of felines regardless of size or superficial differences. That sociability is based on the matriarchal bond, the long-term affiliation between a mother and successive generations of her female descendants. The extent to which this natural 'matrilineal' social organization is permitted to occur depends upon how much food is available, and it only occurs when food is readily available and where adult mortality is low, in other words in moderate-sized colonies. When more than, say, fifty cats gather around a food source, what is created is not a single colony but rather a confluence of many colonies or social units. A colony itself consists only of females, female descendants, juvenile male descendants and one or two males.

The dramatic differences in the social behaviour of the solitary feral female cat in New Zealand and the group member in the public gardens of Rome raise the question of whether cats can swap cultures; whether they can move from one set of behaviours to another. This question was answered by an observation of the social behaviour of cats in the crofting communities of the Hebrides islands of Scotland.

There, in the summer, females become solitary rabbit hunters, each with her own overlapping home range. In winter, however, they move back into crofts where they live on hand-outs from the crofters. Kittens are moved into crofts when they are about eight weeks old, but male cats remain in the fields throughout the year.

It seems, then, that feral cats have a dramatically variable range of social and territorial behaviours which are completely independent of their relationship with us and that their social system depends upon factors such as density of numbers, age, ecological conditions and genetics. Kittens grow up to conform to the social traditions to which they are exposed when they were very young, but what makes the cat so excitingly different from other animals is its social versatility. When other animals – dogs, horses, pigs, goats, sheep or cattle – return to a feral existence, they either fall back on the social systems of their wild ancestors or create impoverished versions of these. But not so cats. When cats revert to a feral lifestyle, they create enriched social systems that are both quantitatively and qualitatively more profound than that of their closest relative, the North African wild cat. Although cats have depended upon us to take them to all corners of the world, once they arrived in different hospitable and inhospitable locales they were able to develop or adopt an increasing variety of group activities to meet the new conditions to which they were exposed. They did so on their own, without our intervention, and in that sense it is true to describe them as self-domesticated. But of the 400 million cats in the world today, almost 200 million either live with or are at least peripherally cared for by us. How have we affected their social and territorial desires?

RANKING AND TERRITORY IN PET CATS

Soon after their eyes open for the first time kittens start to compete with each other. And although the litter is so well organized that they seem to be living together without friction and with equal rights, those first clumsy but already aimed paws blows at the heads of competing littermates are signals of the ranking disputes and territorial demands that will continue to develop as the kittens mature.

Just as feral cats have their own territories, so too do our pet cats, although in the latter's case these are sometimes no more than favourite sleeping places. A pet cat's home area is usually the house in which it lives and some surrounding territory, a home range that includes favoured places for sunbathing, dozing and sleeping, or simply for sedately watching the world go by. The shape and extent of the home range depends, as it does with feral cats, on the sex and age of the cat, on the number of neighbourhood cats, on the food supply, on the individual temperament of the animal and also on whether it has been neutered, as well as the neuter status of its neighbours. Females and neutered cats usually occupy small, well-defined territories – just as we do, with our fences and hedges. Taking their cue from us, cats often establish territories that conform to our own and will generally defend with vigour their own small areas against other feline intruders.

Unneutered pet tomcats, a relatively rare species, command home territories that are perhaps ten time bigger than those of females. These larger territories have less well-defined borders, but fights still regularly occur when strange cats enter them. Beyond the home territory, and for those that wish to indulge, is the hunting territory, an area linked by specific and often circuitous trails around territories defended by other cats.

In almost all circumstances, cats are entirely familiar with the nooks and crannies of their immediate home territory. They have their resting areas, sunbathing areas, observation posts and larder. Beyond the immediate home area are paths leading to places for hunting, courting, fighting and other activities. There is usually more than one path leading to each of these areas, but the areas between the paths are rarely used at all. Jurisdictional disputes rarely occur because cats are careful to avoid meeting each other on these routes, and fights very rarely happen. If two cats do meet unexpectedly, rank order or simply whoever arrives first decides who should proceed. If rank has not already been determined, a fight might ensue. In disputes of this type it is rare for there to be more than one serious fight between two adult animals. At a different place and at a different time, however, the results of a fight might be different too, for the confidence and courage of a cat increases the closer it is to its own home territory. Leyhausen has coined the term 'relative rank order' to describe the fact that rank hierarchy in cats is not rigid, as it is in other animals such as dogs. In border areas it may simply be the case that the cat who arrives first is the dominant one. This is not always true, for in practice I see (and treat) neighbouring cats who appear to have an unmitigated, irreconcilable mutual hatred and who tear into each other at any given opportunity.

As previously mentioned, cats will mark their territory with their urine and faeces, but no cat has ever been observed to go up to a urine scent post, sniff it and then retreat. What they almost always do is sniff the mark in a leisurely manner and either continue on their way or leave their own mark on it. Scent marks are not intimidating. They only serve to help cats avoid unexpected encounters and sudden clashes; to tell who is further ahead on the path and when he passed that way.

As cat keeping becomes more popular, so too the number of housebound cats grows, but even in these artificial habitats cats will set up their own territories and can viciously defend a favourite sleeping spot on a sofa, for example. However, when the number of cats within a home reaches a certain level – and that level will vary with the size of the home and the temperaments of the individuals – a point is reached where the territory is no longer large enough for the resident population. When this happens a profound change in social structure occurs. At its simplest level, fighting among the cats increases dramatically because there are not enough hiding places for the subordinate animals; in its extreme manifestation, certain cats are treated by all the others as outcasts, pariahs that can literally be hounded to death.

In a typical multiple-cat household there are one or two 'top' cats

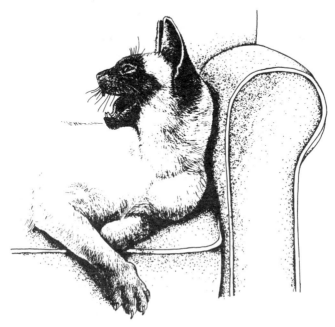

All cats need their own personal territory even if it is only a favourite resting place.

who, either by physical force or by mental aptitude, have come to occupy the best areas of the territory. These get the best resting places and are often first at the food bowl. If there are several food bowls available, they are often left alone at the bowl of their choice while the others gather round the rest. 'Top' cats will ritually bat the faces of the others in a simple gesture of dominance.

Ranking in pet cats is not as pronounced as it is in many other species. For example, when cats are very hungry, they will forget their rank and will all gather around food when it is offered, with the subordinate cats backing away only after they have satisfied their initial hunger. In a similar fashion subordinate cats are happy to occupy the dominant cat's resting position until the latter returns, at which time the place is quietly vacated.

Pariah cats, which can be male or female, are attacked mercilessly by the other household cats when they leave their hiding places. Paul Leyhausen once described one of his cat communities of twelve in which two were treated as pariahs and were forced always to remain perched on the central-heating pipes close to the ceiling. Whenever they ventured down, they were savagely attacked by all others and were so abused they let their urine and faeces simply drop from above. They were permitted to descend to eat only if Leyhausen was there to defend them.

In most of the multiple-cat households with which I am familiar there are no well-defined 'top' cats and pariahs. The residents seem to be mostly co-equals, but a closer examination of these groups reveals that even here there is a pronounced social order. Altercations do occur but are often misinterpreted by us, for the cat that strikes first is not necessarily the superior animal. A lower-ranking cat will often take a swipe at a more dominant individual and then withdraw. And in a similar sense, a great display of aggression such as hissing and laying back the ears shows resolution but does not necessarily indicate rank. The mutual toleration and respect that cats have developed for each other in multiple-cat households can be upset by the arrival of a strange feline. Because of their inherent nature, females are less tolerant of the introduction of new females into the house than are males. When a long-standing community is upset by a new arrival, the existing members of the household will sniff each other, usually nose to nose, and members who are already on unfriendly terms might start to fight. More likely, they will attack the newcomer.

Pet cats create a ranking hierarchy among themselves, but it is neither as obvious nor as well defined as it is with pet dogs. A narrow passage might 'belong' to the 'top' cat, yet if another cat is already in it, he or she is allowed 'right of passage'. A sofa might be the 'top' cat's favoured resting place in the morning, but the same sofa might become another's favoured resting place in the afternoon. In a practical sense, the artificial territory of the human home, or even the home and garden, provides a finite area in which cats can carry out their natural behaviours. Because of the plastic nature of their social behaviour a number of cats can be kept in such an artificial environment but a point is soon reached when the introduction of a new cat breaks down the social order. Despots emerge and pariahs are created. Behavioural problems involving eating, urinating, defecating and fighting filter to the surface. Play behaviour stops. Exercise is reduced to a minimum and hissing, growling and fighting replace the previous calm. These are man-made problems: we inflict upon cats a man-made environment in which they are deprived of the ability to act independently, to simply run away as they would in a natural environment. (These and other behavioural problems are discussed further in Chapter Thirteen.)

When we move house our pet cats often have difficulty establishing a new territory. The garden of the new home might already be incorporated into another cat's territory. Fights ensue and I'm asked to treat the resulting abscesses. An owner often puts a cat flap in the back door only to discover that his or her cat has been chased through the flap and up the stairs by the resident territory owner. Other owners tell me of toms coming through their cat flaps at night and urine marking inside the house. These confrontations are inevitable and the ferocity of the altercations depends upon the sex, age, strength and personality of both your cat and its opponent. Just as feral cats do, females will fiercely defend their home territories. Fortunately neutered females will defend less vigorously and consequently are less frequently injured. Males will defend larger territories and inevitably have the battle scars to show for it. Neutered males still fight but are more likely to defend their immediate territory rather than that of the extended harem of the intact male.

All cats, regardless of sex or neuter status, use the same type of psychological warfare. They employ vocal and visual threats. They bluff and they appease, all in an attempt to keep the actual fighting to a minimum. Fights themselves rarely go on for any protracted length of time and the winner usually chases the loser off the territory. Because of the density of pet cats in urban, suburban and rural areas, if they were to fight each time strangers met all their energy would be used in what would be wasted endeavours. Instead, cats have developed what can euphemistically be called a 'highway code'. When setting off on a trip through its territory, a cat checks the paths ahead. If another cat is crossing the path or even using it, the resident waits at a 'stop' signal until the right of way is free.

Another method of avoiding fights is through time scheduling. Cats have excellent time sense and can set up routines by which several cats can share the same territory simply by not being in the same place all at once. If a confrontation does occur, however, there are still ways of deflecting it. Cats will stare each other down and usually one will, slowly and with great dignity, turn its head and move away. Sometimes both will retreat. If this doesn't happen, the full-scale threat ritual ensues. And only if that doesn't work will a full-scale fight be entered into.

CAT DUELS

Cat fights are vicious but short. And although claws and paws are actively used, the teeth are a cat's main weapons. In a slow and seemingly calculated manner the dominant cat approaches its target. All its legs are straight and, as the hind legs are longer than the forelimbs, there is a downward slope from the hind end to the front of the body. The pupils of the eyes are not dilated. In fact, if anything, they are slightly constricted, indicating that what follows is not provoked by fear but rather is a preplanned aggressive act. The hair on the cat's back is erect right up to the ears, as is the hair on the tail which he carries straight back. The tip of the tail bends down at right angles and it might twitch back and forth. The ears are not flattened back but rather are turned in an outward direction so that the cat's opponent sees a very pointed triangle.

As the cat moves in almost slow motion towards its opponent it howls, mews and growls – all pure threat. The cat might be salivating and if it does so excessively it has to swallow. At the same time the tongue moves rhythmically forwards and backwards and the jaws chatteringly open and close slowly. When the cat is less than a yard from its opponent, it raises its head and tilts it at a 45° angle sideways to its body but keeps its eyes on its opponent.

If the opponent is of equal strength or resolve, it will have behaved in exactly the same way, but now, face to face, both cats may remain motionless, only inches apart, for many minutes while they grunt

Duals between males are vicious but usually short.

their battle chants and howls. Suddenly one will lunge at the other's neck and in the same instant the defender will throw itself on its back, fending off the attacker's fangs with its own, using its forelegs to hold off the attacker while scratching and beating violently with its hind legs. When this happens the attacker has no choice but to do the same, and both animals end up rolling wildly on the ground, all the time shrieking and screaming. Then, just as suddenly as they started, they break the clinch, separate, leap away from one another and instantly face off for another threat and fight. This continues until one cat gives up. The victor continues to threaten and might chase the loser hundreds of yards, all the time uttering piercing howls. More often the victor simply continues to threaten, but does not attack again. And in a rather disdainful way it may half-turn away and sniff the ground. This 'alternative' movement seems to be provoked by the now defensive attitude of the opponent, who remains motionless, crouching, protecting its neck by pulling in its head, flattening the ears, hissing and, if the attacker comes close once more, striking out with a forepaw. If possible, the defensive animal will try to get higher than the aggressor. (Cats climb trees for fun or to get away from predators or other cats.) The winner, with its ears still in the 'threat-to-bite' position and its hair still on end, turns and moves away, and only when the victor is a good distance away does the loser slink off.

Adult tomcats meeting for the first time invariably fight, regardless of the season, but once it has been decided who is the stronger they settle arguments and confrontation by ritual display rather than through further fighting. In this way cats that 'pass the test' and are not reduced to pariahs are allowed to join the establishment and live unmolested in a large communal area. They gather in what appears to be friendly convention and even during the mating season will not fight with each other but rather simply line up in a silent, unblinking queue to service the female.

Although the victor is the first to leave the battlefield, the territory is his, and when our pet cats come home with bite marks around their faces they will have endured just such a conflict. Abscesses around their tails mean that they have been attacked while running from a fight. The tears to eyelids and ears are caused by claws, but the punctures and abscesses to ears, face, neck and limbs are bite wounds. The aim of an attack is to bite the nape of the neck in the right place, which is why male cats have evolved such thick neck skin.

Although females have the muscles, co-ordination and vocal abilities to duel in this way, they very rarely do so. Both intact and neutered females will ritually threaten and attack, but do not repeatedly duel as will male cats. Fights themselves are usually between cats of the same rank or between a resident and a stranger. Male cats usually won't pick fights with females, but neutered males are just as likely to indulge in territorial fighting as are intact males. What they are less likely to do is engage in rival fighting for females. And because of their size and strength, neutered males are very successful at keeping strange cats from their territory. Some breeders have used this fact to permit their breeding females to freely run in the garden. Visits by undesirable males are prevented by keeping a big, burly, neutered tom in the garden who sees off all other males, and other females for that matter.

In any given pet cat population over 70 per cent of all individuals, be they indoor or outdoor cats, are neutered. The social behaviour of these cats has recently been investigated and has been found to be strikingly similar to that of feral groups. Hierarchies form in which the 'top' cats are net recipients of social interactions and those at the bottom are givers. What is different is the frequency with which behaviours occur. Mutual grooming, for example, is virtually absent among groups of neutered feral cats.

Activity levels also vary according to social level, sex and status of the cat. In a major Swedish study of both feral and free-ranging pet cats all were active on average about 50 per cent of the time. Females and very young males (novices) were the least active (41 and 45 per cent respectively) and the outcasts were the most active (65 per cent of the time). Regardless of season, the peak period of activity for all cats was between 6 and 9pm. In a similar study of female cats on a Welsh dairy farm, they spent 40 per cent of their time sleeping, 22 per cent resting, 15 per cent grooming, 15 per cent hunting, 3 per cent travelling, 3 per cent feeding and 2 per cent on other activities.

The ranking behaviours, creation and defence of territories and social activities of domestic cats are much more varied and colourful than those of their immediate forebear, the North African wild cat. Household cats can develop close social ties with other cats, and with humans or even other animals too. My cat Millie has formed strong social bonds with the two golden retrievers she lives with. She bats their faces, swings from their tails, rubs herself against their legs, sits between them as they watch their meals being prepared and curls up and sleeps with them when the spirit moves her. She grooms them and in turn they lick her. My family takes these behaviours for granted, but they indicate the amazing versatility of which the cat's mind is capable. Millie has been conditioned to live with dogs and with people in her territory. But private territory is still important. With or without our involvement, cats need territories they can call their own. For free-ranging cats the territory is both home and a restaurant. For males it is also a brothel. But even for Millie her own territory means places to hide, sentry posts and observation platforms, eating areas and play and rest stations. All cats need this uncrowded minimum if we are to provide them with stimulating lives.

Chapter Seven

Sexual Behaviour and Maternal Activity

Desmond Morris once calculated that, given optimum conditions, a single breeding pair of domestic cats could produce 65,534 descendants in the course of five years – a grim and apocryphal scenario for gardeners and mice. Accidents, disease, lack of territorial space, competition and extensive neutering of pet cats keeps populations under control, but in many countries, including the USA, Britain, Sweden, Norway, Denmark, France, Italy, Spain, Germany, Japan and the USSR, the pet cat population is increasing yearly.

Left to themselves, not all sexually mature cats are capable of breeding. Pariahs, either male or female, virtually never breed, nor do novice males. Outcasts don't have the opportunity to breed either. Among feral and free-ranging cats, those most likely to breed are

During courtship the female presents herself while the male 'flehms' her urine scent.

group females or male members of the roaming 'brotherhood', and they go about it this way.

Breeding involves three distinct phases, a courtship, mating itself and then some specific post-mating activity. Although, when they are six months old, tomcats may start the sex-related activities of spraying urine or 'flehming' (sneering at the scent of female oestrus cat urine), and show sexual activity when they are about a year old, they don't reach full physical and sexual maturity until closer to eighteen months of age, which is when they are more likely to become successful breeders.

Feral females may not reach puberty until over a year of age, but pet cats usually achieve it by seven months. Puberty means sexual maturity, so they are ready to be mated. Some breeds, such as the Siamese and Burmese, are sexually more precocious, sometimes reaching puberty as early as the age of three and a half months. (With their loud and plaintive yowling, writhing on the floor as if in agony and desperate desire to be near 'their' owner, Siamese have probably prompted more late-night distress telephone calls to the vet by their tormented, sleepless owners than any other breed. These callers plead for advice as to what they should do with their over-sexed felines: as the recipient of such requests, I have varied my answer according to how late at night I have been awakened!) Others, like the pedigree long-hairs, may not become sexually mature until over a year of age.

The actual onset of puberty, the time when the female's ovaries and the male's testicles begin their production of eggs and sperm respectively, will vary more with the size of the cat than with its age. Bigger, healthier cats reach maturity faster than their smaller or malnourished cousins. And as puberty usually occurs in the spring, females born late in the previous year might reach sexual maturity earlier than females born early in the preceding breeding season.

Wild cats have distinct breeding seasons that start in the spring. Feral cats often have seasonal heat cycles as well, but these begin somewhat earlier, usually in late winter, and because of the seasonal nature of their cycles these cats are described as 'seasonally poly-oestrous'. They have multiple heat cycles but only at certain times of the year, usually from spring until autumn. These cycles are stimulated by the increasing daylight of late winter and early spring, an environmental change that heralds the increasing food supply of spring and summer, when prey will have to be found for the new litter.

The actual production of eggs usually begins soon after daylight starts to increase, but regular cyclical activity does not start for another month or two. Experimentally, if female cats are kept in an environment where light is provided at a constant fourteen hours per day, their heat periods continue throughout the year. This type of exposure to light changes the body's biological rhythms. Specifically, melatonin production is altered. Because so many of our pet cats are housed indoors and exposed to artificial lighting, some of them don't exhibit the seasonal polyoestrous activity of feral or free-ranging cats. Although some breeders are convinced that their pure-bred cats breed year round because they are biologically different, the real reason is in their housing rather than in their genes.

Cats are induced ovulators. Unlike female humans, cattle, dogs and most other female mammals which release eggs at certain times in their oestrous cycles, cats release eggs only after they have been mated. Sexually experienced male cats will mate year round, although there is some evidence that males also have a seasonal sexual cycle similar to that of females.

In female cats each cycle lasts for two to three weeks, and within each cycle the prime period for mating (oestrus) lasts on average for seven days. In pure-bred cats there seems to be a difference in the length of oestrus itself. Oriental cats seem to have shorter cycles but longer oestrus periods within the cycle. And as the cycles continue, the periods between cycles grow shorter until it seems that the female is constantly calling her availability. With Siamese and Burmese that's some call! Persians and British shorthairs appear to cycle less frequently than 'moggies', a fact that leads to seemingly more restrained sexual behaviour.

During the receptive (oestrus) phase of her cycle the female cat's ovaries actively produce the sex hormone oestrogen and she will be sexually attractive to males. The major oestrogen produced by cats, estradiol-17beta, can actually double in quantity within twenty-four hours, which is why sexual behaviour can begin so abruptly. Estradiol production continues on average for ten days. Cats are unusual in that, even if they have successfully mated and have started to produce progesterone, the hormone of pregnancy, they will still continue to mate.

Mating itself triggers ovulation and is usually entirely under the control of the female. As her receptive period approaches, her personality can change dramatically. Dignified reserve gives way to restlessness, an increased appetite, more frequent urinating and the plaintive repeated monotone of the 'call'. Housebound females sit piteously at the window, ineffectively howling their availability. Females become more affectionate with 'their' people, but also with strangers. They rub against objects, roll on the ground and miaow constantly. They rhythmically tread with their forepaws while raising their rumps and deflecting their tails to the side, a posture called lordosis.

Naturally, if a female behaves like this outdoors, she soon has a male congregation surrounding her, attracted by the scent of her oestrous urine, by the changes in her glandular secretions and by her voice. During the courtship and mating that follow, although she might appear to be behaving like a hussy, she entirely controls the situation, allowing the males to mate only when she wants to. Many do so, and there is a curious biological reason for these multiple matings.

The female's control of mating begins when she starts increasingly to scent mark. This attracts many males and reduces the likelihood of a chance mating with an inferior male. According to Eugenia Natoli, who has studied the mating behaviour of feral cats in Rome, during a single oestrus period a female was courted by up to twenty males and mated with up to sixteen of them. Even with multiple matings such as these, there are still losers.

Natoli discovered that males followed two different courtship strategies. Some spent prolonged periods close to the female and others did not. Yet the amount of time spent close to her did not guarantee mating, for other males were quite successful, using more of a hit-and-run tactic. 'Slam, bam, thank you ma'am' was equally successful. These 'mobile' males would bypass the queue, yet never used aggressive behaviour to do so.

Experienced males are more successful at reading receptivity in the behaviour of the female. Courtship between unacquainted cats may last several hours before mating occurs and if a premature attempt to mount is made by the male he often gets viciously beaten up by the female. During this prelude the male will sniff the female's genitalia and will 'flehm'. He might sit still, staring at her, or circle her, but if she turns in his direction he freezes and 'plays statue'. She might hiss and spit, but he chirps a curious noise and eventually, with her acquiescence, he grasps her neck with his teeth and mounts with his front legs. The bite might look savage but in reality he is only protecting himself. Females can be ferociously aggressive towards males, but just as picking up a kitten by the scruff immobilizes it, so a bite on the neck does the same. (In fact that is how I hold cats when

Withdrawal by the male induces the female to cry out and often to attack.

I spray them for fleas – although I grasp them with my hand rather than my mouth.) As the male mounts and holds the female by the neck, she crouches down. He then straddles her with his hind legs and makes stepping movements while she treads. Then, as he arches his back and makes pelvic thrusts, she swings her tail to the side and raises her hind end. All of this might take a few minutes. Copulation itself lasts only for seconds. Intromission and ejaculation occur. She screams and then turns on him to bite him. The scream is prompted by the fish-hook-like barbs on the male's penis, but these serve a sound biological function. Receptors in the female's vagina are stimulated by these barbs and the consequence is a cascade of hormonal changes that eventually lead to ovulation. The receptors trigger a release of gonadotrophin-releasing hormone in the hypothalamus. This hormone stimulates a release of luteinizing hormone (LH) from the pituitary gland. Once LH reaches a high enough level, eggs are released. And this cascade of events is also why cats indulge in multiple matings, for one mating alone is often not enough to trigger these hormonal changes.

Even though mating seems to be painful to the female, she is soon at it again. Within half an hour she is once more interested in sex and repeats the entire curious cycle of preventing mating, enticing mating, then screaming and aiming a blow at the male. And as the repeated matings continue she increasingly croons, writhes and rubs.

Ovulation in cats is an 'all-or-none' phenomenon. Either all the ripe eggs are released or none of them are, and the most important factor in guaranteeing egg release is multiple matings. The actual time course for LH release is quite short – about ninety minutes – and that is why the multiple matings must be in quick succession. There are biological reasons, too, for these feline sex orgies. First of all, if multiple matings with different males produce a single litter sired by different males, this leads to a genetic diversity that might be advantageous. It seems strange but scientists still don't know whether a single litter has several fathers, although some evidence points strongly to the fact. But even if this is not the case there is still a biologically sound basis for multiple matings, for they ensure that only the healthiest sperm are successful. Although cannibalism of kittens by male cats has been reported, it is certainly very rare. I have never personally heard of such a happening, but this too could be a reason for multiple matings. By increasing paternal uncertainty the female might succeed in reducing male aggressiveness to her offspring.

Following mating, the female goes through a series of post-copulation behaviours. In a state that is seemingly more excited than her normal one, she rolls on the ground, rubs her head on any convenient object, licks her genitalia and is soon inviting further mountings from the congregated males. And, as successive matings occur, the initiative for mating seems to pass from the males to the female until finally it is she who makes the advances, rubbing against a rather nonplussed male and taking up the mating position in front of him. Some writers have said that catnip causes females to behave in the same way, but that is only partly true. Catnip induces some cats to body-roll and head-rub, but it doesn't cause foot-treading, vocalizing or vulvar presentation, all central aspects of sexual behaviour. While the female rolls, rubs and 'whispers sweet nothings' after mating, the male simply sits near her, often licking his penis and forepaws. Experienced pairs might mate ten times in an hour, but if the male is in a strange location it takes him much longer to get into action. This is why breeders usually suggest that the female is brought to the male's territory rather than vice versa. Once mating has occurred the male might stay around for a day or so, but he plays no further role either during the pregnancy, the birth or the upbringing of the kittens. All of these roles are the total responsibility of the female.

PREGNANCY

You cannot tell whether a mating has been successful until at least three weeks later when the veterinarian can first feel the developing foetuses and the female cat's nipples become somewhat firmer and change from a dull to a more pink colour. Progesterone, the hormone of pregnancy, rapidly increases and remains at its highest level until around the thirty-fifth day of a sixty-three-day pregnancy. It gradually decreases, falling precipitously during the last week until it returns to its baseline level in the last days of pregnancy. This is necessary to permit the uterine contractions of delivery.

At around thirty days the cat's belly begins visibly to get rounder, and during the last three weeks you can actually see and feel on her abdomen the movements of the kittens in the uterus (womb) inside. Pregnancy can be as short as fifty-seven days or as long as seventy, with the developing kittens growing on average about $\frac{1}{8}$ in (3 mm) per day.

BIRTH

One or two days before birth the female cat becomes restless. Pregnant females choose all sorts of different sites for whelping dens. Free-ranging cats look for shelter, but those attached to people might prefer the wide-open spaces of their owner's bed. Cats often search for an appropriate spot for days and frequently change sites. You can help by providing a newspaper-lined box in a warm, dry, draught-free, dark, quiet and (from the cat's viewpoint) easily guarded location, such as under a bed or in a cupboard.

As labour begins the mother-to-be claws and rearranges her bedding, lies down, gets up, visits the litter box but doesn't use it, lies down again or paces restlessly. If you have more than one female, you might find that the other comes over either out of curiosity or actually to act as midwife, helping to chew through umbilical cords and lick new-born kittens. If the first water has not yet broken, it will now, and soon afterwards the first kitten, still enclosed in its amniotic sac, is pushed out by the strong contractions. The mother bites through the sac, the remaining fluid inside flows away and she licks the new-born baby clean (which stimulates it to take its first breath). After another few contractions the afterbirth or placenta is passed and usually eaten, together with the birth sac. In this way the mother tidies up the birthing den but also provides herself with useful nourishment. For the next few days she will not leave the kittens and this is her only meal.

Between births the mother cleans herself, and as each kitten is delivered she (or her feline midwife) chews through the umbilical cord and vigorously licks each new kitten. Young, naive mothers sometimes need help, as do mothers who as kittens were taken away from their own mothers at a very early age. Birthing usually lasts for a few hours, but in older females it might take a whole day. Cats seldom have physical problems in giving birth as dogs do, simply because we haven't produced feline anatomical misfits as we have with certain canine breeds – bulldogs, for example. The only feline breeds moderately prone to birth difficulties are the Persians or long-hairs. Because of their broad heads, kittens of these breeds can some-times be more difficult to deliver.

Mothers often purr through the entire birth, a behaviour that is immensely soothing to human observers. After the last kitten is born the mother gives herself a final wash, then settles down in a crescent around her new brood, another behaviour that reduces our blood pressure, skin temperature, heart rate and general state of arousal. Even the most burly tattooed truck driver turns to jelly at the sight of the warm and secure mother surrounding her new-born brood. There the mother will stay for the next few days, devoting her entire attention to her offspring, leaving for only a few minutes to empty her bladder and bowels, have a short stretch and possibly take some food and water. Her body produces the hormone prolactin for the next month, stimulating milk production. As long as the kittens suckle, this hormone suppresses oestrous activity, but after a month, or sooner if the kittens aren't suckling, her prolactin level drops rapidly and heat activity returns. If the kittens don't suckle at all, she can be calling again within seven days of delivery.

MATERNAL BEHAVIOUR

Many aspects of maternal behaviour have already been touched upon in Chapter Five, but I would like to expand on a few of them. For the next two months the mother is responsible for feeding and maintaining her brood, defending them, educating them and finally disbanding the family unit. She is responsible for making and then breaking the family ties.

One of her first objectives is to keep the litter together. To do so she retrieves errant kittens by grasping them by the neck just behind the head and carrying them back to the nest, or to a new nest for that matter if she is moving house. As frequently as you move a kitten away from the nest, the mother, responding to her baby's cry, will fetch it back. This is an instinctive or 'prewired' behaviour and is most important when the mother changes nests, for although cats are brilliant mothers they can't count.

When changing nests it is dramatically important that no kittens be left behind. And, to complicate matters, the distance from the old nest to the new is sometimes so great that the mother has to park her kittens at intermediate stages. In these circumstances, after she has removed the last kitten from either the nest or the kitten park, she always goes back once more to check that none is left.

Most pet cats are content to have only one nest for the duration of mothering and some kittens are so secure in the nest that they are reluctant to leave it. In these circumstances a mother has been seen to grasp her three-week-old young by the nape of the neck and to drag them out of the nest. She then watches over their perambulations and makes sure that they keep within her predetermined range of safety. If they try to go further, she picks them up and carries them back to the nest or its vicinity. Some mothers continue to do this for some weeks, exhausting themselves as they try to drag their hulking and now self-reliant progeny back to the den.

Kittens start following mother as soon as they can walk. They run after her, but when she stops they usually keep on running to explore what's ahead. Although they are mobile, they are still completely defenceless, yet under these conditions the mother, contrary to what she or any other cat would usually do when faced with a superior opponent, will not back down or flee but instead will stand her ground and fight tenaciously. This is maternal aggression, a defensive form of attack, and perhaps the most uninhibited type of feline aggression. Mothers with broods will attack other cats, dogs or people over far greater distances than they would otherwise do and at incredible speed. With experience even the most physically powerful tomcat has overwhelming respect for the ferocity of maternal aggression and avoids nursing mothers if he can. And even when the kittens are quite large and have virtually finished nursing, the mother will still protect them in the same way, hissing at them and cuffing them back into their den when she senses danger, then growling menacingly at the incautious dog or human who has the temerity to approach her nest.

As I have mentioned previously, the mother initiates feeding for the first three weeks, but soon the kittens are asking to be fed. By the time they are five weeks of age she is teaching them how to kill and shortly afterwards how to hunt. (Chapter Eight describes this in more detail.) She also teaches them much more besides. Numerous scientific studies have demonstrated that kittens can learn to open door latches or negotiate obstacles if they are first given a 'demonstration' by their mother. Without a demonstration they either can't perform or do so only by chance, and if a cat other than their mother is the demonstrator they do not learn as quickly. Mother cats educate their young. They teach them how to use litter trays through example. They teach them how to use cat flaps through example. They can even teach their kittens which human sex to prefer by example!

The disbanding of the family more or less coincides with the mother's milk drying up. Progesterone, the hormone of pregnancy, and prolactin, the hormone responsible for milk let-down, have both returned to their base-line levels and with the reduction in these hormones has come the concomitant reduction in 'mothering'. Large litters of five or six are usually disbanded by six months, but smaller ones of two or three might stay together for another two months. This is possibly related to the amount of suckling that still goes on. Because of the kittens' sharp teeth, suckling hurts the mother, and when they try to suck she hisses and cuffs and bats them away. The more kittens there are, the more hissing, batting and cuffing, and this leads to the family break-up. If a mother has only one kitten, or if all but one are removed, the remaining kitten, on its own, is not enough of a nuisance to provoke maternal violence and irascibility. In these circumstances the mother often lets the kitten continue to suckle long after her milk has dried up and might even try to carry the fully grown 'kitten' into the nest. If the mother is a member of a feral or free-ranging colony grouped around a large food source the kittens will remain longer, but eventually the males will be forced to emigrate and try their luck joining the surrounding male 'brotherhood'.

Good mothering behaviour is not 'prewired'. Cats that have been well mothered produce kittens that grow up to be good mothers. In fact a statement by the paediatric psychiatrist Robert ten Bensel of the Mayo Clinic in Rochester, Minnesota, about human baby behaviour seems to have equal application to cats. He said, 'The proper time to influence the character of a child is 100 years before he is born. In each of us lives our own childhood and the values of past generations.' Good mothering depends upon skills that are learned both before and after birth, not on instinct alone. In that sense, early weaning of kittens is counter-productive for it denies them the continuing opportunity to learn from their mother and siblings. Misguided genetic selection for such dubious qualities as hairlessness doesn't help either, nor does human intervention in helping the litters of poor mothers to survive. Some bright-spark animal behaviourist might one day set up an ante-natal clinic for felines to help them learn to be good mothers. In the meantime they are more natural than almost any other domestic species and still outstandingly successful at reproduction, unless we interfere. And we certainly do interfere. Today in Europe and North America over 70 per cent of female cats and 90 per cent of males have been neutered. What effect does this have on their minds?

NEUTERING

Ovariohysterectomies (or spays) and oophorectomies (or castrations) are the most common operations that veterinarians perform. I've done at least one and usually several every single day of my working life, and although owners like to feel they are having this surgery carried out to prevent unwanted pregnancies it is equally true that neutering operations are requested to alter the behaviour of their cats. Owners simply don't want to put up with the fighting, roaming, spraying and unpleasant urine odour of intact toms, nor do they want to hear the plaintive cries or receive the pelvic presentations of females in heat. But how effective is neutering, and if it is to be carried out when is the best time for the surgery to be performed? And are there less dramatic alternatives?

Ben Hart at the University of California veterinary school at Davis was the first to investigate the value of neutering male cats. He interviewed cat owners twenty-three months after their cats had been castrated. The owners reported that in nine out of ten animals neutering reduced fighting, roaming and spraying. Sometimes the change took longer than in others, and by Hart's definition a 'rapid decline' meant within three weeks of neutering and a 'gradual decline' meant one that took up to four months. His findings were as follows:

Fighting	– rapid decline	53%
	– gradual decline	35%
	– no change	12%

Effectiveness – 88%

Roaming	– rapid decline	56%	
	– gradual decline	35%	
	– no change	9%	
			Effectiveness – 91%
Spraying	– rapid decline	78%	
	– gradual decline	9%	
	– no change	13%	
			Effectiveness – 87%

Hart noted that it was not the most experienced fighters, roamers and sprayers who continued their activity but rather the most vigorous ones, and he attributed this variation to both inheritance and early learning. He also noted that a rapid decline in one behaviour did not necessarily correspond to decline in the other two behaviours. Some cats would stop spraying and roaming but continued fighting. Others stopped fighting and spraying but continued roaming. Finally, and importantly, he observed that there was no relationship between the age at which a tomcat was neutered and the rate of decline in any of these behaviours. The cats in this study were all between one and seven years old and the effect of neutering was the same throughout the various ages.

Neutering reduces male spraying, fighting and roaming.

Castration will almost immediately eliminate what is to the human nose the unpleasant odour of tomcat urine. And, contrary to what some owners believe, if it is carried out after five months of age it will not result in a smaller urethra (urine passage) or contribute to urethral blockages in cats. Castration does not affect either fear aggression or predatory aggression but significantly reduces male dominant aggression and territorial aggression. Most cats will stop breeding within two weeks of surgery but some experienced males will continue to mate with oestrus females for as long as a year. Although domestic cats usually reach puberty before they are a year old, it often takes another year before they fully develop all their secondary male characteristics, such as bulky muscle mass and a thick neck. From what we know about the effect of castration, regardless of age, owners who want their tomcats to develop these secondary sex characteristics can wait a little longer before having them neutered, but they should remember that there is a high likelihood that their cats will start spraying, wandering and fighting.

Neutering females does not result in such dramatic changes as it does in males. It simply terminates oestrous cycles. It does not affect either predatory or any other type of aggression. If a female house cat has not permitted another female on her territory before, she is unlikely to do so after surgery either.

In reviewing the literature on the behavioural consequences of neutering cats, I was struck by the lack of statistical information on the subject. Like other veterinarians I had my own feelings on the matter, but rather than rely solely on those I carried out a simple survey by sending a questionnaire to one hundred practising small-animal veterinarians, asking them questions about ten different behaviours in male, female and neutered male and female cats. This was a 'forced evaluation' survey, an exasperating form to complete, but one that is scientifically valid if a large enough number respond. Well over two thirds did so almost immediately.

The survey compared the behaviour of intact males and females and yielded the following results. Females are more playful, demand more attention, are more hygienic and are friendlier to other household cats than are males. They are also slightly more affectionate and excitable. Entire male cats are slightly more active and more destructive than entire females and both are equally vocal and tolerate handling. These behavioural difference can be graphically portrayed in this way:

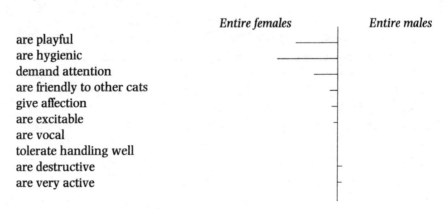

	Entire females	Entire males
are playful		
are hygienic		
demand attention		
are friendly to other cats		
give affection		
are excitable		
are vocal		
tolerate handling well		
are destructive		
are very active		

The survey asked about behaviour changes in both males and females as a consequence of neutering. Neutered males are much more hygienic, are much friendlier to other cats, tolerate handling better, give more affection, are more playful and demand more attention than entire males. Entire males are more active and more vocal. Neutering has no effect on excitability or destructiveness. Once more, these changes can be described graphically in the following way:

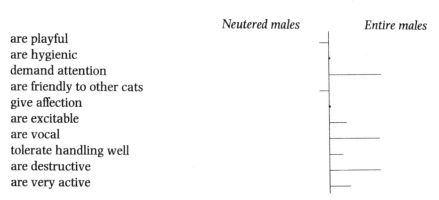

The same questions asked about the behavioural effects of neutering females produced results that were not as dramatic as those reported when males were neutered. Neutered females are slightly more playful, are friendlier to other household cats and tolerate handling better than entire females. Entire females are more vocal and more active, but neutering has essentially no effect on hygiene, demand for attention, giving of affection, excitability or destructiveness. These changes are represented graphically as follows:

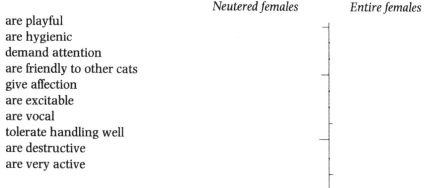

Finally, and perhaps most importantly, the survey compared the behaviour of neutered male and neutered female cats. The results

show that there are very few and only minimal differences in behaviour. Neutered males are very slightly friendlier to other household cats, are slightly easier to handle and give a little more affection
than females. There is no difference in their demand for attention,
hygiene, level of activity, destructiveness, use of voice, excitability or
playfulness. Graphically the changes look like this:

	Neutered males	*Neutered females*
are playful		
are hygienic		
demand attention		
are friendly to other cats		
give affection		
are excitable		
are vocal		
tolerate handling well		
are destructive		
are very active		

These results conform well with the anecdotal comments of professional cat breeders. Whereas the difference in behaviour between
male and female dogs remains significant after neutering, this is not
the case with cats. In fact there is some evidence to suggest that as
far as friendliness to other cats, ease of handling and giving of affection goes, neutered males actually make easier pets than do neutered
females. In any case our personal biases and preferences usually
decide what sex we choose to keep as pets. The evidence shows that
we should not use our knowledge of sex differences in dog behaviour
when making decisions about cats. The consequences of neutering
are dramatically different.

Finally, are there any safe alternatives to neutering that avoid
surgery but prevent unwanted litters and social behaviours? The
answer is a very qualified 'yes'. Both males and female cats can have
their 'tubes' tied, surgery that does not interfere with hormone production but that simply prevents eggs or sperm from getting where they
are most useful. Neither operation can be seriously recommended as
routine because they don't resolve what is for many owners the
major inconveniences of their cat's sexual behaviour, urine smell,
spraying, fighting and calling. Because all of these behaviours are
hormonally influenced, other hormones given either in tablet form or
by injection have been used for almost twenty years to counter
sexual behaviour. Oestrus can be suppressed in cats by the administra-
tion of progesterone or a related progestogen, the hormones of preg-

nancy. Progestogens are also used to treat spraying and aggression in tomcats or neutered males and females, although their use is based on clinical experience rather than on controlled trials. The actual mechanism of action of progestogens still isn't known, but they can have a potent effect on modifying various feline behaviours and may act centrally on the brain. These hormones also have an anti-inflammatory effect, causing adrenal gland suppression, and this too might result in behavioural changes. The down side is that, although oestrus can be suppressed by these hormones, there are possible side effects including weight gain, lethargy, loss of hair, womb infections, adrenal gland suppression, diabetes and mammary gland development. Some cats develop a pot-bellied appearance. Others suffer a heavy moult *after* the hormone treatment has been stopped. My clinical advice is that hormones are excellent for use in short-term therapy but have too many potential side effects to warrant their use as a replacement for spaying or castrating.

Chapter Eight

Predation, Eating and Elimination

PREDATION

In North America cats eat rabbits and mice, ground squirrels, chip-munks, flying squirrels, gophers and deer mice, but they don't appear to like the taste of jumping mice which they kill but don't eat. In Europe cats eat rabbits, mice and voles, small rats and birds, yet don't seem to care for the taste of shrews and moles which are preyed upon but not eaten. In Australia the introduced European rabbit is important prey, but remains of the common ringtail possum are present in 56 per cent of cat droppings in north-east Victoria. Australian cats also eat at least forty-four different species of reptiles, including at least two venomous elapid snakes. On sub-Antarctic Marrion Island, as well as on Dassen, Little Barrier, Stewart, Hog and Macquarie Islands, they eat penguins, terns and noddies. Young cats eat spiders, moths, craneflies and bluebottles. But nowhere do they particularly eat fish or frogs. Cats are opportunist hunters that catch prey to satisfy their hunger but also hunt for the sheer pleasure of it. More often than not, pet cats will chase and capture prey, not to eat it but to bring it back and deposit it on our carpets or beds. Most of the cats I see in practice are kept for companionship or because of their attractiveness, but it was for their rodent-hunting ability that they were first domesticated and accepted into human habitations. Selective breeding has produced cats of varying colours, body shapes and dispositions, yet the urge to hunt is so integral to the cat's make-up that it still exists in even the sweetest-looking fashion adornment. Predatory behaviour and the death bite are 'prewired' or inherited actions. They can be modified one way or the other by early experi-ence but not eliminated.

As we know, all kittens stalk and pounce on each other, on their own tails or, in the case of my cat, on my dogs' wagging tails. They bat at flies and scoop at toys, throwing them high in the air. They hide in ambush, waiting for littermates or our feet to pass by, then lunge at them, mock-biting, kicking and chewing. These are inherent behaviours that do not need to be learned, but with the right mother a kitten soon learns to apply these actions to the capture and despatch of fresh meals.

Cats hunt in two different ways. They stealthily stalk prey, exploiting available cover, which is necessary for capturing birds, or they sit and wait at burrows, waiting for mice, small rats or rabbits to emerge. A typical hunt is carried out in this way. The cat leaves its home in what appears to be a purposeful way and walks or even trots along paths or roads to a specific area which is often different from the surrounding land, usually within a few hundred yards of home. For example, if a field of hay has been freshly cut, the cat is more likely to go to that field than to the surrounding ones. Feral females spend almost half the day hunting, while female house cats spend only one quarter of the day doing so. Dominant toms spend much less time hunting than do outcast tomcats, who spend around one third of each day doing so. Cats that know each other will hunt in the same field within sight of each other, but they always hunt alone, and some dominant cats will forcibly exclude subordinates from particularly good areas.

Once a cat has arrived at its hunting territory its movements slow down and it begins a close-to-the-ground search. According to scientists, experienced cats follow the urine trails left by mice; others have seen cats carry out an almost geometric zig-zag search of a field; and others say that some cats go directly back to where they have had previous success. Whatever the method, eventually an interesting place such as a burrow is discovered and here the cat intently stands, sits or crouches, keeping its unblinking eyes on the burrow opening. Should a mouse appear, the cat waits until it has moved away from the burrow entrance, then pounces. If the cat is confident, it throws itself on its side, rakes back with its hind feet and uses its forepaws to pin the prey for the death bite. If less confident, the cat releases the prey and attacks again. Whether or not it is immediately eaten depends upon whether the cat is hungry or whether it is a mother with a litter at home. Mothers will often bring live mice back to the den for their kittens to kill, 'educating' them in how to apply the death bite. If the pounce is unsuccessful or if prey doesn't emerge, the cat will give up that location and search out another attractive one.

Experienced cats wait until mice have moved away from the burrow entrance before pouncing.

Bird catching requires a different strategy, and by their nature cats are nowhere near as good birders as they are mousers. Many birds have close to 360° vision, so cats must use stealth to creep up on them. Prey is located by sight or sound and the cat, running silently with its stomach to the ground, draws near. Advancing under cover, it slink-runs, pauses, then slink-runs again. It moves either extremely slowly or extremely fast until it is close enough to pounce, then it waits. This wait is characteristic of the cat's bird-hunting behaviour, as is the wait when a mouse leaves its burrow, and many birds simply fly away oblivious to the danger they have been in. The consequence is that many cats give up birding because of their low success rate, although some individuals eventually become specialists and lethal bird killers. One of my childhood cats was such a hunter and I remember counting 128 bird carcasses in her larder under the redundant 1938 Dodge in our garage behind the house.

Feral cats can become moderately successful at hooking fish out of shallow water, although fish is rarely a natural and integral part of their diet. With the exception of Van cats from Turkey, felines generally don't like water and avoid it whenever possible.

If a cat has a bird in its sights and the bird doesn't fly away, excitement mounts and the cat begins to quiver. The hind legs tread quietly and the hind quarters might sway from side to side. The cat also moves its head from side to side in a way that helps its excellent binocular vision judge the exact distance of the prey. The tail twitches, then the cat lunges at the bird, forepaws extended, but with the more powerful hind legs remaining firmly on the ground to give stability if the prey is awkward. On rare occasions the cat might actually leap in the air. Then, once more, the prey is killed and eaten, or killed and taken home for us, or, if the hunter is a mother, killed and taken home for the kittens to eat. Pet cats are just as likely not to kill the prey but to play with it, either at the site of entrapment or at home, seemingly torturing it over a prolonged period.

When house cats stalk birds on the open lawns of our gardens, they frequently twitch their tails, a body-language signal of conflict. Cats will naturally stalk birds only from cover, but as so many modern dwellings are mouse-free, and as cats instinctively have the need and desire to hunt, birds are their only option. They want to creep up on birds undetected, but well-manicured lawns offer no hides. The consequence is a feeling of conflict between wanting to stay still and not be noticed yet wanting to rush forward to capture the bird. Tail twitching is the only outward manifestation of that conflict.

If cats do catch prey, they often indulge in a cruel game of trap and release, prolonging the excitement of the capture of the rodent or bird until the prey either dies of shock, dies from its injuries or escapes. When prey is played with, stalking, watching, creeping, pouncing, seizing, carrying away, plucking and tossing might all occur but not necessarily in a fixed order and not necessarily culminating in a death bite. Cats carry out these movements with a little extra gusto and exaggerated exuberance. They 'play baseball' with mice, batting and catching them, and 'badminton' with birds, swatting them into the air. With either closed or spread paws they propel their prey along, intermittently grasping the poor creature with their paws. If the prey is carried by the teeth, it is usually grabbed in some innocuous place and rarely injured by the bite. Killing is inhibited. Some cats will literally dance around their prey, taking high, curving, pantomime leaps. Cats will also do this after they have killed large and dangerous prey, such as adult rats. Paul Leyhausen calls this 'overflow play', a sudden release from the pressure of the chase, and says that it rarely occurs in feral cats but rather more frequently in free-ranging animals. He believes that it is a result of the retention of juvenile behaviour in domesticated house cats. The killing or death bite matures to full strength relatively late in young cats and if their natural behaviours are modified through their relationship with us, the killing bite can become, using Leyhausen's word, 'retarded'.

The hunting drive is independent of hunger and a successful capture is so intensely rewarding that cats will often roll with excitement. The very thought of capturing prey can cause housebound cats to behave in ways we consider to be anti-social. At the sight through windows of potential prey some incarcerated cats will urine-spray. Others chatter their teeth in a staccato-like fashion, mimicking their behaviour in performing the death bite.

Cats usually kill long-necked prey such as pigeons with a bite to the nape of the neck. This either severs or crushes the spinal cord and death is instantaneous. They 'feel' their way to the spot using sensitive touch receptors at the base of their teeth and with their whiskers. Cats with damaged whiskers are less successful with their death bite. Small prey with a short neck is usually bitten on the breast and shoulder. If a cat is not too impetuous and misses with the first bite, it flips the prey in its mouth so that it can grasp it behind the head, then bites home. In any attack on prey the teeth are used for seizing and killing while the forelimbs are used only to grasp the prey and hold it down. Cats are highly successful with the killing bite. The shape of their teeth, the muscles and position of the jaws, the ligaments, tendons and nerve supply are all such that there is a high probability that only one bite is needed to kill. Their canine teeth in particular are well suited for forcing things apart rather than for crushing.

Cats are opportunistic predators. They prey upon what is available: mice, penguins, possums, gophers, songbirds, grasshoppers – whatever is at hand. Small mammals are caught using the 'sit-and-wait' technique. Rabbits are more often ambushed and small songbirds are caught by stalking and pouncing. Experiments with laboratory cats have shown that cats can systematically carry out searches. Some always search hides from right to left and others from left to right and it is assumed that cats can do likewise when hunting. They are also supremely successful. Most field studies reveal that one out of every two to four pounces will capture prey. But which are better at hunting, males or females?

Most studies show that feral cats are more successful hunters than house cats, a logical fact, for the former depend totally on hunting and scavenging for their meals. Studies of the stomach contents of cats in Germany killed in road traffic accidents showed that country cats had eaten at least fourteen different species of animals, but city cats' stomachs held only tinned food and a grasshopper. Dennis Turner's studies in Switzerland strongly suggest that when rodents are the main game, mothers with kittens are more successful hunters than non-mothers. Mothers took on average 1.6 hours to capture a rodent while non-mothers took on average 11.2 hours. Mothers travelled faster than non-mothers, didn't sit as long at burrows waiting for prey to emerge and, after an unsuccessful pounce, moved on to another burrow faster. They required fewer pounces to catch a meal. Other studies in southern Sweden suggest that when rabbits are prey, male cats are more successful than females. Rabbits took five times longer to capture than mice but one rabbit weighed ten times as much as a rodent. Mothers might simply not have enough time to spend catching such lucrative meals and so restrict themselves to rodents. No one knows whether neutering alters a cat's hunting success rate. As many pet owners are aware, neutered cats do catch and eat prey as well as bring it home to their owners.

If prey is eaten, it is entirely consumed. Birds are de-feathered first but small mammals are eaten whole. Both are swallowed with, as opposed to against, the grain of the prey's hair or feathers. Why so many house cats bring their prey back home is a question upon which I can only speculate. Both males and females do it, so it isn't a 'bring-it-home-for-the-kids' phenomenon – male cats play no role in the feeding or teaching of kittens. There is some evidence that when cats were first domesticated they were used to retrieve hunted game. Dropping frogs on their owner's pillows might be a vestige of that behaviour. Equally it may simply be that the house cat with a full stomach catches prey because it is 'prewired' to do so, then doesn't know what to do with it so brings it home. Bringing maimed birds, rodents and reptiles home to their owners may simply be a way in which cats resolve the conflict of the situation in which they find themselves.

Predatory aggression, grasping and killing prey are all 'prewired' behaviours. If a certain part of the brain, the anterolateral part of the hypothalamus, is electrically stimulated, cats will perform the death bite on whatever is available. But, as I mentioned in Chapter Five, mothers are very important in teaching kittens how to catch prey and what to catch. Cats are better at catching prey if they have had experience as kittens and their specialization as mousers or birders is based upon previous experience. Experiments over fifty years ago showed that kittens raised with a mother who killed rats in their presence killed rats at their first opportunity. Kittens raised alone seldom did and kittens raised in cages with rats never did. Cats become good ratters and will keep premises rat-free as long as all adult rats are eliminated first. Domestic cats willing to take on full-grown adult common Norway rats are rare but they can be very adept at killing juveniles weighing up to $10\frac{1}{2}$ oz (300 g).

Specialization is an adaptive behaviour passed on from generation to generation by cat mothers. To ensure becoming a good and success-ful predator, a kitten needs a mother that brings home prey, needs to observe its mother's and its siblings' behaviour with the prey and must be allowed to manipulate the prey itself. Competition with siblings might be useful too, and adult experience certainly is. Gen-etics probably plays a role and although one gene alone does not control predatory behaviour, when the cat genome is eventually mapped out it may be possible to breed killing and non-killing cats.

EATING

If you feed a cat a piece of meat that is roughly the size of a mouse, the cat will not eat it immediately unless it is terribly hungry. Instead it will pull it off the plate, paw it, shake it, possibly throw it in the air or even hide it. It might gulp it down and regurgitate it, or 'defend' it from other cats by hissing and spitting. These certainly are not the behaviours of Millie, my pet cat. She sits silently as she watches the can opener at work, then darts over to her food bowl, crouches down and quietly, intently and almost delicately eats a small portion of the offered food.

Mice rank high on the cat's natural menu although they will satisfy their hunger by eating almost any living creature and will prepare their natural meals according to their individual idiosyn-crasies. Small rodents are eaten head first, but some cats first make an abdominal incision and remove the gall bladder and intestines. Larger rodents are eaten from the forequarters to the back. Most cats eat the intestines and stomach but some pull these organs out and squeeze out their contents before eating them. They do this by squeez-ing a section of intestine with the tongue against the palate and pressing out towards the incisors, then moving on to the next section. Small birds are plucked a little, then consumed, but bigger birds like pigeons require more clinical plucking because their feather shafts are so strong. When plucking a pigeon, the cat holds the carcass down with its front feet, grabs feathers in its mouth and yanks them out. Some cats simply skin birds before eating them.

Paul Leyhausen once carried out eating experiments with his cats by making fur-covered sausages, some with heads sewn on and others with tails. All of his cats started eating them head first. But when Leyhausen sewed heads on the 'wrong' end of the sausages, against the grain of the fur, the cats started eating from where the head should have been.

It would be gratifying to assume that cats eat different foods to satisfy their specific nutritional needs. Liver and brain, for example, organs that most cats relish, are excellent sources of essential fatty acids and of vitamin D. I've seen too many instances of self-induced nutritional deficiencies in house cats that restrict their food intake to a single item to accept this hypothesis. Cats hunt because they enjoy it and eat foods that taste, smell, look and feel good to them. When offered commercially produced cat food, most cats will choose it over their ages-old 'natural' diet.

Over 30 per cent of the dogs that I see are clinically over-weight, yet the percentage of over-weight cats is much lower, closer to 10 per cent. And while anorexia is only a problem in certain individual small-breed dogs, it is considerably more common in cats.

When allowed to eat according to their own choice, cats will eat ten to eighteen meals evenly distributed throughout a twenty-four hour period, regardless of whether it is day or night. Cats are not diurnal eaters, consuming food at dawn and dusk as was once assumed. When dependent on their own hunting ability, the food intake of feral cats is predominantly mammals, although reptiles are a consistent part of the Australian cat's diet. The results from various surveys are tabulated as follows:

Mammals	55–88% of diet
Birds	trace–8% of diet
Reptiles	1–11% of diet
Kitchen waste	trace–26% of diet
Vegetation	trace–6% of diet

The previous eating experiences that a cat has had are strong factors in determining what it will eat in the future. In one study new-born kittens were fed either soya beans, mackerel and rice or a variety of foods. Six months later they would consume only the diets they had first eaten. The animal behaviourist Roger Mugford could not repeat this experiment but he fed different diets at weaning age rather than at birth. When diet selection is not as artificially altered, cats select food according to its aroma, consistency, texture and taste as well as their previous experience. Protein alone is not the most important factor.

Cats are much more finicky eaters than are dogs. Cats like fresh-tasting food, not carrion, and although the cat does not have a sweet tooth it prefers sucrose to either saccharin or cyclamates in dilute milk. Cats are also highly successful at coercing their owners to feed them to *their* schedule and according to *their* specific likes. I hear it all the time: 'But he'll only eat Pacific prawns ... iced ... at dawn ... on a silver platter ... fed by hand.'!

In one study cats preferred cold rats to warm rats, meat-based cat foods to rats, and salmon to the meat-based cat food. Cats easily develop food fixations if their diet is not varied at an early age, but Roger Mugford and Chris Thorne's work has shown that they generally prefer a new food to the one with which they are familiar as long as the new food is equally palatable. In other words, they enjoy variety. If a new food is less palatable, it will be eaten only for a few days or eaten only in small quantities. If the animal is under emotional stress, in a new home, at a cattery or with new animals, it will prefer the diet with which it is familiar rather than the new one.

According to one study, the average cat prefers beef, lamb, horsemeat, pork, chicken and fish in that order. According to another, the average cat prefers fish to meat. The average cat does not like the taste of cured meats but in practice there are few average cats. Cats that I hospitalize prefer a brand of rabbit-based tinned food made from wild rabbit from China. And Millie would kill for crispy bacon and smoked salmon. Certain factors, however, are known to increase the palatability of a food. Warming food to around 86°F (30°C) enhances its taste and odour. Salt can increase palatability, as can brewer's yeast or garlic powder. Slightly sour, bitter or acid tastes are generally preferred to sweet tastes unless the cat has been previously conditioned to enjoy sweet. Early studies concluded that cats couldn't detect 'sweet', but later studies contradict this. All that can be presently said with justification is that cats show no preference for sugars. Cats prefer denser foods to lighter ones and whole milk to dilute milk. They eat more chunky food than powdered food and prefer pelleted foods to fine ones.

Small rodents, the historic staple of the cat's diet, have a very high fat content, almost 40 per cent dry weight, and in feeding tests cats do prefer one fat to another, but they don't show a preference for foods with the same fat content as mice, being equally happy eating diets with 15 per cent fat as they are with diets containing 45 per cent fat. Left to their own common food sense, cats are able to and do regulate their energy consumption, which is why obesity is not a great problem.

Cats naturally lose and gain body weight in cycles of several months and will increase their food intake when the water content of canned food is increased. In a similar fashion cats increase the volume of food they eat when the caloric density of it is decreased. The female hormone progesterone stimulates the appetite and as progesterone and other progestogens are used to treat a wide range of behaviour disorders from spraying to aggression, weight gain should be expected when they are used. The benzodiazepine tranquillizers such as Valium are also used to treat feline behavioural disorders and these stimulate an increased food intake as well. So too does housing cats in groups rather than individually. Finally, when we interfere in their behaviour, for example by restricting them to an indoor existence, we interfere in their activity and as a consequence some cats eat in excess and get fat. Spaying and castration may lead to increased weight in some cats, although the low rate of obesity in cats combined with the high rate at which these procedures are performed indicates that neutering is a very minor cause of weight gain.

At varying times of the year the 'set point' for the body weight of cats seems to fall. Anorexia and weight loss follow, with some cats losing several ounces. There is still no scientific explanation for why this happens, and although it can be distressing for owners, the anorexia is not persistent and feeding always resumes.

Cats are opportunistic feeders that evolved in circumstances where they had little control over the timing and size of their meals. They have a relatively simple digestive system capable of dealing with large quantities of food in a short period, but given free choice they will nibble several small meals throughout the day and night. Even so, they are excellent at adjusting their energy intake so that it is roughly equal to their energy expenditure. That's why they don't get fat. Most of our cats are dependent upon us for both the timing and the size of their meals, but in laboratory experiments where cats have to work in order to obtain food they quickly learn to take larger meals so that they don't use up lots of energy working for many small meals.

Meat is the staple of the cat's diet. It is high in protein which is made from amino acids. Meat contains essential amino acids and animal fat contains essential fatty acids that cannot be found in any other source – the reason why cats can't survive on vegetarian diets. They do, however, survive on much less water than many other animals and can survive waste levels in their bodies brought about by dehydration that are two and a half times higher than those that would kill us. Cats can survive on the fluid in meat or fish alone and dissipate excess heat through panting at 250 pants per minute, a rate similar to that of normal breathing, so it isn't energy-consuming.

And they lose as much fluid each day through self-grooming as they do in their urine.

Water is the best liquid to give to cats and it should always be readily available, especially if dehydrated or dry foods are offered. When cats are young they can digest milk but later on some have difficulty digesting the lactose in it and this causes diarrhoea. It you want to provide dairy products for your cat as a source of calcium, try feeding yoghurt or cottage cheese as the lactose in these is used up in the souring process.

An enigma as yet to be solved is what effect, if any, does diet have on the cat's mind? Certain theoretical and irrefutable facts are known. The essential amino acid tryptophan, provided in meat, is the precursor of the brain hormone serotonin which is involved in mood, sleep, wakefulness and body rhythms. In turn, serotonin is the precursor of melotonin, produced in the pineal gland and involved in seasonality and the body's sensitivity to increasing or decreasing day length. What happens, then, if there is not enough or indeed too much tryptophan in the diet? This is a poorly studied area, although one veterinarian, Professor Ballarini of the University of Parma in Italy, has coined the term 'psycho-dietetics' to describe it. Ballarini argues that quality of food is related to animal well-being. He states that some foods have simple nutritional value and others are pharmacologically effective, acting as naturally occurring antibiotics, hormones or pheromones. He certainly has a point when you consider the behavioural effect of catnip. Not only domestic cats but lions, leopards, jaguars and snow leopards respond sexually to it by rolling; adult tigers don't, however. Immature tigers actually show violent alarm when they sniff or eat it and beat a hasty retreat. Catnip acts on the central nervous system and causes pronounced mood shifts. It might also cause longer-lasting physiological changes to the nervous or endocrine systems. Is it possible, then, that other chemicals, pheromones, hormones or hormone-like substances in food, can alter the cat's behaviour although in less obvious ways?

Recent research has shown that animals remember better if they are fed straight after performing a task. Is this related to diet in general or to specific components of the diet? Ballarini argues that the quality of protein in the diet influences the cat's neurohormonal system, a seemingly logical argument but one that is exceedingly hard to prove. He states that serotonin, produced from the amino acid tryptophan, inhibits aggression in cats. Others have argued along similar lines in the attempt to control aggression in dogs. William

Campbell has claimed for over fifteen years that a high-protein diet – containing lots of tryptophan – is beneficial in reducing canine aggression.

Anatomical evidence also suggests that Ballarini might be on the right track. In cats the hunger centre and aggressiveness centre in the brain are so closely related that it is difficult for one to be electrically stimulated without the other being activated. In a similar way the satiety centre is closely associated with the part of the brain that inhibits aggressiveness. Ballarini's final argument is perhaps his most intriguing. He notes that nutrition has an effect on early learning in cats because nutrients can pass from the blood directly into the brain and influence its development. The blood-brain barrier develops later and prevents chemicals, including many therapeutic drugs, from crossing from the bloodstream into the brain. But in young cats and dogs this barrier is still immature. Could it be that poor nutrition or wrong nutrition at a very early age has a direct physical consequence on the cat's mind?

Eating Behaviour Problems

Compared to dogs, cats suffer from few eating problems. Coprophagia (eating their own or other animals' droppings) is exceptionally rare as is pica (the eating of inedibles such as stones). Obesity occurs less frequently, but when it does and it is not caused by an under-active thyroid or by behaviour-altering drugs, it can usually be attributed to feeding excessive amounts of highly palatable foods and to boredom. Treatment simply involves altering the cat's lifestyle so that it is more active, or cutting back on its energy intake either by feeding less of what it is eating or switching to a less calorie-dense diet. Anorexia is suffered more frequently and can occur after a cat has experienced an upper respiratory tract infection. Eating is initially stimulated by odour, and if the nasal passages are impaired cats readily go off their food. Other diseases and injuries cause anorexia but so too will diet changes that cats dislike or psychological stress. In these circumstances it is important to determine the specific cause and alter the diet or alleviate stress. When it is impossible to do the latter, the use of Valium-like sedatives as appetite stimulants is often effective.

Many cat owners feel that grass eating is abnormal, but in fact only excessive grass eating is cause for concern as it usually suggests abdominal discomfort. In the absence of grass, however, many cats eat house plants, some of which are toxic. As wild carnivores, cats never needed to take great care over what they ate as none of their potential prey, other than some unusual toads, was poisonous. Consequently they will willingly eat almost any plant, sometimes with lethal results. The problem can be avoided by providing house cats with planters of succulent, fresh grass. If the problem continues, their access to house plants can be prevented through simple or devious means. One effective way involves aversion therapy in which the cat comes to associate plant eating with an unpleasant experience. Placing set mousetraps under single layers of newspaper around the plants in question is quite effective. When the cat steps on the newspaper, its foot pressure sets off the traps which fly up under the paper. The paper protects the cat from injury, but the startle often stops the damage. And if your cat seems to have a passion for your young spider plant, remember that to cats the newly formed leaves of the plant contain an hallucinogen which has a similar action to that in catnip. It acts like a narcotic on the central nervous system, and prolonged chewing of spider plants leads to a chronic dull state. As with most behaviour problems in cats, the best treatment is prevention.

Abnormal sucking activity occurs occasionally in cats, although it is never seen in dogs. Prolonged or adult sucking is most likely in orphaned kittens or those that have been weaned too early. Females normally wean kittens at eight to ten weeks, but for some reason, possibly related to our attitude to dog weaning, we often arbitrarily change that to six weeks of age. Early-weaned cats will continue to suck other cats, dogs, us or themselves, often accompanied by a kneading motion with the forepaws. Just like thumb sucking in human beings, it is a self-rewarding behaviour and, as with thumb sucking, taste aversion is the best way to alter the behaviour if you choose to do so.

Another more interesting form of unusual sucking behaviour is wool eating and wool sucking, a problem that occurs mainly in Siamese and Siamese-crosses. These cats are primarily attracted to blankets and sweaters and are especially attracted to human sebaceous gland smell, so they suck the under-arms of sweaters and dirty socks. Many head straight for the armpit itself. This type of wool sucking begins after weaning. And, once again, the best treatment is to avoid the problem by removing all suckable wool articles. If your Siamese makes a bee-line for your armpits, try using under-arm deodorant.

Most cats enjoy chewing on wool but in some Siamese and Siamese crosses this can become an obsessive activity.

Prey-catching behaviour is completely normal, even vital to the life of the cat. It keeps the mind active and alert, but many pet owners are embarrassed or concerned about the killing. In the absence of prey some cats vent their energy by attacking their owner's or guests' ankles. These cats have excess energy and very little to do. If you are worried about your cat decimating the surrounding wildlife, equip it with a bell on its collar. If the cat learns to move silently without ringing the bell, add another. De-clawing is of no value whatsoever as the claws have a minor role in predatory aggression. If your cat is an ankle attacker, it needs something else to do. Invest in wind-up furry toys. At least one zoo has installed perspex tubes along the floors of its large-cat enclosures and runs clockwork rodents through them. If the cat reaches the end of the tube before the mechanical rat does, the cat gets a food reward. That is the type of inventiveness for preventing boredom and associated behaviour problems that we should be showing with our own pet cats.

ELIMINATION

Cats are inherently tidy with their urine and faeces, using natural latrine sites for both. In both urination and defecation most cats follow the same sequence of events. They go to the latrine site, an area where the soil is relatively loose, dig a small hole in it with the forepaw, squat over the hole and urinate or defecate, then turn, sniff the hole and rake earth over it, again using the forepaw. This naturally sanitary behaviour is why so many millions of us are content to share our homes with felines.

There are, however, two other natural variations of elimination we don't particularly admire. Some tomcats don't restrict their defecating to latrine sites but will apparently pass their droppings anywhere and other males and some females will spray their urine against objects rather than into natural latrines. Dominant male cats use their urine and faeces as territory markers. Unburied faeces are usually left as a potent sign to other cats (and to us) that a boss cat has occupied the territory.

Both males and females can spray urine either to mark territory or to indicate a state of anxiety.

Spraying

Cats, both male and female, usually spray from a standing position. They back up to a vertical object such as a fence post (or a curtain), hold the tail stiffly to attention while at the same time tensely twitching it at high speed, and pulsate urine on to the object behind them.

They might simultaneously shift weight between the hind legs. If, however, they want to spray an object that is not vertical, they take up the squatting position they use when they urinate normally. This is an important fact to understand, for if you have an elimination problem with your cat it is quite imperative to know whether he or she is simply emptying the bladder or specifically spraying an object, and he or she will sometimes use the position of the former behaviour to carry out the latter.

Dominant male cats scent mark their territory by spraying urine, but in behavioural studies 10 per cent of neutered males and 5 per cent of neutered females continue to spray urine on a frequent basis. As already mentioned, the age at which the cat is neutered is not a factor. Castrating a male at any age will eliminate spraying in nine out of ten males. The others remain a problem.

Spraying in intact females sometimes occurs when they are in oestrus, but usually only in the absence of males. The reason for this essentially male behaviour is unclear, although studies in rats have shown that female foetal rats growing adjacent to male rats in the uterus (or womb) are predisposed to male-like behaviour. Males are masculinized in the uterus. Male foetuses actually produce the male sex hormone testosterone, but females do not produce the female hormone oestrogen and they remain sexually 'neutral' until puberty. Recent studies in California, however, have ruled out location in the uterus as the reason for spraying or fighting in female cats.

Although spraying is a territory-marking behaviour in males, it is also a stress-related activity in both sexes and in neutered animals. It is a common cause of house soiling, one that must be differentiated from simply missing the litter tray, and as house soiling is the most common feline behavioural problem reported to veterinarians it is important to know exactly what is happening before you try to correct the situation.

Cats will spray for a variety of reasons. Some are simply genetically predisposed to do so. Others might have medical problems, such as a sub-clinical bladder infection. Intact males and females in heat sometimes spray, as might cats receiving the hormone testosterone for medical reasons. But cats can also spray when the new baby is brought home, when you move house, when the garden furniture is brought in at the end of summer, when a guest comes, when a feral cat walks through the back garden, or when you decide to increase the size of your feline family. Spraying in these circumstances is stress-induced and it can be precipitated by odours, sights and sounds.

Spraying can occur anywhere in the house and its location is an important clue to the cause of the feline anxiety that has provoked it. If the intruders are people, the mark is often left in the room they occupy or on objects associated with them – a chair, clothes or even, in one instance in which I was asked for advice, the briefcase of the visitor. This is why spraying seems 'spiteful' to some people, but in fact it is the result of anxiety, not spite. In its extreme form it can result in cats spraying the pillows and beds of the people they associate with their anxiety, and in these circumstances their spraying position looks more like the normal urinating position and is frequently misinterpreted as such. The incidence of spraying increases in multi-cat households, and it seems that once a population threshold has been reached, spraying begins. Again, spraying in these circumstances must be differentiated from simply avoiding the use of a litter tray soiled by the urine of too many other cats.

Urine sprayed near a window, especially the one at which the cat usually sits watching the world go by, suggests that some outdoor event has triggered the behaviour. Often it means that your cat has seen another in the garden and is reacting to its presence. This is most likely to occur in spring, even in neutered cats, for although neutering removes the ovaries or testes, the hormonal changes in the hypothalamus and pituitary gland that are precipitated by increasing daylight still occur and even without gonads some cats will still have the hormonal desire to roam, create territories and mate. And if they can't because they are locked up in the luxurious, full-comfort cells we provide for them, they might begin to spray. As a general rule, the most likely cause of spraying is a change of routine for the cat. Look for that before attempting to correct the problem.

Treatment of Spraying

The best treatment, as always, is to try to avoid the problem happening in the first place. If a new cat is about to join a household in which there is already a resident, anticipate that the event might cause distress to your resident by sequestering the new arrival in its separate room with food, water and a litter box. This accomplishes two things. It allows the newcomer to search out and find good hiding places; to establish its own small territory. It also gives the resident cat a chance to scent the new odour and hear the new sounds without direct visual or physical confrontation. Open the door to the new cat's room after a few days and let them find each other. When you move house, use similar tactics. Always let your cat settle into a small territory before exposing it to the larger one. And if you see cats in your new garden, keep the curtains closed for a few days while your moggy settles in.

The same simple treatment can be used for cats that spray when they see other outdoor cats. Removing the source of the problem in this case is impossible, so simply draw the curtains or restrict your cat to the parts of the house where it won't be able to see other cats. If spraying in these circumstances is seasonal or a consequence of moving home, the problem will often naturally resolve itself with time.

When the cause of spraying cannot be eliminated, there are other methods that can be used to diminish the problem. Naturally, neutering is the most important consideration for unneutered sprayers. If you have a neutered tom which continues to spray and also have unneutred females, neutering the females will usually solve the problem. And if you have increased your cat population past the 'magic number' and spraying has commenced, reducing back to the level at which the colony had reached a *modus vivendi*, or specifically finding the spraying cat a new home, are the most successful options.

If a cat is spraying only one or two locations, clean them thoroughly and try converting them to feeding stations. Biological washing powder and water with a little vinegar added is still perhaps the best cleanser, although there are special urine-odour eliminator products available that seem to be quite effective. Whatever you do, avoid any cleanser with ammonia in it as it smells like urine to the cat and will actually attract it back to the spraying site. Cats don't like to void themselves near their food and this change in their environment often works. If, for practical reasons, it isn't possible to feed the cat at its spraying site, cover the site with mothballs; or, if you want to be more effective, crinkle aluminium foil and spread it over the area. Most cats don't like the sound that is made when they stand on it. To be most dramatic you can hang aluminium foil food containers over the sprayed area. This acts as aversion therapy because cats don't like the noise of squirted urine hitting aluminium. You get your own back, too, for the urine gets deflected back on the producer, something the cat will find unpleasant.

Finally, drugs can be very effective in overcoming this problem, either progestogens such as megestrol acetate or benzodiazepine sedatives such as Valium. In my experience Valium given as a short course is the safest and most effective medical treatment for spraying.

Urinating and Defecating Problems

Although most cats are inherently hygienic, some are not. Dominant males don't bury their faeces, and some subordinate males and females don't either. Owners try showing them how to do so by scratching their cat's paws in the litter, but if a cat mother has not instructed her kitten in this behaviour and if that kitten grows up to be disinclined to bury its faeces, there are no reliable ways of successfully training it. Other cats seem to have a poor aim when using the litter tray. They get in, scratch it, then perch on the side and defecate over the edge. The simplest treatment in these circumstances is to invest in an enclosed tray. Some cats prefer to defecate in the earth in flower pots rather than in their trays, but these are usually indoor-outdoor cats who defecate in earth outdoors. This problem is easily overcome either by keeping them indoors or by adding earth to their litter trays while covering the flower-pot earth with pebbles, bark or even mothballs or aluminium foil. If a cat is urinating but not defecating in its tray, consider that it might be associating rectal or anal discomfort with the tray. Impacted anal sacs and constipation are causes for cats to stop defecating in their trays.

The feeling under the feet is one of the most important factors in a cat using or not using its tray. Most cats need a 'substrate' they can dig in as they do in earth outdoors, but some actually prefer hard or semi-hard surfaces, such as vinyl tile or carpet. Some cats won't use litter trays that are too clean. Others won't use them if even a little dirt remains. Cats don't like their trays to be in busy areas or in places that are difficult to get to. They don't like changes in litter either. Studies done at the Texas A&M Veterinary School cat colony indicate that 50 per cent of cats will not immediately accept an abrupt change of litter type and half of these cats will still not completely accept the new litter even after a week. If you want to change litter types, do so gradually, a third at a time over three weeks. We might like the newer, odour-absorbing and scented litters, but that doesn't necessarily mean that cats do. Cats like to smell cat urine and faeces, not lavender and pine. If your cat has stopped urinating in its tray after you have switched to these, think about reverting to the cat's favourite litter and simply cleaning it more often.

If you have to move a litter box from one location to another, do so slowly, inches per day, rather than abruptly. And always keep it on the same storey of the house as the cat, in a quiet and 'private' area. Don't be over-fussy about cleaning the tray. Faeces should be removed daily, but the litter itself need only be changed around twice each week. Always use the same litter as the cat used before you acquired it, and when first bringing the cat home bring a little of its soiled litter with it so that it can scent where the new litter tray is.

Treatment of Problems

Kittens come ready-packaged with a strong drive to use a latrine as their toilet area, to dig holes, urinate and defecate in them and then cover them. Elimination itself is stimulated by the smell of previously soiled areas, by feeding, drinking and exercise. When bringing a new kitten home, restrict it for the first few days to a single room in which it is provided with food and water at one end and a litter tray, preferably with some of its previously soiled litter, at the other. Once you see that the kitten is using the tray, allow it more freedom to explore but always make sure the tray is accessible. If you live in a house rather than a single-storey flat or a bungalow, you might need a litter tray on each floor.

If your previously litter-using cat has stopped using the tray, look at the following four possible causes:

1. The Litter
Make sure that the litter is not too dirty, not being used by other cats and of the type your cat is willing to use.

2. The Litter Tray
Make sure that the tray is the right shape and size for your cat and is in an appropriate location, easy to get to but offering privacy. If your cat is soiling in a specific place, try moving the litter tray to that location. If it is soiling over the edge, either build a frame or invest in a covered tray.

3. The Cat
Have your veterinarian medically examine your cat for all of the potential clinical causes of not using the litter tray. Once again, sub-clinical bladder infection is an under-estimated cause of house soiling and is easily treated by diet change and antibiotics.

4. The Environment
Clean up all areas that have been soiled. Carpet can be difficult to

clean, so after cleaning spread crushed mothball crystals in the pile. Tiles can be cleaned with soap and water or disinfectant, but cement is virtually impossible to clean as the scent of urine and faeces penetrates the pores. The only sure way to eliminate the scent is to clean the area as effectively as possible, use a carpet deodorant and then paint the area. Cats that urinate in flower pots can be prevented from doing so if you cover the earth in the pots. Some cats prefer using sinks or bathtubs. This is often a sign of cystitis, but if it is strictly a behaviour problem simply leave 2–3 in (5–7.5 cm) of water in the sink or tub as cats usually dislike standing in water. For cats that perch on the edge of the sink, Bonnie Beaver, behaviourist at Texas A&M Veterinary School, suggests leaving a cactus plant in the sink: mean but effective!

If your cat is urinating on your bed, simply keep it out of your room. If that is impossible, Don McKeown, behaviourist at the Ontario Veterinary College in Canada, suggests leaving a sensitive burglar alarm on the bed. One touch to the duvet and the cat disappears. After cleaning a soiled area, use it as a feeding station, because cats are reluctant to soil where they eat. And if this isn't possible, try spreading a little dry pelleted food on the area or covering it with aluminium foil or crinkled plastic film. The covering should remain in place for at least two months. If you have a cat flap, consider securing it while the problem continues so that your cat is forced to use the tray rather than avoid the confrontation by going outdoors. Punishment never works and is counter-productive. If caught in the act, your cat should be picked up and calmly put in the litter tray.

But even if you carry out all of these procedures, some adult cats will continue to urinate and defecate outside their litter trays. Should this happen, all you can do is confine your cat to a small training pen large enough only for sleeping quarters, an eating station and a litter tray and then, over a period of four to five weeks, accustom it to the use of the tray. The cat should not be allowed out of the pen for the first week and then only under your supervision and into one room for short periods of time. If you don't have a pen, use your smallest uncarpeted room. Place the litter box at one end and the cat's food, water and bed at the other. But as well as filling the tray with litter, sprinkle some over the floor. Then the cat cannot avoid the feel of litter under its feet no matter where it voids itself. After a week, push the litter farthest from the litter tray towards the tray, clearing about a quarter of the floor but still leaving the rest feeling 'gritty'. Then, week by week, and as long as your cat is performing as you want it to, clear further quarters of the floor until, during the fourth week, only one quarter is litter-covered. During the fifth week leave litter only in and immediately around the tray, and in the following week only in the tray. If your cat is using the tray, keep the tray where it is but allow the cat to leave the room, gradually increasing the area of the house to which it is allowed access. If you are willing to do this rather than get rid of your delinquent, you are a prime candidate for feline sainthood!

Chapter Nine

Fear and Aggression

When as a kitten Millie first found herself on the kitchen floor being sniffed from above by my two querulous golden retrievers, she stood her ground and arched her back. Her hair stood on end (piloerected) and she spat hot cat breath at them. Both dogs retreated. Though she was only nine weeks of age and less than $2\frac{1}{4}$ lb (1 kg) in weight, a simple and ritual display of aggression was sufficient to protect her from animals thirty times her size. It wasn't 'aggressive' aggression: it was fear-induced aggression, but there was no way my dogs would know that fact.

When my kitten first met my dogs a simple threat display caused them to withdraw.

Just as dogs do, cats display many different forms of aggression and, in spite of the multitude of scientific papers that have been written on the subject, there is still no universally accepted definition of the word itself. There are distinct and defined categories, however, and they include the following:

1. Inter-male aggression: aggressive behaviour between males, especially during the mating season.
2. Territorial aggression: cats of either sex carry this out to protect a territory that usually includes a sleeping location and an eating station.
3. Competitive aggression: called dominance aggression in dogs, this is less distinct in cats but defines rank when several cats co-exist in the same territory.
4. Predatory aggression: stimulated by the sight, sound or smell of prey.
5. Play aggression: in the absence of prey, cats can act aggressively towards non-prey objects such as passing ankles.
6. Fear-induced aggression: when a cat is confronted with a frightening situation it may use a display of aggression to warn or actually to attack the intruder.
7. Redirected aggression: the cat does not direct its aggression at the cause of its discomfort but waits, then later slashes out at an 'innocent'.
8. Learned aggression: some cats learn to control situations by using aggressive tactics and can do such things as tease dogs or demand feeding by their owners in this way.
9. Petting aggression: this occurs after a period of petting. Mixed feelings cause the cat to attack the hand that is petting it.
10. Sexual aggression: some male cats bite the female's neck excessively during coitus. Females often viciously attack males after coitus.
11. Maternal aggression: females with litters may launch fearsome and frenetic attacks on other cats or other animals who venture near the nest.
12. Paternal aggression: there are reported incidents in domestic and other cats of males killing litters sired by other males.
13. Pain-induced aggression: injured cats, or even those that are simply on the receiving end of unpleasant intramuscular injections, may react aggressively.
14. Disease-induced aggression: epilepsy, under-active thyroid activity, rabies, general irritability or simply the aches of old age can all invoke aggressive behaviour.

Aggression is the second most common feline behaviour problem presented to the veterinarian (after elimination problems) and so, even though many of these forms of aggression have already been discussed in previous chapters, it is useful at this point briefly to recapitulate.

Several forms of aggression involve ritualized forms of body posture. By using a specific set of signals or body language, one cat can tell another what is on its mind. Needless to say, other cats are usually better at interpreting these signals than we are. The first three forms of aggression in the above list all use ritualized body language and, although all three are classically directed at other cats, the second, territorial aggression, can be directed at us.

Inter-male Aggression

In inter-male aggression ritual threat is almost always employed. This includes the stare, piloerection (raising of the hair), arched back, a lateral body posture, growling or caterwauling and drawn-back lips revealing the weapons. The cats face off, slowly approach each other on tiptoe and direct the attack towards the head and neck, wrestling, biting and clawing. The toms often walk slightly past each other before one will spring and try to grip the other's neck. After a struggle, an interlude occurs during which they stare each other down once more and then, as if in slow motion, set themselves up for another action replay. This behaviour is both inherited and learned and is influenced by environmental circumstances. Although it usually occurs between intact males, it may also sometimes be witnessed between neutered males.

TREATMENT
The best method of control is castration. If this is not possible, try to separate the gladiators. If this is impossible, the use of previously mentioned drugs might be helpful.

Territorial Aggression

As a classic independent individual, each cat needs its own personal space. Outdoors the personal space requirements of the intact male are considerably greater than those of the female and both have diminished territory requirements after they are neutered. But regardless of whether domestic cats are housed outdoors or indoors, and regardless of their neuter status, each cat still needs its own personal space, even if that territory is simply a sofa or a shaft of sunlight. When the cat feels challenged on its territory it responds aggressively.

This aggressive behaviour is most evident when a new cat is brought into a home, and cat owners are often amazed and distressed at how long the animosity between the resident and the newcomer continues. In a classic situation this is what happens.

The cat that knows its way around the house considers this to be its territory and often without threat launches a direct attack on the intruder. Not only does this happen when a new cat is brought home, it also happens when a resident cat returns from boarding or hospitalization. For unknown reasons, perhaps because of strange odours clinging to it, the returning cat is not apparently recognized and is attacked. In colony cats, as kittens mature they too may cease to be tolerated. The older cats behave in a territorially aggressive manner with their offspring and drive them away with attacks, chases, howls and paw blows.

Territorial toms sometimes sexually posture over other cats that enter their territory, as if mounting an oestrous female. The mounted cat, male or female, responds with sounds of indignance and a lowered body posture, then escapes when possible, often lashing out as it does so.

In the absence of other cats, residents can behave in a territorial manner with cat-surrogate humans. Some owners are threatened when they try to remove the cat from its favourite resting place. Others are growled and slashed at if they approach the cat while it is feeding. These are variations of territorial aggression.

TREATMENT

Although it is an intense form of aggression, this form of territorial behaviour can be avoided, altered or eliminated through careful introduction of new cats into the environment, as previously described, or by acclimatizing the resident to the new animal. Hormonal therapy, effective in other forms of aggression, is of no value here. Letting the cats simply fight it out may not work either because it can lead to fear-induced aggression (see page 149). The best treatment is gradual exposure of the strangers to each other. The cats should be kept in separate rooms with no visual contact but fed near the door that separates them. An excellent alternative is to train them to eat in cages by putting each cat in its own cage for an hour each day and feeding it there. After they are used to being fed in their cages, alternate the cages so that they become familiar with each other's odours, but in the pleasant context of eating. Finally, bring the cages (and their contents) in sight of each other while feeding the cats and then very gradually move the cages closer to each other daily over a period of several weeks. In the meantime always keep the cats completely separated. After, on average, four to six weeks, the territorial aggression of the original resident cat will have diminished sufficiently for them actually to meet.

Competitive Aggression

Cats don't have a well-defined dominance hierarchy. If two cats – a resident territorial cat and a stranger – meet on a trail, the fact that the stranger has got there first is often sufficient to give it right of passage. In many other species the animal's position in the pecking order dictates who is aggressive and with whom. But in cats the following is a typical scenario.

When two cats meet, one is usually dominant. It might be dominant because it knows the locale, or has been successful in previous encounters, or simply got there first. Depending upon its innate temperament, the dominant cat approaches the other, usually in a slow and crouching manner but tempering this with an air of assurance. The other cat might try to avoid the encounter. The dominant cat tries to sniff the anal region of the other, but this is rarely permitted and the stranger half-turns, hisses and strikes out in defence. But if, for example, the stranger immediately leaps on to a chair, the situation abruptly changes. In competitive aggression, the cat that wins 'King of the castle' cancels the dominance of the other. It can be that ephemeral. The previously dominant cat will now approach reluctantly if at all and the stranger is much more assured in its behaviour. And if the stranger stares at the resident, the stranger becomes the dominant cat. Competitive aggression is often much more subtle than territorial aggression and is rarely directed at us.

TREATMENT

Cats of similar age, sex and size are more likely to fight physically than are cats that are more strikingly different from each other. When there is an obvious difference between cats, they settle competitive aggression through ritual display. Cats that are more equal share the dominance position and may battle intensely and competitively for top position. Because of these circumstances the best treatments involve increasing the 'emotional distance' between two cats who think of themselves as equals. We should determine which is inately more dominant than the other and treat it as such. If a top cat is treated as a top cat, it is possible that, with assurance, it will need only ritual display rather than brute force to maintain its position. The cat elected as the 'submissive' one can be made more submissive through the use of hormones. This might sound cruel because our instinct is to always support the underdog, but if we do in this case we might unwittingly be creating more mayhem.

Predatory and Play Aggression

Although the forms of aggression already described all involve ritual forms of body language, neither of these does. Whether a cat is stalking a mouse or a visitor to your house, the attacks are carried out without the distance-increasing body signals or adrenal-gland responses associated with territorial, competitive and inter-male aggression. The attacks are without warning.

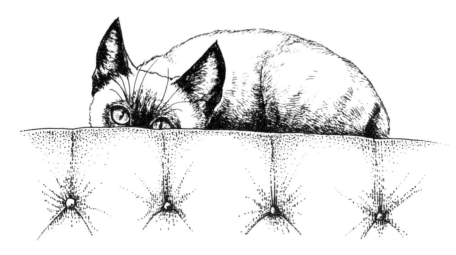

Some cats enjoy stalking and pouncing on their owners.

Play aggression is a major component of play behaviour. Kittens stalk and pounce upon each other and inflict controlled 'killing bites' to the nape of the neck, or anywhere else they can bite for that matter. Play aggression allows kittens to develop the motor skills and co-ordination that are necessary if they are to become successful hunters. Initially the various components of adult predatory aggression are carried out in a fragmented way. Predatory aggression involves five phases: alerting to prey, stalking, pouncing, killing with a neck bite and eating. Kittens will carry out these activities but not necessarily in the correct order. With time, however, the order is learned and by six months of age, kittens can become quite aggressive in their play-fights. At the same time, play-fighting with humans can lead to more serious biting.

All cats have the potential to become successful hunters, but because our intervention and selective breeding of them has not placed a high priority on hunting skills, there is now a considerable variation between felines where these abilities are concerned. Compounding this fact are the millions of cats that lead sedentary, indoor lives and which never have the opportunity to practise their predatory skills. They don't use up the energy that would otherwise be invested in hunting. These cats have energy to burn and one consequence is that any moving object can trigger predatory behaviour. Some ruthlessly stalk their owners or visitors from the time they enter the front door, slinking furtively from behind sofa to behind chair until the prey is within range and the angle is attacked. A veterinary colleague of mine once had a Siamese that perched on the sill above the door to the living room, waiting for unsuspecting prey to wander into his trap. From his 'hide' he silently launched himself on to the neck of unwary visitors while his owner gleamed with unmitigated pride.

TREATMENT

Kittens that over-indulge in play aggression should be treated as other cats would treat them, with a quick and well-aimed thump on the nose. Picking them up by the scruff of the neck, staring directly at them, then ignoring them for a few minutes is also effective.

Cats that attack human feet simply need more exercise and mental stimulation. Spend more time playing with them and in your absence provide them with toys that move and swing. Table-tennis balls, especially ones covered in wool or fur, are cheap and effective toys.

Some owners don't want their cats to show predatory aggression towards living creatures, particularly birds. Hunting is a learned sequence of behaviours that is based upon the cat's 'prewired' hunting instinct. Kittens learn how to hunt and what to hunt especially from their mothers, although half of the kittens that do not learn how to hunt from their mothers will still learn how to do so on their own. Raising kittens in an environment in which they are exposed to the type of prey you don't want them to attack can be useful. Our parrot was allowed to continue to fly from his perch to the front window during Millie's first few weeks at home and when she showed a gustatory interest in him she was firmly reprimanded. She was similarly reprimanded when she eyed him in his cage. Now, when he takes off on his evening flight through the living room, Millie's response is one of nonchalance, similar to that of the dogs.

It is difficult to overcome the predatory behaviour of outdoor cats. Aversion therapy, by which the cat associates its activity with something unpleasant, can be effective but it means that you always have to be there, high-velocity water pistol or noise maker at hand, when it stalks birds. As I've mentioned, prevention is easier than cure. Add one or more bells to the cat's collar so that it loses the advantage of stealth when it stalks prey.

Fear-induced Aggression

Fear is common in all cats and manifests itself in two different ways. The most obvious is 'fight or flight'. When the cat is confronted with what it perceives to be a dangerous situation, it flees if it can, but failing that it becomes 'defensively aggressive', alternately approaching and withdrawing, howling, spitting and hissing, swiping with the forepaws while showing the teeth. This is the behaviour of feral cats when they are 'rescued' and brought to me for medical treatment.

There is also an alternative method by which cats more accustomed to handling show fear. Rather than fight or flee, they simply crouch down, avoid eye contact and stay perfectly still. Some behaviourists call this the 'conservation-withdrawal' response to a fearful situation.

Fear-induced aggression stimulates a combination of attack and defence behaviour. Rather than launching the confident attack of the dominant aggressor, the fear-induced aggressor attacks with its head drawn back to protect its neck and hits with its paws instead of biting. Paul Leyhausen describes it as 'sword-and-shield' behaviour. The attack with paw blows indicates that the cat is defensive, which is why veterinarians and their nurses get scratched much more frequently than they get bitten. The most common type of aggression I see at the clinic is fear-induced aggression.

The defensive cat presses itself close to the ground. Its ears don't stand out and back as in attack but are pulled down sideways with the back edge folded and are virtually invisible from the front. The eyes are widely dilated, indicating the surge in adrenal-gland activity, and all the hair on the body bristles.

When confrontation continues, the abjectly fearful cat rolls over on its back but does so head and forequarters first. This leaves the hind legs firmly planted for leverage but frees the forepaws (and the teeth) for defence and attack. The upside-down fearful pose often slows down the attacking cat, and if it comes too close it gets a vicious swipe of unsheathed claws on its nose. If the attack goes on, the defensive cat rolls completely over on its back and parries with all paws.

If an attack is sudden and powerful, however, the defensive cat alters its tactics and, instead of boxing with its forepaws, uses them to hang on to the attacker while trying to drag the attacker towards its open jaws, all the while scratching and slashing with its hind paws. Any veterinarian with substantial clinical experience has been a victim of this form of fear-induced aggression and will know that it induces the 'attacker' to let loose and defend himself or herself. This form of aggression is accompanied by howling, hissing, spitting and growling, but not the caterwauling of the purely threatening inter-male aggressive encounter.

The defensive posture of fear is not submissive as it is in dogs. It does not offer up the groin for sniffing or the nape of the neck for biting. When cats assume a defence posture, it is simply that – a posture from which they try to defend themselves against further attack – although in certain circumstances it will lead to a counter-attack. This means that, unlike the dog, the more a cat defends itself the more likely it is to counter-attack. This is why cat fights are not as potentially lethal as dog fights. Attacking cats are cautious when confronted with fear-induced behaviour for they know that this behaviour leads to counter-attack. This is one reason why a victor does not always pursue a retreating rival and it is also why cats are unwilling to fight opponents that are fully prepared to defend themselves. Chase occurs only in territorial fights or in the form of mock pursuits in play or in mating behaviour.

Concisely, when cats are fearful they know that attack is one of the best forms of defence and so attack is what they will do when confronted with a villain who is infinitely superior, a dog or a veterinarian, for example. This approach can surprise or baffle the 'enemy', giving the cat a chance to escape. The behaviour of the mother cat protecting her young is classic unalloyed fear-induced aggression. When frightened by an intruder – a dog, for instance – she will without warning shoot towards the intruder and rain fierce unsheathed paw blows on him. In most cases the stranger turns immediately and runs away, often pursued for some distance by the dilated-pupiled, screaming mother.

In other circumstances the fearful cat will give a display of aggression. It pulls itself up on fully stretched legs and arches its back in the shape of an inverted U. Cats kept in isolation as kittens will arch at humans, as will feral cats. Kittens will arch at almost anything that surprises them, including their mirror image when seen for the first time. The stiff legs tell us that the cat is angry, while the arched back indicates fear. Together they produce a bigger cat. (The straight back of anger and the crouch of fear would most certainly not create the impression the cat wants to make.)

Assuming the 'arched' position, the fearful cat will often stand broadside to its opponent and hiss, snake-like and ominously. The hiss turns to a growl which becomes a spit. If the enemy comes within a critical distance, which varies with differing circumstances and with the temperament and individual experiences of the cat, an attack follows. If the enemy is hesitant, the fearful cat will still usually attack. Inexperienced and fearful cats will try to escape more frequently than experienced ones.

Trial and error has evolved this type of fear-induced aggression, for if a cat were to run away from another predator, a dog for example, it would trigger the dog's urge to chase and the cat would most certainly lose. But frightened as the cat is, if it makes a stand it gives none of the normal prey signals to the dog.

TREATMENT

Fear-induced aggression can be inherited. It can also be learned from early experience or lack of it, and can be learned through later experience. It is certainly possible with foxes to 'breed out' fearful behaviour in a few generations and, as I mentioned in *The Dog's Mind*, many breeds of dog have been unwittingly bred for enhanced fearful behaviour. Fear of pain or perceived pain causes this form of aggression. A mother's fear of danger to her kittens will also precipitate an aggressive response. These are circumstances where prevention of fear is more important than the treatment of its consequences. In a similar way, threats imposed by a new environment, a new animal or baby in the house or from excessive restraint should all be anticipated rather than treated. Fears that are learned later, however, such as fear of children because a child has caused previous pain to the cat, can be treated.

With time, fear of specific locations or objects that the cat associates with a traumatic incident will subside, but this can be accelerated by associating those places, objects or people with pleasant experiences. When fear is of a low intensity, a cat can be counter-conditioned by appropriate playing, grooming and feeding. These procedures should gradually be carried out by the person who causes fear or in the location where the cat is fearful. Sometimes drugs such as Valium are useful in conjunction with this training.

As fear is one of the cat's most common and expected responses to a visit to the veterinarian, there are also ways to try to minimize this aspect of its behaviour. In the cat's mind, the sights, sounds and odours of the veterinary clinic mean pain, distress or discomfort. Many cats quickly learn to relate the cat basket to the subsequent visit to the veterinarian and will fight viciously and fearfully to prevent being put in it. Others go into hiding at the first sight of the basket and the truly impressive disappear as soon as they hear their owners utter the syllable 'vet'.

Visits can be made as unthreatening as possible by first training your cat to associate the cat basket with pleasant activities, such as feeding and sleeping. Forward-thinking owners put bedding and food in their baskets and train their cats to sleep in them and to take food from them. In that way you eliminate the first fear, that of the basket.

Many cats seldom leave home other than to go to the cattery or the veterinarian's clinic. They never travel by car or public transport. These are fear-inducing experiences for unsophisticated cats, but the fear can be diminished if a cat goes on an occasional journey while still a kitten and is rewarded with food and affection for not showing signs of distress. Depending on the individual temperament of your cat, some like fully-enclosed baskets from which they protectively peer and others enjoy the 360° vision offered by perspex or wire carriers. Generally speaking, enclosed carriers are best for cats with a withdrawn personality and open ones for their more gregarious cousins.

Once you are at the veterinarian's it is up to him or her and the staff to minimize the fear of the visit. Where space is available, some clinics offer separate dog and cat waiting rooms, although to have that amount of space is for me an enviable luxury. Cats should be allowed to explore and investigate clean examining rooms while the veterinarian talks to the owner. The minimum amounts of restraint necessary should be used when examining the kitten or cat and diversions such as vitamin tablets or food offered when potentially painful procedures such as injections are given. As most cats that are used to humans will show their fear through 'conservation-withdrawal' rather than 'fight or flight', they simply withdraw to the back of their carriers. For simple procedures it is often possible to treat them in their cages. Most house cats feel more secure with their owners but some can curiously behave in a more fearful way. When this happens it is better for you to leave the room and let the veterinarian and a nurse carry out any necessary treatment.

Redirected Aggression

When a cat becomes agitated enough to lash out at what bothers it but is prevented or inhibited from doing so, it can sometimes vent its anger on someone or even something else. In a typical situation a cat is brought to me for examination and treatment. I examine its ears with an auroscope, take its temperature with a thermometer, pry its mouth open with my fingers to look inside, stare into its eyes, sometimes with the assistance of a bright light, hold it by its hind legs to feel the pulse and probably inject the cat with a vaccine or some other drug. When I'm finished the owner tries to gentle the cat, but as soon as it is free of me and safely in the owner's hands it hisses and slashes at him or her. Sometimes the cat remains restrained and saves its venom for home where it attacks as it is taken out of the carrier. The cat's victim is not the appropriate recipient of its aggression but is simply the first available one who comes along. In a similar way, cats upset by one member of the family might attack another if they feel they can get away with it. In some families a cat may attack only one specific person, not because that person is unpleasant to the cat but because it is he or she whom the cat feels is safest to attack.

Redirected aggression is induced by an incident that frightens the cat and is augmented by an increasing level of excitement. It is an offensive form of aggression, sometimes almost premeditated in its intensity, and can cause considerable damage.

TREATMENT

Cats that are agitated or frightened should be approached with care and caution, even by their favourite people. In some circumstances it is best to remove whatever has frightened the cat and wait until its state of arousal has diminished before approaching. Aggressive experiences between two cats can cause one of them to redirect its aggression at a human member of the family, and if this is the case the treatment that has been described for territorial aggression (see page 144) will treat the primary cause of redirected aggression. If, on the other hand, the aggression is fear-induced, follow the method described for de-sensitizing against that form of behaviour (page 149). In both circumstances sedative tranquillizers such as Valium can be useful.

Learned Aggression

Some cats learn that they can use aggressive behaviour to control situations. An initial encounter with a dog might stimulate fear-induced aggression but the cat 'wins'. The dog backs off or runs away. Over a period of time fear-induced aggression diminishes until it ceases to be an adrenalin-releasing incident filled with fear. Instead it becomes a premeditated act of aggression, a technique used to control and manipulate the dog. Although cats are usually much smaller than the dogs they live with, most pet owners concede that 'cats rule dogs'. Because Millie has been raised with dogs, and teases them by batting their faces, chewing their limbs, swinging from their tails or using them as climbing frames – all activities that the dogs accept with resignation – she has never developed a fear of dogs. When guests visit with their dog, Millie stands her ground, walks up to the newcomer and bats its face. She does not know the potential danger she is in with some dogs but has learned that she can control a dog's responses by behaving in this way. Other cats learn that if they use aggression on their owner at certain times – for example, if he or she is late wielding the can opener – they can influence the outcome of their owner's behaviour. This could be called a variation of play behaviour or it could even represent a form of irritable aggression, but in either case it has been learned and is used to effect a specific outcome.

TREATMENT
Learned behaviours can be unlearned. All that is necessary is to create situations where the outcome is not the positive one that the cat expects but instead is negative. If I brought a dog into my house that simply thinks cats are there for the chasing, Millie would rapidly learn that boxing a dog's face is not acceptable behaviour. I might, however, be creating a highly dangerous situation for Millie. It would be safer for me to intervene when she boxes dogs, with a stern voice,

a loud noise, a well-aimed cushion or water pistol, or any other inventive form of aversion therapy whereby Millie would associate her aggression towards dogs with something unpleasant. In a similar and easier way, cats that attack their owners when they have not been fed at the appointed hour should not be fed for their actions. That simply rewards the aggression. Instead, discipline your cat with stern words, a shake by the scruff and disinterest, and only later, on your terms, put down the food. Don't let the cat think that its arrogant behaviour is the reason for the meal.

Petting Aggression

Your cat is on your lap almost dozing and you are absently petting it. It is a gratifying behaviour on your part because it lowers your blood pressure, your skin temperature and your heart rate. When you behave in the same way with your dog, it too goes into a state of near-reverie and if you stop it nudges you with its head or uses its paw to convince you to continue, for it too benefits from the contact comfort you are offering it. All social animals engage in mutual grooming and benefit both psychologically and physiologically. But suddenly your cat bites your hand and jumps down. Why do some cats behave in such an apparently insincere way?

If stroked too much cats might bite.

There are several possible reasons for this unpleasant behaviour. Dogs are pack animals that sleep together in physical contact, think together as a team and develop a dominance–subdominance–subordinance hierarchy that they rigidly conform to and demonstrate by kowtowing to the leader and licking his face. Physical contact is a common theme in many of their behaviours. Cats mutually groom each other, but on closer examination it is usually only females who groom and they do so only in conditions where colony life occurs, when a large food source is nearby. When they groom each other, they do so for limited lengths of time. Otherwise physical contact is kept to a minimum. With the exception of those inhabiting certain cold sub-Antartic islands, feral cats do not sleep in physical contact with each other. That behaviour is a consequence of early learning in house cats and has been accentuated by selective breeding.

Contact comfort is enjoyable to cats. That's why they rub against our legs when we come home. But too much of a good thing can lead to aggression. The cat's mind enters a state of conflict. On the one hand the cat enjoys physical contact; on the other it is an independent animal which seldom has natural physical contact with other animals except when fighting or mating, and even when mating there are mixed emotions and fighting. The cat controls this contradiction within itself when its owner is showing it affection until suddenly and impulsively it feels irritated, bites and jumps down from the lap where it had seemed settled.

Dr Bonnie Beaver feels that petting aggression might be a form of fear-induced behaviour. She says that because of cats' world-class ability to catnap, they might fall asleep for a few seconds while being petted. They then wake up to the sensation of something causing physical contact, in most circumstances a sign of danger. They instinctively bite and jump down, but even on the way down to the ground they have become conscious enough to realize there was no danger and upon landing show no further signs of fear.

TREATMENT

The best method of controlling this form of aggression is to control your urge to pet your cat for prolonged periods of time. Single, short strokes that mimic the licking of another cat's tongue are the best and these should be restricted to a length of time shorter than that which you know provokes this seemingly irrational behaviour.

Sexual, Maternal and Paternal Aggression

Sexual, maternal and paternal aggression are described in Chapter Seven. Maternal aggression is hormonally controlled and influenced by the presence of young kittens. All mothers can react in the same way, and when one new-born kitten utters a distress call all other mothers that can hear it become alert and try to investigate. The kitten might be rescued by another mother who carries the kitten back to the nest, almost eagerly attacking anyone or anything that gets in her way. After only a few weeks, however, this impressive form of protection diminishes. Male sexual aggression simply occurs when the male bites the female's neck too harshly during mating. He has to hang on, though, because the barbs on his penis are like fishhooks and when he withdraws after mating he induces enough pain in the female for her to try viciously to bite him. If he hasn't got a good grasp on her she does so, and can follow up her attack with a chase. Paternal aggression against kittens fathered by another sire is rare in domestic cats, although it has been reported frequently among lions in Tanzania and Uganda. When a new lion takes over a pride, he is likely to kill and possibly consume kittens fathered by the previous male of the pride. Abhorrent as it sounds, this is a behaviour of many wild carnivores, but I have no personal experience of its having occurred with house cats.

TREATMENT

Treatment is not necessary for the sex-related forms of aggression, although sex-related aggression can rarely be directed at humans. I have been told by several clients that their neutered male cats have stalked and attacked them on a monthly cycle. On one occasion the owner had lived with her cat (and her husband) with no problems until she stopped taking her birth-control pill. Shortly afterwards her cat attacked her for the first time, and eventually she realized that she was being attacked almost monthly and the attacks were occurring around the middle of her menstrual cycle. This coincides with ovulation and maximum production of the hormone oestrogen. After a year off the pill, the woman's marriage faltered and she resumed taking birth control pills. The cat's attacks stopped as abruptly as they had started.

Pain-induced and Disease-induced Aggression

These forms of aggression are discussed in more detail in Chapter Twelve under the sections dealing with behaviour changes of the ill and in old age. When cats are irritated by pain, they vent their anger through aggression. Old age is often accompanied by some body discomfort, arthritis, muscle pain and/or anal-gland inflammation. The consequence is that previously benign cats can now become fitfully aggressive. They want to be left alone and indeed they should be.

Cats will be aggressive towards the source of what has pained them. If a small child pulls the hair of a cat, the animal will naturally lash out with claws and teeth. Whenever cats attack unsupervised children we should always assume the likelihood that the attack has been provoked through pain. Pain-induced aggression is a 'one-off' form of aggression and usually doesn't alter the relationship that has previously existed between the person causing the pain and the cat. Owners often feel their cats will hate them forever after I ask them to hold their pets while I give an injection. In such a case owners might become the recipients of a little redirected aggression, but the situation ends there. Cats don't permanently associate their owners with the pain unless the exercise is frequently repeated.

TREATMENT
Simply avoiding pain and fear is the best method of preventing the aggressive consequences of these sensations – though, of course, it should be remembered that these sensations are also necessary for cats to develop other normal behaviours.

All forms of aggression in cats can be dramatic, but some are easier to treat than others. The general rules for treating aggressiveness in cats include the following:

1. Avoid early learning or conditioning that leads to aggressive behaviour.
2. Whenever possible, counter-condition or 'unteach', but never use punishment as it is counter-productive. Aversion therapy, on the other hand, through which the cat associates an unpleasant experience with its aggression, can be a successful means of counter-conditioning.
3. Diet may have a role in aggressive behaviour. Some argue that, because serotonin inhibits aggression and because high-protein

diets increase brain serotonin levels, high-protein diets inhibit aggression. At present this is no more than a theory.

4. Drugs can alter aggressive behaviour. Tranquillizers such as Valium and progestogens such as megestrol acetate can have a potent effect on reducing certain forms of aggression.

5. Neutering in both males and females dramatically and precipitously reduces some forms of aggressive behaviour.

6. In certain medical situations where aggression is caused by space-occupying lesions in the brain and by other physical disorders, the only acceptable form of treatment is euthanasia.

Chapter Ten

Individuality and Behaviour Towards Humans

It is a curious truth that many cats enjoy warmer, more convivial, even affectionate relations with humans than they could ever do with fellow felines. If I might bore you with Millie once more, this morning she has been fed, has climbed a tree where she eyed some blackbirds, played with the dogs' tails and performed a few somersaults in a pile of laundry, but chose to lie herself on my lap as soon as I sat down to write. Her body is limp. One forelimb is stretched out while the other is slightly retracted. Her tail is hanging over the edge of my leg (and as it's a very long tail it looks like a furry divining rod pointing out a hidden treasure in the floor below). She is, to put it simply, behaving in a warm, relaxed, friendly and perhaps even affectionate way with me, in a way that she would never behave with another cat.

Millie is a recent manifestation of this cross-species behaviour, for even Muhammad, as the story tells, cut off the sleeve of his garment to avoid disturbing his sleeping cat. If you ask me to describe Millie, I would say she is a playful, active, curious and equable but relaxed cat who is very sociable with people and dogs. In other words, she has a distinct personality, an individuality. But, as I speculated in the Introduction, can I really use these words to describe cat behaviour?

Although all cats share behaviours with all other cats, the majority of my clients, and I imagine most cat owners, feel as I do, that their cat is an individual with a distinct character. Some people refer to their cat's personality, others to its temperament, but all are saying the same thing: that their cat is a unique individual. Scientists do the same. In one paper in the journal *Animal Behaviour*, three scientists studying cat behaviour stated, 'We felt that each animal in our laboratory colony had a distinct personality in the sense that the sum total of its behaviour gave it an identifiable style.' This is as good a definition of individuality as I have read.

Just as I have described Millie, other cat owners describe their cats to me as 'friendly' or 'nervous' or 'shy' or 'bold' – all descriptions of human behaviours or traits. A client might describe his or her cat to me in a very specific way, but when I hospitalize it, my nurses use different adjectives. In other words, our very perception of the cat's mind is influenced by our own inter-actions with that individual and indeed by our knowledge of other animals. It leads back to the perennial question. Does Millie lie on my lap out of affection or simply because I'm warm? It's a question that science is trying to answer.

The origins of individuality rest in the genes. The behaviourist Bonnie Beaver has noted, for example, that in some lines of blue-eyed white cats, the females are unusually timid. Selective breeding in silver foxes, on the other hand, has eliminated timidity within only a few generations. One of the precepts of the domestication process has been to reduce or eliminate fear of humans in domestic animals, but in doing so with cats in particular we have created a unique situation where we can live side by side with another species and watch its natural behaviour at first hand. Domestication has done more. It has allowed cats to express their potential variations in behaviour in more ways. And some of those variations are seen most clearly in their relationship with us.

Researchers have recently explored who influences whom in the human-cat relationship. At the University of Zurich in Switzerland it has been observed that the breed of cat has no influence on the amount of time owners spend with their pets. Pure-breds might look like fashion accessories but they are treated no differently from their back-alley relatives.

Conforming to old-fashioned scientific principles, the Swiss researchers set up several experiments. In one study they engineered 240 controlled first encounters between people and cats who had never met each other, observing the cats' behaviour in half of the encounters and the humans' behaviour in the others. Humans took, on average, fourteen seconds before they made a social contact with the cat, sixty-four seconds before they spoke to it and seventy-four seconds before they touched it. But when the results were looked at in more detail, it was found that 98 per cent of adults spoke before touching while only 38 per cent of children did so. Adults always used complete sentences but children often used only single words or sounds. Both, however, were equally successful at gaining the cat's attention. There were no appreciable differences in the way men and women approached the cats.

When people were asked not to act spontaneously with the cats, it took on average five minutes before the cats made contact with them, but once the people were permitted to inter-act the cats became much more active. The behaviourists stated that by far the most important factor influencing cat behaviour was the animals' individuality. They noted, 'We were able to differentiate qualitatively between shy and trustful individuals, initiators of contacts and more reserved cats and individuals having a preference for body contact or play and those showing no preference . . . each cat reacts consistently in its personal way.'

What, then, creates individuality? In the 1950s investigations began into the effect of early experience and handling on the developing personality of animals. Handled animals showed accelerated development and maturing of the central nervous system. They grew faster and were more resistant to emotional stress. Handled Siamese kittens opened their eyes earlier and emerged from their nest a few days sooner than non-handled littermates. They even developed their Siamese coloration faster. I have already mentioned these effects of early experience on the cat's mind, but as well as accelerating learning they are also integral in creating individuality. More recent work from the Department of Ethology at the University of Zurich has shown that feeding a cat plays an important role in establishing a relationship between a human and a cat but is not sufficient to maintain it.

Scientists have three methods for measuring individuality in cats. The first and perhaps the most common involves observing a cat's behaviour in a free and uncontrolled situation. Those who watch feral cats stalk penguins on sub-Antarctic islands are using this method. A second method is to create specific test situations, observing for example how long it takes a cat to learn to use a maze. The third allows two or more observers who actually know the cat independently to score or rate the individual according to very specific behaviourally defined categories.

There is also a fourth category, under-used but invaluable, and that is cat-owner observation. If I may perpetuate a stereotype, dog owners are active and cat owners passive. Dog owners want to do things with their dogs, want to play, command and inter-act. Cat owners are natural observers, good at nuance and detail. There is often understanding, perception and clarity in how they describe their pet's behaviour when they visit me when their cat is unwell. Cat-owner questionnaires are an under-used method of investigating the eccentricities and quirks of cat individuality as well as their uniform behaviours. And if I may continue on this tangent, so too is anecdote. Science loves hard fact. Two out of fifty-six cats finding their way through a maze in thirty-six minutes is a hard fact. My cat actively choosing to snooze on my lap is an anecdote. I think both are equally important, although one behaviour is observed under rigid and controlled conditions and the other is not. Anecdote, or even the image of cats in literature and art, is important because it tells us of our expectations of cats. And what we expect of them influences how we treat them and how we treat them affects their individuality.

In the late 1970s researchers learned that talking softly to kittens from shortly after they were born until weaning caused them to be more attentive to the talker, to leave the mother while nursing and approach the talker and to make more friendly approach sounds and gestures. (Millie's friendly approach sound is an abrupt 'brp' with a rolled Scottish 'r'.) The paediatrician Berry Brazelton has noted that human babies are influenced in the same way while still in the womb. Later on, Eileen Karsh, carrying out her work on socialization periods in kittens, observed that certain activities such as vocalization that started at a very early age persisted into adulthood. Active kittens grew up to be kinetic cats, while reserved kittens grew up to be retiring individuals. Pavlov, in his work with dogs over sixty years ago, had noted a similar effect and divided dogs into two categories, excited and inhibited. He described excited dogs as energetic and highly reactive, while inhibited dogs were melancholic or phlegmatic. By their behaviour shortly after birth, cats too have been classified under two headings, the 'quick-noisy' and the 'slow-quiet'. The 'quick-noisy' were described as the most responsive to human companionship. As previously mentioned, Hans Eysenck's classifications of introvert and extravert can equally apply to cats, and in defining individuality these dual descriptions seem an apt starting point. They become even more useful when you are choosing the right individual for your lifestyle, and this too is an area that has recently been investigated.

Once more, the ever-active workers at the University of Zurich carried out studies of how people behaved with their cats and how cats behaved with their owners in their own homes. Claudia Mertens spent 500 hours in fifty-one different homes. Much of what she observed confirmed the obvious. Cats spend most of their time with the person who is at home the most. As most of these households were 'conventional' in that the man went out to work and the woman stayed home, they consequently spent most time in the presence of women and least time with men. Children aged eleven to fifteen ranked in between. On average, cats spent 27 per cent of their time in the presence of 'their' human and in close proximity 17 per cent of the time. Average petting time, however, was 3 per cent and playing time less than 1 per cent. But if the owner was a woman with no children, her cat spent on average 6 per cent more time in its owner's presence. And if a cat was strictly an indoor animal, it spent 8 per cent more time inter-acting with 'its' human than did cats allowed outdoors. In other words, as the environment changes the cat alters its behaviour. Its individuality is affected by the circumstances in which it finds itself.

Owners' behaviour with their cats was also found to be influenced by 'ecological' circumstances. Generally speaking, women were more likely to comply with the demands of cats with access to the outdoors and single women were less likely to accede to their cat's requests than women living with partners. This becomes an important factor when behaviour problems are encountered but also has a direct bearing upon any studies on how we behave with our pet cats.

Several years ago I carried out a questionnaire survey of 500 Saturday-morning-TV-viewing cat owners. Virtually all of them talked to their cats and most played with them daily. Play is a reciprocal activity – an inter-action occurs. Most owners shared their food with their cats and just over 50 per cent allowed their cats to sleep on their bed. Many celebrated their cat's birthdays and some confided in their cats. Most looked upon their cats as members of the family and treated them as children. One third felt that their cat offered protection by its sensitivity to noise. Most believed they understood their cat's moods and the majority felt their cat understood their moods.

Using this and other information, Michael Mendl created categories to rank individual behaviour. These include:

Aggressive	Playful
Agile	Sociable with cats
Curious	Sociable with people
Equable with cats	Solitary
Excitable	Tense
Fearful of cats	Vocal
Fearful of people	Voracious
Hostile to cats	Watchful
Hostile to people	

Using mathematical principles, three behaviour categories were then created:

Alert = active + curious
Sociable = sociable with people – fearful of people – hostile to people – tense
Equable = equable

These three groupings seem to be independent personality dimensions, an enlargement of the previous two of Pavlov, Karsh and others. Employing this method, behaviourists are now trying to use ordinary subjective personality descriptions to describe individuality in cats. I personally prefer the simpler two categories: 'sociable, confident and easy-going' *versus* 'timid, shy and nervous'.

Over half of all surveyed cat owners allow their pets to sleep on their beds.

Although cats seem to possess defined individual personalities, the question remains why they will behave with us in a more relaxed, equable and physical manner than they will with others of their own kind. While I have been sitting writing this, Millie has got up several times, reached up and head-rubbed against my face. That's a simple behaviour signifying we're on friendly terms with each other. She is probably anointing me with her scent, saying in her feline way that I am a member of her group. She has walked back and forth across the keyboard of my word processor, miaowing constantly and inadvertently rewriting the chapter, but is such a champion time waster that I have simply stared back at her as she has implored me to be more active – to *do* something. Failing with me, she has launched herself on Libby, my retriever, lying on the floor beside me, pouncing on the dog's forelimb, throwing herself on her side and then chewing the limb while her forelimbs hold and her hind legs kick. This is simple behaviour too, social behaviour transferred from the natural recipient, a littermate, on to another furry animal she has grown up with and considers to be very much like a cat, even more so than humans. But why will she lie on my lap? Why, when I feed her, will she start to eat, then come over to 'speak', then return to her food? Why, when the back door is open, the sun is shining and birds are everywhere, does she climb three flights of stairs and actively search me out, only to lie down either near me or actually on me? Why will she be friendlier to me than she will ever be to another cat?

The eminent observer of feline behaviour Paul Leyhausen has replied with the most plausible explanation. In his work with a wide variety of cat species he observed that cats with an even more solitary lifestyle than the domestic feline, species such as the ocelot, are able to establish a close, one could say almost affectionate link with humans. In the cat's mind, we humans are almost ideal social companions because we don't represent competition. We don't compete for food, territory or sex, all factors that seriously inhibit affectionate relations between adult cats. Adult cats rarely sleep together, but in my TV survey and in similar American surveys over 50 per cent of cats actively choose to sleep on their owners' beds. Leyhausen states that the constant antagonism towards other cats that is generated in territory protection and defence, in vying for sexual supremacy and in protecting resources, leaves no room for the perpetuation of the more sociable aspects of juvenile behaviour. Because, in cats' relationship with us, none of these antagonisms is raised, their juvenile social behaviours are not crushed.

It is certainly true that in many other species – wolves, for example – juvenile behaviours never completely disappear; they are simply submerged, but in adulthood they will readily emerge if circumstances permit. I mentioned in *The Dog's Mind* the observations of David Mech, watching adult wolves on an island in a lake in British Columbia, Canada, play 'King of the castle' for five continuous hours for no apparent reason other than the sheer pleasure of doing so. Feral adult cats are occupied by guarding territory, defence, rivalry and mating. They retain a residual ability to behave in a juvenile manner but are seldom given the opportunity to do so. By the nature of their lifestyle, domestic cats, raised in secure proximity to us, look upon us as 'conspecific' enough to treat as fellow cats (which is why Millie will head-rub me or play-fight with my dog) but sufficiently different not to be a danger. The result is that genuine and lasting friendships, of a kind that would never develop between feral cats, and that would seldom develop between even neutered housebound domestic cats, are possible between them and us. To answer the question as to whether it is affection and security or simply warmth that draws cats to us, the answer is affection and security.

Chapter Eleven

Breed Differences in Behaviour

In the previous chapters I have reviewed the various factors that affect the cat's mind. Its age, sex and early experience are three components. So too are later learning, whether the cat is neutered and, as just discussed in Chapter Ten, its individual personality. But there is still one more factor that has a bearing on the cat's behaviour and that is its breed.

Unlike with breeds of dogs, virtually no research has been carried out on possible behavioural differences between cat breeds. Ben Hart at the University of California, quoting a very brief survey he conducted of the opinions of four cat-show judges, stated that Siamese cats, for example, are outgoing, demanding of attention and vocal. Domestic longhairs (Persians) are lethargic, reserved and inactive. Abyssinians are shy, fearful and nervous of children.

Individual breeds are a result of natural or manipulated restricted breeding. The Norwegian Forest Cat and Maine Coon are classic natural breeds, survivors of matings between cats from different origins brought to Norway and the East Coast of the United States respectively. Both of these examples are probably mixes of the domestic (British) shorthair and longhaired cats from Turkey. The Somali, another increasingly popular breed, is a mix of the Abyssinian and a longhair, but in this instance premeditated, with the longhair gene intentionally added by breeders to alter the look of the cat.

To our eyes the colour of the cat's coat is the most important characteristic we look for. In one study of university undergraduates, grey was the most popular colour, followed by black, then striped and black. Orange was the least preferred colour and calico cats had second lowest preference. We selectively breed for coat colour, coat length and eye colour, but seldom for personality. Unwittingly, however, as Bonnie Beaver observed in noting timidity in blue-eyed white cats, personality and coat type or colour are genetically linked. When the ethologist Dennis Turner at Zurich University asked independent observers to rate female cats and their offspring at two research colonies according to their friendliness to people, he found that most of the cats rated friendly came from the same father, although none had ever had contact with him. The trait of friendliness to people is at least partly genetic and might be perpetuated through selective breeding with the right fathers.

Although there is virtually no scientific documentation on breed differences in behaviour, anecdote should never be disregarded and there is plenty of this sort of information in the descriptions of temperament in the breed standards for cats. These descriptions say as much about our expectations as they do about the cat's mind (all describe their specific breed as 'intelligent'), but they still provide a good starting point from which to look at breed differences in behaviour. Because the breed standards are concerned with expectations, it can be more accurate to compare the temperament descriptions in more descriptive texts. One such, *The Ultimate Cat Book*, has used these words to describe the behaviour of various breeds:

Siamese – extravert, devoted, intolerant of other cats. [From clinical experience I would add that they reach sexual maturity sooner, have larger litters and live longer than other breeds.]
Abyssinian – sweet-tempered, obedient.
Somali – good-tempered, shy, unsuited to entire outdoor life.
Burmese – affectionate, loves people.

Each colour of longhair or Persian cat has its own descriptive adjectives:
Black longhair – loyal, suspicious of strangers.
White longhair – calm.
Cream longhair – even-tempered.
Blue longhair – gentle.
Red-self longhair – polite.
Bicolour longhair – placid.
Smoke longhair –relaxed.
Cameo longhair – langorous.
Tabby longhair – equable.
Tortoiseshell longhair – good mother.
Tortie and white longhair – calm and sweet-natured.
Colourpoint longhair – gentle but spirited without being demonstrative.

Pewter longhair – exceptionally affectionate and even-tempered.
Chocolate and lilac longhair – more outgoing and inquisitive.

Almost all the descriptions of longhairs include 'affectionate', and from these a composite picture emerges:
Longhairs (Persians) – placid, quiet, adaptable, affectionate. [From clinical experience I would add that they have smaller-than-average litters and seemingly moult more than other cats.]

Other longhaired cats have varying temperament descriptions:
Turkish Van – lively.
Birman – civilized, amenable.
Ragdoll – extremely tolerant.
Balinese – less loud and boisterous than the Siamese.
Angora – fun-loving, friendly, gentle.
Maine Coon – companionable, given to much 'chirping'.
Norsk Skaukatt (Norwegian Forest Cat) – friendly, playful, hardy.

British shorthaired cats are also described individually by colour:
Black shorthair – good-natured.
White shorthair – street-wise and friendly.
Blue shorthair – particularly affectionate, hankering for the quiet life.
Blue-cream shorthair – lively.
Tabby shorthair – good-natured.
Tortoiseshell shorthair – sharp-witted.
Spotted shorthair – affable.
Bicolour shorthair – even-tempered, friendly.
Smoke shorthair – pleasant-natured.

The American shorthair is a descendant of British imports, but just as the Maine Coon has evolved its own breed personality, so too have the resident shorthairs:
American shorthair – energetic, robust, hardy.

Other shorthaired cats are described in these ways:
Russian blue – shy, quiet.
Korat – sweet-natured.
Tonkinese – ultra-affectionate, loves people.
Bombay – craves human companionship, dislikes being left alone.
Burmilla – even-tempered.
Rex – playful.
Egyptian Mau – good at learning tricks, enjoys walking on a lead.

Once more, virtually all of these descriptions include the words 'intelligent' and 'affectionate'. Some subtly suggest the author's and editor's painful search for synonyms. The Japanese Bobtail, for example, is described as 'brim full of personality', a neat way of saying nothing. Nevertheless they are excellent descriptions and in a scientific context would be described as 'forced evaluations' in which an individual or group of individuals is 'forced' to not vacillate but make a descriptive decision.

With that in mind, but in view of the lack of published information on breed differences in behaviour, I surveyed one hundred practising veterinarians, asking them to rank six different breeds or colours of cats according to ten different personality characteristics. Because it can be irritating to complete 'forced evaluation' surveys, I made the questionnaire as simple as possible. A fault in this method is that the terms are not defined. What does 'friendly to people' really mean? When ethologists carry out personality assessments, they define it to mean 'a willingness to initiate proximity and/or contact'. In my survey I simply left it to the veterinarians to interpret the behaviours. Seventy were willing to do so and return completed forms.

Some cats are more demanding and outgoing than others.

I included the most popular breeds of cats, the Siamese and the Burmese, and grouped the Persians under the single 'domestic long-hair' heading. Because the Somali is a genetically altered Abyssinian with a longhair gene, I grouped these two breeds under one heading. And because the population geneticist Neil Todd speculated that it was owing to their ease of handling that non-agouti-coloured cats were more readily transported great distances from their place of origin, I included the black shorthair as the representative non-agouti and the blotched tabby as the classic agouti-coloured cat.

Veterinarians were asked to insert 'always', 'frequently', 'sometimes' or 'never' alongside the following statements about each breed:

(Breed name, e.g., Siamese) demand attention
                         tolerate handling well
                         give 'affection'
                         are very active
                         are destructive
                         are friendly to other household cats
                         are vocal
                         are excitable
                         are playful
                         are hygienic

As a matter of interest, the veterinarians were also asked to insert 'always', 'frequently', 'sometimes' or 'never' alongside similar statements about each sex: male, neutered male, female and neutered female.

The results of the survey which conformed surprisingly well with previous descriptions of each breed and sex, were as follows (the graphs show sex differences in behaviour):

Attention Demanding

All cats demand attention and, according to my results, the Oriental or foreign shorthairs, the Siamese, Burmese and Abyssinians, demand significantly more than do either domestic shorthairs or Persians (domestic longhairs).

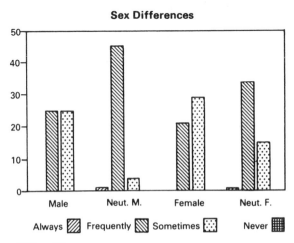

Toleration of Handling

Domestic shorthairs tolerate handling more readily, while Siamese tolerate handling less than other breeds.

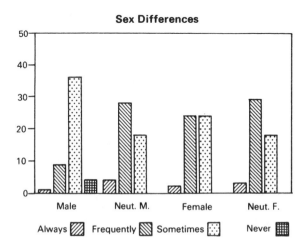

Giving 'Affection'
All breeds give affection, although the Persian (domestic longhair) is
the least inclined to do so.

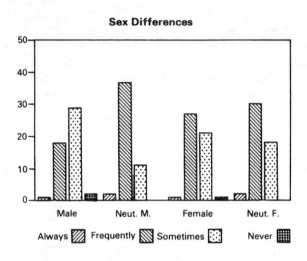

Amount of Activity
The Oriental shorthairs, the Siamese, Burmese and Abyssinians, are
the most active breeds and the Persian (domestic longhair) the least
active.

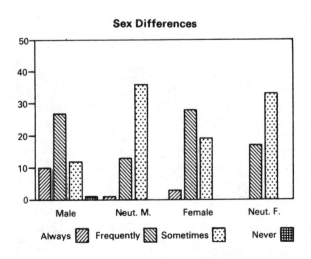

Destructiveness
Cats are not very destructive but the Oriental shorthairs and especially the Siamese are more destructive than domestic shorthairs. Persians (domestic longhairs) are the least destructive.

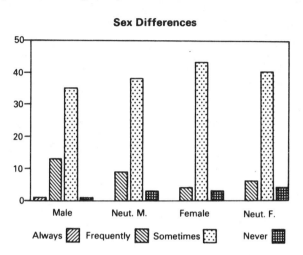

Sex Differences

Friendliness to Other Cats
Domestic shorthairs are the friendliest to other cats, while the Siamese and Burmese and to a somewhat lesser extent the Abyssianians are the least friendly.

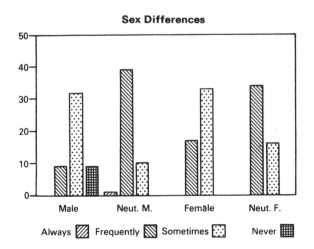

Sex Differences

Siamese and Burmese cats are more likely to resent the introduction of other cats into their homes.

Being Vocal

The Siamese is dramatically the most vocal. The Burmese and Abyssinians are also very vocal, while the Persians (domestic longhairs) are the least.

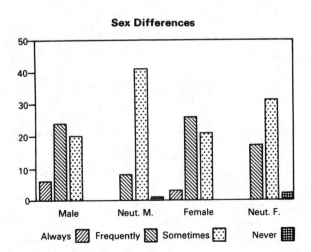

Excitability

Generally speaking, cats are not very excitable animals, although, once again, the Siamese is the most excitable, followed by the Abyssinian and the Burmese. Domestic shorthairs and Persians (domestic longhairs) are equally calm.

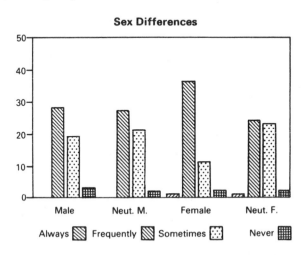

Sex Differences

Always 🔲 Frequently 🔲 Sometimes 🔲 Never 🔳

Playfulness

All cats are moderately playful, although the Persian (domestic longhair) is the least and the Siamese the most.

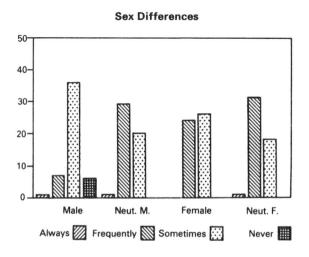

Sex Differences

Always 🔲 Frequently 🔲 Sometimes 🔲 Never 🔳

Hygiene

All cats are almost equally hygienic, although Persians (domestic longhairs) are less so.

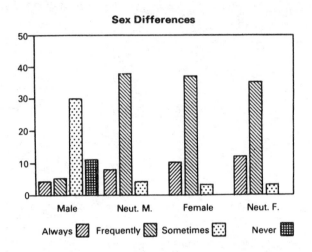

Sex Differences

Always ⧄ Frequently ⧅ Sometimes ⸬ Never ▦

From the viewpoint of Neil Todd's hypothesis on the domestication of the cat, the survey failed to reveal any real differences between the perceived behaviour of black or tabby cats.

Although this was a simple and basic survey, it does reveal significant breed differences in behaviour. I chose to survey practising veterinarians because I had easy access to them and knew that their judgements would be less biased than those of, say, breeders, who are often most familiar with only a few breeds. Vets' opinions are based upon what they are told by their clients, on their personal experiences as cat owners and on their experiences while examining cats at their clinics.

It is, of course, only logical to assume that there are breed differences in cat behaviour, but because so many of us still think 'generically' of cats, we often don't consider it when selecting pets. Equally important, now that breeds are being 'genetically engineered' in the sense that breeders are actively cross-breeding to produce new coat colours and textures, the temperament of the offspring should be considered. Depending on where the breeder's priorities lie, this is not always the case. At one end of the spectrum the hairless cat, the Sphinx, has been perpetuated for its oddity value. Although it may have a pleasant personality, it suffers from the overwhelming genetic flaw of hairlessness that should be eliminated from the gene pool rather than perpetuated. At the other end is the Burmilla, the result of an un-authorized alliance between a Burmese and a Chinchilla longhair. This accidental breeding was continued by a client, Miranda von Kirchberg, because, in her words, 'the most compellingly attractive characteristic was their charming personality. They were "human-oriented" to an astonishing degree and at a very young age. They also demonstrated that most engaging characteristic in both felines and humans – a willingness to capitulate. Playful, fighting games never became too boisterous.'

I have seen many of the descendants of the original accidental mating and agree with the Baroness's description. Others obviously do too as Burmilla breeding programmes are now under way in Britain, France, the Netherlands, Germany, Switzerland and the United States of America.

Just as in the case of dogs, as the role of animals changes from utilitarian to social and psychological, we should pay more attention to breeding for temperament rather than simply for eye and coat colour. Natural selection has given us good building blocks. The British shorthair is a robust, sturdy, muscular animal with short legs. Its American descendants are larger and leaner with longer legs, but they are also more energetic and active. Similar differences apply to the Persian or domestic longhair and its very close relative, the Maine Coon. Persians are placid and slightly aloof. Maine Coons are more active, are keen hunters and, speaking as an addict, I can confirm that perhaps their most important characteristic is their constant 'chirping'. Their 'brp' is a compelling, happy noise, and if the pet cat's role is to amuse and make you forget your worries, there is no better sound in all of catdom – unless it's a 'brp' combined with a purr.

Chapter Twelve

The Mind of the Ill and the Elderly

'He's not acting himself,' I'm told. 'He didn't go out this morning,' or 'He hissed at me,' or 'He's always been independent but suddenly he's become friendly.' Just as paediatricians must rely upon the initial observations of parents for a description of what is wrong with a child, veterinarians rely upon cat owners to notice illness in their pets and what they often notice first is a mood change. The first words of a medical history frequently describe the cat's behaviour, and the most common words I hear are 'lethargic', 'listless' and 'dull'. These changes are not, however, caused by the illness itself but are more likely behaviour changes, changes in the cat's mind, that have evolved over the millenia to help the cat overcome its illness.

From the time, billions of years ago, when multiple-celled organisms first evolved, all living creatures have been under constant and remorseless attack from viruses and bacteria. (Viruses have been so successful that remnants of their ancient ancestors still exist in almost every cell of our bodies.) One of the consequences of this incessant exposure was the development of the immune system, the system that helps to prevent infection or, if infection occurs, helps to contain and destroy it. (Feline leukaemia and feline immune deficiency viruses are dangerous to cats because they reduce the efficiency of the immune system.) But other methods of fighting disease also evolved and one of these is behavioural. Dullness, lack of appetite, reluctance to move and even irritability in the sick cat all occur *before* the immune system has a chance to come on stream and fight the infection. These are life-protecting mood changes.

When a cat suffers an infection, its body temperature rises. Certain circulating white blood cells release a substance called interleukin-1 which acts on the thermostat in the hypothalamus of the brain, effectively raising its set point. This is beneficial because many viruses and bacteria thrive best at normal body temperature, but interleukin-1 is also probably important in depressing the cat's appetite. Certainly in laboratory animals it is interleukin-1 rather than hyperthermia (fever) that induces loss of appetite, and this reluctance to eat can be life-saving in two ways.

By not eating, the sick cat might starve the invading bacteria of the minerals they need. Much more important, however, is the fact that if the cat does not eat, it does not hunt, and if it does not hunt, it does not use up precious energy looking for food. The cat can find a hiding place, conserve energy, reduce heat loss and fight the infection. The cat can be so efficient in this that it hisses or spits at anyone who comes near, behaviour resulting in much worry on the part of its owner – but neither this behaviour nor a temporary lack of appetite should cause concern. In fact, experiments with mice have shown that forced feeding during a fever can actually be harmful. Mice that are force-fed during a bacterial infection have a decreased survival time and an increased mortality rate compared to mice that are allowed to eat as they wish. Mice that are deprived of food for two to three days before a bacterial infection have greater survival rates than do well-fed mice.

As all veterinarians know, the majority of cat infections are not potentially lethal. For millions of year cats have overcome most of their infections by using their superb immune system and adopting the 'withdrawn' behavioural strategy. The cat's problem, however, is that its body can't differentiate between less serious and more serious illnesses. Its response to both is the same. And as the cat's mind has naturally evolved from that of the lone hunter to that of the more sociable animal, dangerous transmissible viruses such as peritonitis virus, leukaemia virus and immune deficiency virus have found it easier to spread simply because cats now live in closer proximity to each other, either in natural colonies around large food caches or in breeding catteries.

The conclusion we can draw from recent research findings is that we should respect the cat's natural evolutionary response to disease, but only to a point. Cats should not be force-fed initially unless there are specific clinical reasons for doing so. If fever is present it should be reduced only if it is seriously high, for it acts as an excellent barometer of a cat's state of illness. (And always avoid aspirin. It takes four days for the cat's liver to remove just a quarter of an aspirin from the bloodstream. Giving more than that amount can be toxic and potentially lethal.) Treatment should be directed at removing the cause of the illness. Antibiotics, for example, should be used when a problem is bacterial.

Not all illnesses cause dullness and depression. The very opposite can occur, and with increasing frequency I see skinny elderly cats because their owners are worried they are *too* active. Any dramatic mood change should be a cause of at the least interest, and sometimes concern. An over-active thyroid gland will make a cat compulsively active. It can't sit still, constantly wanders, frequently vocalizes, and demands copious quantities of food (but nevertheless shrinks to skin and bone). In a classical sense its mind is dramatically altered by the influence of thyroid hormone on the brain and the consequent modifications to virtually all of the body's biofeedback mechanisms. When I asked an acquaintance, a human acquaintance I should add, about her hyperthyroid condition, she told me that when she was put on medication to reduce her excessive thyroid activity down to a normal level, she felt as if her soul had been tampered with. Thyroid function can have a dramatic effect on mood and mind.

Diseases can induce dramatic behaviour changes.

There are many other organic and infectious diseases that alter the cat's mind, obvious diseases like rabies and less obvious ones too, such as certain liver or kidney problems. Aggression can be a component of at least three disease states. Epilepsy is one of them. Unlike in dogs where aggression is a rare manifestation of epilepsy, in cats it is much more common (though epilepsy itself is not). Owners will describe the 'funny look' in their cat's eyes just before an attack. The seizure itself is usually quite short and during it the cat is oblivious to everything, including the owner's shouts and screams. This aggressive form of epilepsy usually occurs in young cats, and after an attack the cat might actually come to its owner for attention, although it is equally possible it will try to hide. It is this confusing behaviour, rather than excessive play behaviour, after the attack that suggests epilepsy, and when the incidence of seizures is frequent, medical treatment is necessary.

Grumpiness and irritability can be manifestations of an underactive thyroid gland. Dogs with an under-active thyroid gland simply become corpulent and slothful, but a few cats with the problem gradually become aggressive without the accompanying obesity and skin changes. Simply walking past one of these cats can provoke an apparently spiteful swipe. This medical form of aggression dramatically resolves when the cat is given a thyroid supplement.

By far the most common medical cause of aggression is simple irritability. Cats with blocked anal glands, or bladder infection or old-age arthritis or sore gums all have a rightful reason to be irritable. Minor events become upsetting. Even a change in daily routine is enough to trigger an attack. Clients have told me that being late with a meal can be enough to bring on an aggressive display. The cat that suddenly bites and jumps off your lap might be displaying irritable aggression or petting aggression. Social grooming is a short-term behaviour in cats but not in humans. If we 'socially groom' cats for too long, some of them get irritated, bite and leave. But equally, petting might be painful if a cat has a medical problem and this is what induces the aggressive response.

There are numerous other medical problems that affect the cat's mind, but many of them still don't have defined causes. Excessive licking is perhaps the most common. Although fleas should always be considered when cats lick excessively, there are still more circumstances in which licking appears to be unrelated to any physical cause. The licking can become so excessive that after the hair is lost the skin becomes chronically thickened. Other cats suddenly and almost aggressively bite their feet or tail. They frequently vocalize in a threatening manner as they do so. This can be a displacement activity, brought on by pain elsewhere in the body, the anal sacs for example, but as it responds to mood-altering drugs it is equally likely that it is strictly behavioural. In the same sense hallucinations, or what we assume are hallucinations, might be caused by severe fear, but these too respond to mood-altering medications.

Hyperexcitability is not as great a problem in cats as it is in dogs, although the causes are the same: inheritance, lack of proper socialization and exposure to the environment during the formative first two months of life and then lack of stimulation. Hyperexcitable cats are very active, especially at night, and some will attack people or other animals simply for something to do rather than for territorial or other reasons. This behaviour is very difficult to alter or modify.

The use of drugs in the treatment of other behavioural problems in cats is, however, dramatically increasing. Tranquillizers, anti-anxiety drugs, anti-convulsants and hormones are all used. Well over twenty years ago it was observed that one tranquillizer would subdue both 'pure' aggressive and defensive behaviour, while another only reduced defensive behaviour. Other drugs reduced 'pure' aggression, while not influencing defensive attack behaviour.

In human medicine tranquillizers are differentiated as anti-psychotic and anti-anxiety. For use in animals the distinction is better made by describing them as major and minor tranquillizers. These drugs calm the cat's mind but they also reduce spontaneous activity, a significant reason for avoiding prolonged use. Tranquillizers suppress aggressive behaviour, counter-act fear and anxiety and have a sedative effect. They are often used to reduce activity during car and plane journeys.

Anti-anxiety drugs are often called anti-depressants when used in human medicine and are perhaps the drugs of choice in treating anxiety-related problems in cats. Dr Victoria Voith at the University of Pennsylvania was the first veterinary behaviourist to publish statistics on the success rate in resolving anxiety-related house soiling and spraying in cats. Using Valium for just a three-week period eliminated the problem in just over half of the delinquent cats.

Anti-convulsants are used to treat all epilepsy-like disorders. As already mentioned, cats don't suffer from epilepsy as frequently as do dogs, and anti-convulsants are useful diagnostically in determining the exact nature of a behavioural problem – the difference, for example between 'hallucinations', which most cats seem to have, and true psychogenic epilepsy in which the 'hallucinations' are an unusual manifestation of epilepsy.

Hormones are now the most frequently prescribed drugs for behaviour problems in cats. Progesterone-like drugs are used to treat urine marking and spraying, male aggression towards other cats and people, hyperactivity, 'neurotic' behaviour, anxiety, frustration and excessive sexual behaviour. They are also employed to control territorial aggression, suppress or prevent oestrus in female cats and prevent conception. Outside the behavioural sphere, progestogens are used to treat hair loss, acne, 'stud tail' and numerous different forms of dermatitis. They are used to treat gum inflammations, an eye inflammation called eosinophilic keratitis and a throat inflammation called plasma cell pharyngitis. Progestogens are used for so many different problems that a large number of cat owners know about them and consider them to be the panacea of all problems. A word of caution is needed here, however. The discovery of the therapeutic uses of progestogens has been a delight for veterinary clinicians who treat behavioural disorders. But there are real and theoretical drawbacks. Most cats on this hormone supplement gain weight. They are hungrier, thirstier and urinate more. Although many are friendlier, some appear depressed and others become lethargic. Metabolically, progestogens alter biofeedback. They suppress the adrenal gland and alter carbohydrate metabolism. This can lead to increases of sugar and lipids in the bloodstream and eventually to either transient or permanent diabetes. These drugs alter the lining of the uterus (or womb) and increase susceptibility to uterus infection. They can stimulate mammary-gland enlargement, milk production and mammary tumours in males and females. They suppress the formation of various cells in the body and this leads to skin changes, a change in coat colour or hair loss. From a social-behaviour viewpoint, treatment with progestogens can precipitate a loss of social order in an existing cat colony. As drugs for use in the temporary medical management of behavioural disorders in cats, hormones are major players, but when used for prolonged therapy there should be constant medical supervision.

The female hormone progesterone has been the flavour-of-the-decade drug for the treatment of behaviour disorders in cats. With the recent synthesis of human growth hormone there is the now theoretical potential that this drug will be the panacea of the twenty-first century, a fountain of youth to delay the ravages of ageing.

AGEING

One of the great biological puzzles still to be solved is why we and cats and most other living things grow old, decrepit and die. Amoebae don't. They just keep on dividing *ad infinitum*, never ageing, only multiplying. Sir Peter Medawar, the Nobel prize-winning British biologist, suggested a possible answer in the 1950s. He said that in evolutionary terms, because most animals die from disease or violence before the ageing process begins, genes responsible for ageing are not weeded out by natural selection. A few years later George Williams, the American evolutionary biologist, suggested that genes causing young animals to breed more successfully actually cause ageing. This, he explained, is why ageing is so general. It would also mean that animals breeding early in life age more quickly.

A genetically controlled biological clock probably controls the ageing process.

Researchers at the University of Uppsala, Sweden, recently found this to be true in the population of collared flycatchers they were studying. Early breeding seemed to affect the females permanently rather than simply limiting breeding in the next season. But whether their findings can be applied to cats is another matter. After all, the breed that reaches sexual maturity soonest and is biologically most likely to breed early, the Siamese, also has the longest life expectancy.

It is highly probable that a genetically controlled biological clock controls the ageing process. This clock is possibly located in the hypothalamus and specifically in the part known to control growth hormone as well as the activities of many of the body's hormone-producing glands. Growth hormone, as its name implies, is necessary for growth and development of the young. It is liberated when the kitten sleeps, but even after it reaches its mature size, growth hormone continues to be secreted. An immediate conclusion is that the hormone itself is poorly named as it must have other functions. One of these might be in arresting the ageing process. A pilot study in the United States in 1990, using synthetic growth hormone supplementation on a population sample of elderly men, revealed potentially dramatic findings. All participants said they 'felt' much better while on growth hormone, but as well as the mood change, they had greater muscle mass and increased elasticity to the skin.

Whatever the reason may be, I see cats that are 'old' at nine years of age and others that are 'young' at fifteen. The environment in which the cat finds itself can speed up or slow down its genetically predetermined life span. This is the area that we can influence by providing a stimulating environment, one that keeps the brain active.

Cats are born with a finite number of brain cells. And as they age their brains get lighter as the number of cells falls. By the end of a cat's life its brain is about 25 per cent lighter than it was when the cat was in its prime. The glands in its body have shrunk in a similar fashion. The thyroid shrinks. The adrenal glands lose their ability to respond rapidly. And if the cat is a male and still has his testicles, they produce less testosterone. When a cat is in its prime a single brain cell might have inter-connections with up to 10,000 other cells, but as it ages the wiring system becomes faulty. Chemical transmitters don't reach their target cells. The consequences are poorer senses, poorer reflexes, inefficient hormonal responses and a general slowing-down of reaction time. Different nerve pathways are activated to get messages from one place to another. Cells called 'interneurons' are used to amplify and refine these signals, but in the ageing cat, when these cells are stimulated they remain stimulated much longer than they should. The result is that the first piece of information transmitted temporarily blocks the whole system. Observant cat owners see this happening with their elderly felines. Responses occur almost as if the brain is working in slow motion. And in fact it is.

Other changes also occur. The lungs and blood vessels become less efficient. As a consequence the brain no longer receives as much blood as it formerly did. The membrane around the brain, the meninges, thickens and sometimes becomes hard or even brittle. Microscopic haemorrhages occur in the smallest blood vessels, destroying only a few cells but nevertheless impairing the cat's mind.

At the same time the cat's hearing diminishes and it no longer hears sounds at the extremes of its former range. Its eyes lose both rods and cones and the lenses lose their elasticity and become blue-grey with connective tissue. Taste is affected and saltiness loses its intensity. It isn't just the creaky bones that make the geriatric irritable; it is the general decline in all the body functions that does so.

Because the brain controls or at least influences the ageing process through its control of the body's hormones, it should be possible to delay ageing in cats by providing the optimum environment for mental stimulation. This has certainly been done successfully with rats, in studies at the University of Illinois. Elderly over-weight rats were moved from their featureless, drab and uninteresting cages into 'rat Disneyland' – new homes with slides, swings, ramps and other rats. At first they hid, but soon they started doing aerobics and socializing. They lost their excess weight, became more active, set up territories and, according to the observers, seemed to enjoy themselves more. When brain tissue was ultimately examined, the researchers reported that each nerve cell in the cerebellum had on average 2000 more connections with other nerve cells than did similar cells in rats left in the old boring cages.

The deterioration of the mind is an inevitable fact but it can be delayed by providing a cat with mental stimulation. In humans, the last third of our lives is often referred to as old age, but in cats we see old-age behaviour changes only in the last year or two, in the last 10 per cent of their life. In an ideal situation it would be delightful to co-ordinate mental and physical deterioration so that both occur simultaneously. And how long should a cat live? The answer varies with who it is and where it lives, but there are several hard facts. Indoor cats live longer than outdoor ones. Neutered cats, whether indoor or outdoor, live longer than entire cats. Certain breeds of cat, like the Siamese and Burmese, live longer than moggies, again regardless of whether they are indoor or outdoor animals. Today I expect neutered, vaccinated house cats to live to around fifteen years and Siamese to live to seventeen or more. I'm no longer surprised by twenty-year-olds, although cats older than that are still unusual. And when the end finally comes, their minds probably have one great advantage over ours in that they die without any idea of death itself.

Chapter Thirteen

Behaviour Problems: How to Alter the Cat's Mind

Cats are self-reliant, self-entertaining, self-determining, independent and clean. That's why they make such good pets, but as they increase in popularity so too do their behaviour problems. Until recently most pet cats were outdoor animals that returned home for warmth, security and food, but whose lives were otherwise occupied with normal feline outdoor pursuits – walking, stalking, patrolling and marking. Outdoor cats have few behavioural problems; however, as cats are increasingly being kept as indoor pets, the behaviour problems presented to veterinarians increase in numbers. These are often problems of our making, for some owners fail to understand the natural needs of their pets and interpret their cats' behaviour as abnormal when in fact it is not. In other circumstances we actually create real problems, usually anxiety-related, by not providing natural outlets for our cats' needs.

We also have a tendency to misunderstand cause and effect. Let me give an example. You come home to discover that your cat has jumped up on the kitchen counter and helped itself to your chicken dinner which is now lying partly consumed on the floor. You take a swipe at the animal and shout, 'Bad cat!' The next day you return home and find that it has jumped back up on the counter and has left deep lick marks in the butter. Once more you shout at the cat and give it a swat. The following day you come home and you can see that the cat feels guilty because it hesitates to greet you. Sure enough, the cream has been drunk. You throw a towel at the cat and screech that it'll never be allowed in the kitchen again.

You feel you've been unsuccessful as a cat trainer, but you're wrong. You've been dramatically successful. The problem is that you've been training the cat to be frightened of you when you come home rather than training it to avoid the kitchen counter. Cats learn to associate what they *are doing*, not what they did, but what they are actually doing, with either a reward or a punishment. To be effective rewards need to be given when a cat performs as you want it to and, similarly, punishments must be meted out at the instant the crime is committed.

Cats learn in three different ways, through observation, by classical conditioning and through training (or operant conditioning).

1. Learning by Observation

Kittens are better than pups at learning by observation. They copy their mother's hunting and prey-catching behaviour. In laboratory experiments kittens are adept at watching other cats solve a puzzle and then solving it themselves in the same way. Learning by observation is not frequently seen in adult cats, but because behaviours that are learned at a very early age may not be exhibited until later in life, early learning through observation might lead to what we consider to be behaviour problems.

2. Classical Conditioning

Historically, classical conditioning involves an involuntary 'visceral response' on the part of the animal. Pavlov's dogs salivated at the sound of a bell after they learned to associate the bell with food. Ethologists are now more inclined to think that classical conditioning is not simply a discrete form of learning because the animal might actually *think* 'food' when it hears the bell. It is a form of cat training. The cat that runs away from you when you pick up a newspaper might have been classically conditioned to avoid newspapers because you use them for punishment. Its visceral response involves the activation of its adreno-pituitary axis. The important fact about classical conditioning is that the cat's visceral response is involuntary. It has no control over it.

3. Cat Training (or Operant Conditioning)

The cat's mind is always undergoing operant conditioning although we have little positive influence on this form of learning. The principle is that a certain action, carried out under certain circumstances, is immediately followed by a reward. Jumping up on the kitchen counter in the absence of people leads to an immediate food reward. Jumping up on the kitchen counter in the presence of people leads to a swipe, an immediate punishment, the antithesis of a reward. Unlike dogs, cats respond poorly to training to rewards, but if a reward is potent enough it is possible to train felines this way. For most cats only food is a potent reward. I certainly found it easy to train Millie to return to our back garden by first 'addicting' her to vitamin tablets, then shaking the bottle of tablets when I gave her one and finally training her to come to the sound of the shaken bottle. Some cats will also respond to verbal and petting rewards but this is much less effective in cats than it is in dogs. Cats are simply less interested in pleasing. (Fortunately Millie is responsive to verbal training and also comes to her name.)

Reinforcement
Millie's training was successful because we used reinforcement. In her circumstances we used positive reinforcement, primarily food but also petting and attention. Operant conditioning works fastest when a behaviour is consistently rewarded. The cat that jumped up on the kitchen counter and found food each time was rewarded each time it jumped. In a technical sense it was using a continuous reinforcement schedule to reward the behaviour. This is how many problem behaviours develop. Initially, through continuous reinforcement, the cat learns to carry out a certain behaviour and then through intermittent reinforcement the behaviour becomes fixed in its behavioural repertoire.

Cats can be trained to 'speak' by the use of food rewards.

Just as positive reinforcement creates behaviours, negative reinforcement can be used to retrain cats to behave as you would like them to. This can also be called avoidance learning or punishment.

Punishment does not mean pain, and indeed there is never even the remotest reason to use pain as a punishment in behaviour training. It might give you immediate revenge but will teach the cat only to avoid you rather than to avoid doing whatever it was doing before. Successful negative reinforcement involves either direct or indirect intimidation or association of the behaviour, in the cat's mind, with a fearful stimulus. These include tastes, smells and sounds.

Dogs are fun to train because they are so responsive to positive reinforcement. Food, touch, sounds, play or simple attention from the owner can all be used to correct behavioural problems in dogs. Not so with cats. With these more independent animals, punishments are unfortunately more effective than positive reinforcers. Some of the following training methods might seem cruel but none involves pain. They startle or cause fear and in these ways alter the cat's behaviour.

AVERSION

Taste-aversion is an effective method used to train a cat to stop chewing or sucking on furniture or clothing. Dr Bonnie Beaver suggests loading a 2 ml syringe with hot pepper sauce (she teaches in Texas and so has ample supplies of this commodity stockpiled nearby), letting the cat have a good smell then squirting the contents into its mouth. Needless to say, this is a 'bad experience'. The pepper sauce can then be applied to whatever the cat is chewing or sucking, and it is most likely that the cat will associate its action with the object now smelling and tasting unpleasantly of pepper sauce.

Smell-aversion works in the same way, although it is not as successful and usually is effective only if the cat is doing something like sucking its owner's skin. In these circumstances using a body deodorant spray on the skin can be quite offputting to the cat.

Aversion training can also use sound or movement to shape a cat's behaviour. Indoor cats often chew house plants, some of which are toxic, and a useful but harmless way of putting them off this habit is described on page 132.

INTIMIDATION

Intimidation can be direct or indirect. Direct intimidation involves shouting at the cat, hitting with your hand or a rolled newspaper or, if you live in fly country as I did for most of my life, hitting with the nearest fly swatter, an instrument that seems to have been made quite specifically for intimidating cats. Direct intimidation is the punishment of choice when the unwanted behaviour is either directed towards you or occurs only in your presence. If your cat employs your leg as a scratching post, use direct intimidation to alter the behaviour. Alternatively try using milder intimidation by mimicking the way a mother would treat her slightly delinquent offspring. (And remember, in the cat's mind we are all mothers in that we provide food and comfort for them; quite different from the role we play for dogs when they consider us as members of their pack, sometimes higher but often lower in the pecking order.) A mother cat bats the kitten's nose with her paw. Later, in cat colonies, the dominant cat will use the same behaviour to express authority. Use a mild thump on the nose as a natural form of intimidation, or pick up the cat by the scruff as the mother would when she moves her kittens from nest to nest. Although cats stare at each other as a form of intimidation, their reactions to stares from humans are so varied that it is not advisable to use these as a form of direct punishment. Remember that punishment must occur at the time of the misdemeanour and that direct punishment is most effective for altering oral behaviour problems such as chewing or sucking.

Indirect or remote punishment is probably the most effective way to train or retrain cats. The advantage of remote punishment is that the cat does not associate you with it and statistics from animal behaviourists show that it produces the most acceptable results. This form of training calls for inventive and original thinking on your part, and the best forms of indirect punishment involve the cat associating its unacceptable activity with something it finds unpleasant. As water, especially unexpected water arriving from nowhere, is something most cats loathe, a high-velocity water pistol or a garden squirt-gun set for a solid stream should be an absolute requirement of all owners of indoor cats. If the cat climbs the curtains, it gets shot with water. If it jumps on the kitchen counter, it gets shot. If it uses the leg of the Chippendale chair as a scratching post, wham! Shouting at the same time can double the shock, but remember that cats will quickly come to associate you with the punishment if you shout each time. When a local tom was recently in our back garden sizing up Millie, and I happened to be there with a glass of apple juice in my hand, a simple deluge convinced the tom that Millie wasn't worth it. It might seem a mean thing to do but, at the very worst, all it causes the cat is embarrassment.

A garden spray water bottle is useful as a remote form of instant punishment.

If your cat jumps on the kitchen counter, using direct intimidation or remote punishment with a water pistol will only train it not to jump on the counter when you are there. It will still do so when you are not present. In circumstances such as this you will need to devise other more creative forms of intimidation. Completely covering the kitchen counter surface with pots and pans, boxes and utensils means that when the cat jumps up it is bound to knock something over, or fail to find a footing, or create an unexpected noise. Making sure that no food is left out is equally important, for remember: an instant reward can overwhelm associated punishment. Cats can become used (or habituated) to unpleasant things if there is still a reward to be had. This occurs in two ways, through constant exposure to the unpleasant stimulus (called flooding) or through gradual exposure to it (called systematic de-sensitization). If the cat knocks over a few pots and pans but still gets the chicken, you are habituating it to noise rather than training it to avoid jumping on the kitchen counter.

Many of these forms of training by negative reinforcement use both aversion and intimidation. Mothballs in flower pots to prevent cats from using the earth as a litter tray is classic aversion therapy, while throwing a tin can filled with a few pebbles near to the mis-behaving cat is both aversive because of the noise it makes and intimidating because of its proximity.

In the USA there are more cats than dogs, yet they account for less than one third of all cases referred to animal behaviourists for treatment. In Canada, where cats also exceed dogs in numbers, only one in five cases referred for behaviour problems to the Ontario Veterinary College involves a feline. A similar situation exists in Britain, where behaviourists also see far more dogs than cats. In both North America and Britain male cats account for slightly more cases seen, 60 per cent and 57 per cent of the total respectively. One British animal behaviourist has noted that although only 10 per cent of British cats are pedigree, 47 per cent of his cat referrals were of recognized breeds. The Burmese was the most frequently seen (27 per cent), chiefly for aggression towards other cats and for indoor spraying, while the Siamese (20 per cent), Abyssinian (13 per cent) and Persian (13 per cent) were also frequently referred for anti-social behaviour. In Canada the average age of cats referred for behaviour problems is 4.3 years, while in Britain they are on average referred a little earlier at 3.9 years.

By far the most common complaint of cat owners in North America and in Britain involves elimination behaviour and the second most common is aggression, both of which I have discussed in their respective chapters in this book. Bonnie Beaver at Texas A&M University has recently reported that two thirds of all the cases she sees involve house soiling. About half of all feline cases treated at the Ontario Veterinary College involve soiling and spraying, while Peter Neville in Britain, working out of Bristol University, reports that two fifths of his cases involve what behaviourists like to call 'inappropriate elimination'. Only 10 per cent of Neville's indoor sprayers came from one-cat households; over 47 per cent came from homes with two cats and 17 per cent from three- and four-cat households respectively. Owners of more cats seem to tolerate and even expect a certain level of urine spraying.

Behavioural problems involving aggression account for many other referred disorders, but one in particular, learned aggression, can be surprisingly common in indoor cats, accounting for one out of five referrals seen by some behaviourists. Cats, of course, are not trained to be aggressive as dogs are, yet nevertheless they learn aggression, often as a result of unpleasant or painful experiences unwittingly inflicted by children. The cat rapidly learns that by scratching a child it drives the child away. This can also be a fear or stress-induced activity. It can be brought on by conflicts with the owner, another cat, a change in the environment, boarding, hospitalization, over-crowding and probably countless other reasons, and its treatment involves de-sensitizing and habituating the cat to the person with whom it has learned to be aggressive by having that person feed the cat and reward it in other ways for not showing aggression.

The question still remains why behaviourists see so few cats for referred behaviour problems and why so many of those they do see are pure-bred. The answer probably lies, in part, in the owners' minds. If I were to take the thousands of urban cat owners I have met over the last twenty years as a representative sample of people who are inclined and willing to share their homes with cats, I would describe them as more tolerant of natural cat behaviour than dog owners are of natural dog behaviour. A dog that stalks and kills game is socially undesirable and its behaviour is unacceptable, but a cat doing the same, be it with moths, bluebottles, mice or sparrows, is behaving, in its owner's mind, as a cat. The owner might find it distasteful, but is willing to put up with this unavoidable evil in return for the pleasure of the company of a cat. The cat is simply not referred for behaviour advice because the owner acknowledges that what the cat is doing is perfectly normal.

Pure-bred cats are represented disproportionately in the cases seen by behaviourists, not because their breeding has created more behaviour problems (although the results of my survey of veterinarians strongly suggests that the Oriental breeds such as the Siamese and Burmese are more territorially aggressive than are other cats), but simply because pure-breds are more frequently housed as indoor urban cats. Indoor urban cats are kept in luxurious jails and, as a result of the lack of natural outlets for their energy and needs, will urine-spray or walk on the walls or attack visitors' ankles. Hence it is the owners of indoor urban cats who are most likely to be referred to animal behaviourists for advice.

And is treatment successful? Using simple methods of positive or negative reinforcement, de-sensitizing and habituating, most behaviour problems can be eliminated or reduced. The most recently published statistics state that four out of five such problems can be corrected or ameliorated to a tolerable level. What is equally revealing is that few cat owners opt ultimately for euthanasia when treatment fails. Euthanasia is the most common cause of death in dogs under two years of age and is often carried out for behavioural reasons. Cat owners seem more disposed to cope with their cat's behavioural eccentricities, especially once the origin of the problem is explained. When you understand a little of the cat's mind, it's reassuring to know that you aren't at fault or incompetent at caring for your feline companion.

The cat is the pet of the future. In North America cats now outnumber dogs, and in almost every single country throughout western Europe their numbers are increasing faster than dogs'. By the middle of this decade they are likely to be the most popular pets in most parts of northern Europe. Cats are ideal pets because they need little space, are content with short bursts of exercise and a hedonistic existence, are easily house-trained and relatively clean, can be very affectionate, are inexpensive, mostly quiet and enjoy their solitude. In a curious way they can become closer to us than they could ever be with other cats, but that should not hide the fact that the feline remains a distinct and unique species. In many ways we are good cat substitutes, but rather than looking upon them as furry humans or mobile adornments to our homes, we should take advantage of them for what they really are – our guests, offering us the opportunity to observe untarnished nature at first hand in a way we are seldom permitted to do. The cat's mind works in its own ways and the objectives are not always apparent to us. By understanding the uniqueness of cat behaviour, something that cat owners are often more adept at doing than are dog owners with their pets, we have a better appreciation of nature itself.

Bibliography

INTRODUCTION

The image we have of animals is discussed by Dr Barbara Noske in her book *Humans and Other Animals – Beyond the Boundaries of Anthropology*, Pluto Press, London, 1989 (first published in Dutch as *Huilen met De Wolven – Een interdisciplinaire benadering van de mens-dier relatie* by Van Gennep, Amsterdam, 1988)

Francis Pitt wrote about her wild cats in *Wild Mammals of Britain*, B. T. Batsford Ltd, London, 1938

CHAPTER ONE: THE GENETICS OF THE MIND

Cat genetics, especially the genetics of eye colour and coat colour and texture, is described in depth in: *Genetics for Cat Breeders* (Second Edn), Roy Robinson, Pergamon Press, London, 1977

CHAPTER TWO: THE BRAIN, HORMONES AND BIOFEEDBACK

Colin Blackmore is a cogent writer and editor on matters of the mind. Two of his books are worth reading:
Mindwaves, Colin Blackmore and Susan Greenfield (eds), Basil Blackwell, Oxford, 1989
The Mind Machine, Colin Blackmore, BBC Books, London, 1988

For a comprehensive description of the anatomy of the cat's brain refer to:
Physiological and Clinical Anatomy of the Domestic Animals, A. S. King, Oxford Scientific Publications, Oxford University Press, Oxford, 1987

Further information is available in:
Veterinary Neurology, J. E. Oliver, B. F. Hoerlein, I. G. Mayhew, W. B. Saunders, Philadelphia, London, Toronto, 1987
Manual of Small Animal Endocrinology, Maureen Hutchison (ed.), BSAVA Publications, Cheltenham, Glos, 1990

CHAPTER THREE: THE SENSES

Over the decades some quite unpleasant experiments have been carried out to investigate the cat's senses. Today, fortunately, few of them could be carried out as they would fail to pass the ethics committees at most universities and scientific establishments. It would be foolish, however, if I didn't utilize the information that was gained in these disquieting ways and some of this information forms the basis of this chapter. For detailed reading peruse:

Domestic Animal Behaviour for Veterinarians and Animal Scientists, K. A. Houpt and T. R. Wolski, Iowa State University Press, Ames, 1982

And for a good illustrated over-view of the senses read:

The Book of the Cat, Michael Wright and Sally Walters (eds), Pan Books, London, 1980

CHAPTER FOUR: COMMUNICATION

This information is liberally scattered in many volumes:

Social Odours in Mammals, Vol. 2, Richard Brown and David W. MacDonald (eds), Clarendon Press, Oxford, 1985

The Carnivores, R. F. Ewer, Cornell University Press, Ithaca, New York and London, 1985

How Animals Communicate, M. W. Fox and J. A. Cohen, Indiana University Press, London, 1977

Play behaviour is covered in:

Animal Play Behaviour, Robert Fagan, Oxford University Press, Oxford and New York, 1981

CHAPTER FIVE: EARLY LEARNING: THE INFLUENCE OF PARENTS, LITTERMATES AND HUMANS

The Domestic Cat: The Biology of its Behaviour, Dennis C. Turner and Patrick Bateson (eds), Cambridge University Press, Cambridge, 1988, is the most comprehensive scientific yet readable book on this subject.
The relevant chapters to read are:
'Behavioural development in the cat', Paul Martin and Patrick Bateson
'Factors influencing the mother-kitten relationship', John Deag, Aubrey Manning and Candace Lawrence
'The human-cat relationship', Eileen Karsh, Dennis Turner

CHAPTER SIX: LATER LEARNING: RANK AND TERRITORY

Michael Fox is perhaps best known for his books on dog behaviour, but he is equally prescient on cats. It is worth searching out:

Understanding Your Cat, Michael Fox, Coward, McCann and Geohegan, New York, 1974

Also worth reading is Meredith West's chapter on 'Play in Domestic Kittens' in:
The Analysis of Social Interactions, R. B. Cairns (ed.), Lawrence Erlbaum Associates, Hillsdale, New Jersey, 1979

CHAPTER SEVEN: SEXUAL BEHAVIOUR AND MATERNAL ACTIVITY

Most of the information in this chapter comes from veterinary textbooks and already mentioned volumes. These include:
Veterinary Aspects of Feline Behaviour, Bonnie Beaver, C. V. Mosby, St Louis, Toronto and London, 1980
Cat Behaviour: The Predatory and Social Behaviour of Domestic and Wild Cats, Paul Leyhausen, Garland STPM Press, New York and London, 1979
The Domestic Cat: The Biology of its Behaviour, Dennis C. Turner and Patrick Bateson (eds), Cambridge University Press, Cambridge, 1988

CHAPTER EIGHT: PREDATION, EATING AND ELIMINATION

These are perhaps the most intensively explored areas of feline behaviour, with entire volumes devoted to the subject. The best books are:
Cat Behaviour: The Predatory and Social Behaviour of Domestic and Wild Cats, Paul Leyhausen, Garland STPM Press, New York and London, 1979
Nutrition and Behaviour in Dogs and Cats, R. S. Anderson (ed), Pergamon Press, London, 1984
Nutrition of the Dog and Cat, I. H. Burger and J. P. W. Rivers (eds), Cambridge University Press, Cambridge, New York, 1989

CHAPTER NINE: FEAR AND AGGRESSION

Victoria Voith and Bonnie Beaver are the two veterinary behaviourists who have written most lucidly on feline aggression. Their papers are published in various books and journals. Two of the most comprehensive chapters are in:
Veterinary Clinic of North America, Small Animal Practice (Victoria Voith), Vol. 12, No. 4, W. B. Saunders, Philadelphia, Toronto and London, 1982
The Cat – Diseases and Management (Bonnie Beaver), Robert Sherling (ed), Churchill Livingstone, New York, 1989
There is good coverage of the subject in:
The Behaviour of Domestic Animals, Benjamin Hart, W. H. Freeman & Co, New York, 1985

CHAPTER TEN: INDIVIDUALITY AND BEHAVIOUR TOWARDS HUMANS

Most of the information in this chapter was presented at a scientific meeting held in Monaco in November 1989 and subsequently published in various journals. Once more, the most important books to read on the subject are:

The Domestic Cat: The Biology of its Behaviour, Dennis C. Turner and Patrick Bateson (eds), Cambridge University Press, Cambridge, 1988

Cat Behaviour: The Predatory and Social Behaviour of Domestic and Wild Cats, Paul Leyhausen, Garland STPM Press, New York and London, 1979

Also worth browsing through are:

New Perspectives on our Lives with Companion Animals, Aaron Katcher and Alan Beck (eds), University of Pennsylvania Press, Philadelphia, 1983

The Pet Connection, R. K. Anderson (ed), University of Minnesota, Minneapolis, 1984

CHAPTER ELEVEN: BREED DIFFERENCES IN BEHAVIOUR

Only anecdotal information is presently available on this subject. The popular book quoted from is:

The Ultimate Cat Book, David Taylor, Dorling Kindersley, London, 1990

CHAPTER TWELVE: THE MIND OF THE ILL AND THE ELDERLY

Once more, very little is available in book form on this subject, with most references in veterinary journals. There are several books of interest:

The Cat – Diseases and Management, Vol. One, Robert Sherling (ed), Churchill Livingstone, New York, 1989

Animals, Aging and the Aged, Leo Bustad, University of Minnesota Press, Minneapolis, 1980

The Biology of Aging, J. A. Behnke, C. E. Finch, G. B. Moments (eds), Plenum Press, New York, 1979

CHAPTER THIRTEEN: BEHAVIOUR PROBLEMS: HOW TO ALTER THE CAT'S MIND

Once more the veterinarians Ben Hart, Bonnie Beaver and Victoria Voith have published most extensively in the United States on this subject. In Britain most reports on the incidence and treatment of feline behavioural disorders have come from the pens of behaviourists and psychologists such as Roger Mugford, Valerie Farrell and Peter Neville. There are as yet no popular texts on behavioural problems although I touched upon them in:

Games Pets Play: How Not to be Manipulated by Your Pet, Michael Joseph and Viking Press, London and New York, 1986

The best textbooks remain:
Veterinary Aspects of Feline Behaviour, Bonnie Beaver, C. V. Mosby, St Louis, Toronto and London, 1980
Canine and Feline Behaviour Therapy, Ben Hart, Febiger, Philadelphia, 1985

For the most recent information on feline behaviour the best journals to follow are:
Carnivore
Animal Behaviour

THE DOG'S MIND

by Bruce Fogle

'Every dog that ever followed its master gives an immeasurable sum of love and fidelity' – Konrad Lorenz in *Man and His Dog*.

How do dogs perceive the world about them? How do they see, hear, relate to their owners? How large are their brains, what is their emotional make up? Why do they suffer from stress and how can it be coped with?

Over the last ten years a substantial body of knowledge has been built up about the psychology of dog behaviour. Combining twenty years of practical experience as a veterinary clinician with a personal knowledge and understanding of the latest international research, Dr Bruce Fogle has written the most inclusive and relevant book on how the canine mind works.